CHICAGO SHAKESPEARE THEATER

CHICAGO
Shakespeare
THEATER

Suiting the Action to the Word

Edited by Regina Buccola and Peter Kanelos

NIU PRESS / *DeKalb, IL*

Library of Congress Cataloging-in-Publication Data
Chicago Shakespeare Theater : suiting the action to the word / edited by Regina Buccola
and Peter Kanelos.
    pages cm
  Summary: "Chicago Shakespeare Theater is widely known for vibrant productions that
reflect the Bard's genius for intricate storytelling, musicality of language, and depth of
feeling for the human condition. Affectionately known to natives of the Windy City as
"Chicago Shakes," and now in its twenty fifth season, this vanguard of Chicago's rich
theatrical tradition celebrates its silver anniversary with this bracing collection of original
essays by world renowned scholars, directors, actors, and critics. Bringing together works
by such heralded figures as Terry Teachout, Jonathan Abarbanel, and Michael Billington;
industry giants like Michael Bogdanov, Edward Hall, and Simon Callow; and interviews
with Artistic Director Barbara Gaines and Executive Director Criss Henderson, Chicago
Shakespeare Theater unveils the artistic visions and decisions that helped shape this
venerable institution and examines the theater's international reputation for staging such
remarkable and provocative performances"— Provided by publisher.
  ISBN 978 0 87580 467 5 (hardback) — ISBN 978 1 60909 070 8 (e book)
  1. Chicago Shakespeare Theater. 2. Shakespeare, William, 1564–1616—Stage history—
Illinois—Chicago 3. Theatrical companies—Illinois—Chicago. 4. Theater—Illinois—
Chicago—History. I. Buccola, Regina, 1969– II. Kozusko, Matt, 1971–
  PR3105.C48 2012
  822.3'3—dc23
                                2012045333

Contents

CONTENTS

Acknowledgments

As we write this, scarcely a year has passed since the idea for this collection took shape. One does not make so rapid a journey from inception to execution without incurring more debts of gratitude than can readily be repaid in a few paragraphs of prose. To fail in the attempt, however, seems better than to fail to attempt it.

First and foremost, we must express our gratitude to Chicago Shakespeare Theater itself, which demonstrated once again its unique position in the cultural landscape by virtue of the unique relationship in which it has stood to us and to our contributors, offering free access to archives, artists, and administrators while at the same time agreeing to have absolutely no editorial control over the resulting essays. While everyone at the theater has been tremendously helpful, particular thanks are due to Barbara Gaines, Criss Henderson, Marilyn Halperin, Alida Szabo, Chris Plevin, Elizabeth Neukirch, Julie Stanton, and Jonathan Baude, who gave very generously of their time and energy during a theater season that taxed those resources to an exceeding degree. Any factual errors or other infelicities that remain in the volume are entirely our responsibility, and none of theirs.

Second, all of the contributors to this volume are to be thanked for their strong commitment to the project. The alacrity and goodwill with which everyone assayed the tasks at hand has been remarkable. The tight time line for this project meant that not everyone who was willing to contribute was able; for support, advice, and recommendations of contributors, we are grateful to Will West, Jeff Masten, Garry Wills, Lisa Freeman, Mary Beth

Rose, Suzanne Gossett, Richard Strier, and Stuart Sherman. Beth Charlebois deserves special mention for her thoughtful and protracted e-mail correspondence with Regina Buccola about the PreAmble lecture series.

Finally, thanks are due to our family and friends, who sacrificed a great deal of quality time with us at two major holidays while we wrapped up this project.

To all, thanks, and evermore thanks.

R.B. and P.K.

CHICAGO SHAKESPEARE THEATER

Introduction
Regina Buccola and Peter Kanelos

"THE ACCOMPLISHMENT OF MANY YEARS"

Overcoming the clank of "L" trains, the thunder of overflying jets and even the occasional odors from a nearby back-yard fish fry, 17 performers enact 45 parts and serve up the heroic sweep of a major chapter in English history. Their tiny platform space plays home to battlefield carnage and coy royal courtship, to knavish fooleries and kingly crises, to senseless bloodshed and to lusty victory, all in a production that's as economic as it is well-spoken and affecting.[1]

Sid Smith could scarcely have realized when he wrote his review of the Chicago Shakespeare Workshop's production of *Henry V* in 1986 that he was witnessing the prologue to a major chapter in Chicago theater history. The muse of fire that inhabited that production's director, Barbara Gaines, had provided only a pub rooftop for a stage, enthusiastic Shakespeare greenhorns to act, and adventurous audiences who spent more on beer than they did on tickets (the production was performed gratis) to behold the swelling scene. By 1999 that unworthy scaffold had become a fond memory to the world-class Chicago Shakespeare Theater. To tell that story, we must jump "o'er times, / Turning the accomplishment of many years / Into an hour-glass: for the which supply, / Admit me Chorus to this history."[2]

1. Poster for William Shakespeare's *Henry V* (1986), directed by Barbara Gaines—the production mounted on the rooftop of the Red Lion Inn that launched Shakespeare Repertory Company, renamed Chicago Shakespeare Theater on Navy Pier in 1999.

Chicago Shakespeare Theater is the brainchild of Gaines, who has served as Artistic Director throughout the theater's twenty-five-year history. A graduate of Northwestern University's theater program, Gaines garnered early acclaim as an actress in Chicago before heading to New York City.[3] Gaines returned to Chicago in 1980 and started teaching Shakespearean performance in the basement of what was then the Organic Theater while she recovered from knee surgery in 1983. Gaines started (as she does today) with table work using the texts in the First Folio (1623), the first collected edition of Shakespeare's plays, published by his theatrical partners, John Heminges and Henry Condell. A year later, Gaines and her band of Shakespeare students/actors staged a Shakespeare Showcase at Victory Gardens Theater; by the time of a second showcase at The Second City in 1985, the group had grown substantially, and Gaines had a mission statement:

> Our goal is to establish a world-class Shakespeare Repertory Company and training center in Chicago, which will provide work for our artists and culturally nourish the people of our city.
>
> This theater would become an international center for the arts, attracting talent from all over the world, while always keeping its commitment to and dependence upon the artists, directors and craftsman [*sic*] of Chicago.[4]

What sounded like an audacious set of goals at the time now reads like a checklist of the work that Chicago Shakespeare Theater routinely does today.

To take the fledgling company from showcases to full-length productions, Gaines relied on her extensive network within the Chicago theater community. "I asked Victory Gardens for rehearsal space; they said yes. I asked the Goodman Theater if we could build in their shop; they said yes," said Gaines, ticking off the early supporters on her fingers.[5] John Cordwell, owner of the Red Lion Pub in Chicago's Lincoln Park, agreed to let the Shakespeare Workshop stage *Henry V* on the pub's roof. The lone snag came from the Actors' Equity Association, which refused to let the actors who held equity cards perform without pay. The plan for the production had been to ask the audience only for donations. "I thought 'Gee, that's odd—we're trying to start a theater,'" Gaines recalled. "So, a bunch of actors—I was one—went to a meeting and pointed out that a dark theater is a dark theater. So they reversed their decision; they did the right thing, eventually."[6]

The play ran for two weeks to popular and critical acclaim; standing-room only crowds thronged around the jammed bleacher seating. Gaines swears that the meteorological implications of performing on the roof of a pub did not occur to her until she woke up on the morning of opening night—August 3rd 1986, my mother's birthday—with a chill wondering if it would rain for the next two weeks, because then we wouldn't have a Shakespeare theater in Chicago. Of course it did rain on the buildings next door, but it never did rain on the roof at the Red Lion Pub. Nothing was canceled, all of our patrons saw it, and many of them joined the board.[7]

Although they had passed the hat at *Henry V* like a band of itinerant players, the Shakespeare Workshop did not have to rely for long on what they could pull out of it. As luck would have it, Gaines had, through a friend, a connection with a man who worked at Chase Manhattan Bank. One day, Gaines remembered, "I get a phone call from the New York office: 'We hear you're trying to start a Shakespeare theater; we're going to send you $10,000 in seed money.' So finally we had a bank account. Over the course of the next year, we collected over $90,000—which is a hell of a lot of money."[8] That money went into an account bearing the new name of the company: Shakespeare Repertory Company, or as it would come to be known in shorthand, Shakespeare Rep.

The newly christened company also acquired a new place in which to perform: the Ruth Page Dance Center in Chicago's Gold Coast. Shakespeare Rep's first play in its new home was *Troilus and Cressida*, which premiered in October 1987. Like *Henry V* the year before, the production received many positive reviews. Slowly building momentum, the theater stuck to one production per year initially, staging *Antony and Cleopatra* in 1988, and *Cymbeline* in 1989. In a stroke of fate well suited to the preposterous divine interventions of the play itself, one of the people shut out of the packed house to see *Cymbeline* was Criss Henderson, who had just completed his studies in the Theatre School at DePaul University. Identifying him as the company's "entrepreneurial founding father—a visionary entrepreneur," Gaines lost no time securing him as managing director of Shakespeare Rep.[9] The partnership lasts to this day; Henderson remains at the helm of Chicago Shakespeare Theater as Executive Director.

Within the next five years, the company grew exponentially. First came a pair of two-play seasons: *King John* and *Much Ado About Nothing* in 1991, followed by *Pericles* and *Macbeth* in 1992. In the spring of 1992, Shakespeare Repertory launched "Team Shakespeare," its educational outreach program, which brought a new administrator on board: Marilyn Halperin, Director of Education and Communications. "The best thing I ever did was hire Marilyn," Criss Henderson declared. "We say that Marilyn was the first professional we ever hired; up to that point we just had a couple of kids in an apartment office—I was a kid myself," Henderson laughed.[10]

2. Greg Vinkler and Frank Nall in *King John* (1991), directed by Barbara Gaines. Photo by Jennifer Girard

At Henderson's suggestion, the company downsized back to a single production, *King Lear*, in 1993 in order to brace for the its next leap—to a three-play subscription series in 1993–1994. "We backed up in order to get a running start," Gaines explained. A crucial component of that running start was the performance of Richard Kneeland as King Lear. "I did summer stock with him and Rue McLanahan," Gaines recalled. "When we came to do *Lear*, I'd been following Richard's career but hadn't seen him in years. Miraculously, Richard said yes, and saved the theater's life—his performance was so spectacular."[11] Fans of *Slings and Arrows* know that importing a celebrated elder statesman to play the role of Lear doesn't always end happily. For Shakespeare Repertory, however, the production poised the company for critical and commercial success in its first three-play season, with *Cymbeline*, *The Taming of the Shrew*, and *Measure for Measure*. By 1995, the company had added an abridged production of *Romeo and Juliet* to its three-play season (*The Winter's Tale*, *Troilus and Cressida*, and *As You Like It*); in addition to performances at the Ruth Page, the abridgment toured schools throughout the state.

Before its tenth-anniversary season, the basic elements that would carry through from Shakespeare Repertory to Chicago Shakespeare Theater were all in place: three-play seasons on the main stage; robust educational programming, complemented by plays that catered to student audiences and to the unique demands of statewide touring; and visiting actors and directors of international renown, like Kneeland, and David Gilmore, who directed *As You Like It* in 1994. By its tenth-anniversary season in 1996, Shakespeare Repertory had become Chicago's third-largest nonprofit theater company.

"The nineties was a renaissance in Chicago with respect to arts and culture," Henderson reflected. "[Mayor] Daley's platform, [Richard] Christiansen and the power of the *Tribune*—probably more than any other city, in Chicago there was a disproportionately high number of people going to the theater. People attribute that cultural growth and success to the theaters, but it didn't come from us, actually. It came from the audience."[12]

"We grew so fast," Gaines mused. "We were probably the fastest-growing theater in America."[13] By the mid-1990s, Shakespeare Repertory was in fact expanding so rapidly that it was outgrowing its home at the Ruth Page Dance Center. The administrative offices outgrew the Ruth Page space first and moved to another location a few blocks away. Architectural plans and protracted negotiations with the City of Chicago and the Metropolitan Pier and Exposition Authority began in 1997, ultimately producing a set of agreements that allowed the theater to move to its current location on Navy Pier in 1999, taking on the new name of Chicago Shakespeare Theater. Like every other aspect of the theater's growth, the construction of the six-story theater on Navy Pier moved at lightning speed. The groundbreaking ceremony took place on September 29, 1998. In less than a year, the theater was occupied, with actors rehearsing *Antony and Cleopatra* in their spacious new rehearsal rooms, and administrative staff admonished to wear hard hats into the fifth-floor restrooms as construction crews put finishing touches on the fly system.

Much like the shift from a one-play season to a three-play season, Chicago Shakespeare Theater's move from cramped quarters at the Ruth Page Dance Center to its own six-floor, 75,000-square-foot purpose-built space on Navy Pier was a quantum leap. However, as Henderson observed, the les-

sons learned at Ruth Page served Chicago Shakespeare well when it moved
to its new home on the Pier:

> At Ruth Page we were presenting these works at a high level with such lim-
> ited resources. We developed "producorial" muscle. Once we had the ability
> to produce Shakespeare at that level, then anything we put the artistic enter-
> prise toward was coming out at that high quality, and was being supported.
> It didn't really matter who the playwright was, there was something Shake-
> spearean in the way we were making work. We were not rough-and-tumble.
> There is an aspiration here fueled by the theatrical standard of excellence
> that Shakespeare sets that has contributed to the work every day for the past
> twenty-five years.[14]

While it may not initially seem intuitive to see *Peter Pan* or Steven Sondheim's *Pacific Overtures* on the roster at Chicago *Shakespeare* Theater, the
theater's commitment to producing work that meets a "Shakespearean"
standard in terms of production values and aesthetic sensibilities renders
these choices coherent for the theater. "All of the work that we do—the children's programming, the musicals, the plays by other playwrights—all sits
comfortably together," Henderson explained.[15]

"International, children, Shakespeare—that is it," Gaines summed up
the theater's mission. "I'd close the theater before I'd cut the children's programming and the international work."[16] Children's programming is of vital
importance to Gaines and Henderson insofar as those children constitute
the theater audience of the future. When in July 2011 we discussed the theater's first twenty-five years, Chicago Shakespeare Theater had just begun
previews of its summer production, *Pinocchio*. "You see these kids—four,
five, six years old—and they are seeing their first theatrical production and
falling in love with theater," Gaines exclaimed.

In addition to family-friendly productions like *Pinocchio* (2011) or *Joseph
and the Amazing Technicolor Dreamcoat* (2000), overseen by Rick Boynton,
Creative Producer, in the summer months when many other Chicago theaters are dark, the theater also presents abbreviated versions of Shakespeare's
plays intended for family audiences during the regular theater season. Plays
in the "Short Shakespeare" series are designed to be family-friendly, with run
times of approximately seventy-five minutes.[17] A handful of Shakespeare's
plays logically lend themselves to the "Short Shakespeare" format and re-
cur much more frequently than shows typically return to the main stage.
Macbeth, The Comedy of Errors, and *The Taming of the Shrew* share the virtue of being relatively short plays, requiring fewer editorial interventions to

streamline than other plays in the Shakespeare canon. The tragedies *Macbeth* and *Romeo and Juliet* are frequently assigned texts in middle schools and high schools and therefore also appear routinely, creating a clear connection between preexisting lesson plans and the opportunity to bring a class to the theater for a field trip. However, each reiteration of a Short Shakespeare play involves a new production.

Education programming at the theater divides into three main areas, under the purview of Marilyn Halperin: the aforementioned "Short Shakespeare" productions each season catered to elementary, middle, and high school students; the wide range of support provided to teachers who bring their students to see productions of the plays; and "PreAmble" lectures offered before matinee performances of the main stage shows to general audiences by Chicago-area scholars. Area teachers are supported in three main ways by the theater's ambitious "Team Shakespeare" program launched in 1993: through the wealth of resources in the on-site Teacher Resource Center, through teaching guides and online resources prepared and published by the Education Program's staff, and through "Teacher Workshops" held on Saturdays just prior to the opening of each main stage and "Short Shakespeare" production. The workshops orient teachers to scholarly views of the play and how the production engages with that conversation, offer classroom exercises that can be used to engage students with the play and its language, and provide unique access to the rehearsal process for the production and the director's vision of the play. Chicago Shakespeare Theater offers teachers rare behind-the-scenes opportunities to survey the set and costume design plans, watch the actors in rehearsal, and meet the director for a discussion of the production.

Beth Charlebois, Associate Professor of English at St. Mary's College of Maryland, crafted the genre of the PreAmble lecture at Chicago Shakespeare Theater with the advice of Marilyn Halperin; Charlebois still trains the team of scholars who deliver these preshow talks to greater numbers of theatergoers each season. The thirty-minute lectures are designed to introduce theatergoers to significant aspects of the play and to highlight particular elements of the theater's production, all without "spoiling" surprising plot twists or arresting moments in the staging. "I think the best thing about the PreAmbles is that they give the audience not only a background on the play but a way of understanding the significance of the artistic choices that they are about to witness in performance—as choices that have implications," Charlebois contended.[18] While relevant historical context and issues of scholarly concern (such as the exploration of socially prescribed gender roles in *Twelfth Night* or *As You Like It*) do come in for consideration in the PreAmble format, the main emphasis of the lectures falls on production choices: sound design, costuming, lighting effects, period setting, and significant stage business.

Underscoring the extent to which PreAmbles are not meant to be purely didactic, Henderson stressed, "We didn't want people to have to prepare to come to the show; we're putting on shows for everyday people." He linked the inclusiveness of Chicago Shakespeare Theater's productions to its presence in the heart of Chicago's downtown tourism hub, noting "the good sense that we made of the theater at the center of Navy Pier: the people's theater on the people's pier inspired by the people's playwright. The audience is always part of the process from start to finish. Our goal is not to be revisionist, to show how smart we are in these texts; we're show people—like Shakespeare. I think we're structured differently than people realize. We're just show people putting on a play, like he was."[19]

Chicago Shakespeare Theater has played well on its home turf over the years, frequently nominated in numerous categories for the Joseph Jefferson Awards, one of the highest honors in the Chicago theater community. Moreover, an impressive number of those nominations have yielded awards. In 2011 alone Chicago Shakespeare Theater carted home seven awards, including the top honors for a production, *The Madness of George III*, which also earned the awards for director (Penny Metropulos) and principal actor (Harry Groenor). In the past decade, however, the theater has begun to earn accolades worldwide. Associate Artistic Director Gary Griffin's *Pacific Overtures* toured to London, where it received the 2004 Olivier Award for outstanding musical production. In 2008, Chicago Shakespeare Theater received the Regional Theatre Tony Award, a form of recognition that, paradoxically, renders a regional theater significant well beyond its region.

Chicago Shakespeare Theater has found all the world its stage even as it invites all the world to its stage. Henderson identified its World's Stage Series as "one of the great joys of my work here." For her part, Gaines noted, "I actually wrote into the first mission that we do international work, both touring our own work, and attracting it to us."[20] In 2006, Chicago Shakespeare Theater met the former objective when it took a remount of Gaines's celebrated 1999 production of the two parts of *Henry IV*, which had closed out the company's tenure at the Ruth Page Dance Center, to the Royal Shakespeare Company for its "Complete Works" season.

Meanwhile, Chicago Shakespeare Theater has met the second aspect of its international mission by consistently attracting work of the first order from around the world. "Because Shakespeare is the world's playwright it makes sense to look at the plays of the world, since they have all been shaped

3. Nathan Hosner, Mark D. Hines, and Harry Groener in *The Madness of George III* (2011), by Alan Bennett, directed by Penny Metropolus. Photo by Liz Lauren

or informed in some way by Shakespeare," Henderson reasoned.[21] In the past five years alone, Chicago audiences have been treated to a vibrant array of international productions: Tim Supple's *A Midsummer Night's Dream* (2008), featuring actors, dancers, martial arts experts, and street acrobats from India and Sri Lanka performing the play's text in equal parts English and the seven South Asian dialects native to the cast; *Farewell Umbrella* (*Au revoir parapluie*, 2007), during which an audience seated primarily on floor pillows breathlessly watched an acrobatic production designed by James Thiérrée, Charlie Chaplin's grandson; *Water Fools* (*Fous de bassin*, 2009), which transported the audience to bleachers set up on the easternmost edge of Navy Pier to watch members of Ilotopie (France) ride bicycles on the surface of the lake, occasionally accompanied by an overstuffed taxicab, horn blaring, and a towering bewigged and bejeweled opera singer reminiscent of Marie Antoinette, among other aquatic anomalies; and the National Theatre of Scotland's *Black Watch* (2011) staged at a former armory on the north side of Chicago, where new recruits played pool on a table that metamorphosed into a terrifying cross between the Trojan Horse and a clown car, as a knife sliced through its seemingly solid surface and an impossible number of lethal fighters spilled silently out.

Running through a list of some of his own favorite productions in the World's Stage Series, Henderson marveled, "To have the Comédie Française [Molière's *Le malade imaginaire*], to have the Abbey [*The Playboy of the Western World*] on our stage, Peter Brook's *Hamlet*—I can't help but think that the brick walls of this theater were seasoned by Brook's production."[22] Reflecting on the ghosts of Brook's production moved Henderson to think about the ghosts that inhabited the inaugural production of the twenty-fifth-anniversary season, Gary Griffin's production of Steven Sondheim's *Follies*: "All of those ghosts—I like to think that the spirits of all of the productions live here in a more positive way [than the fractious and troublemaking ghosts of Sondheim's play]—perhaps less scantily clad and with fewer feathers."[23]

4. In foreground, Archana Ramaswamy and P R Jijoy in Dash Arts' *A Midsummer Night's Dream* (2008), director Tim Supple. Photo by Tristram Kenton

5. Kaori Ito in *Farewell Umbrella (Au Revoir, Parapluie)* (2008), directed by James Thiérrée. Photo by Richard Haughton

"The most surprising thing to me is not looking back; it's looking forward—the idea that there is a permanence to what we built is never something that we were looking for. We didn't do any of the work that we did in search of permanence," Henderson concluded. "Now, I'm relatively confident that decades and decades and decades will go by and audiences will continue to have the opportunity to see the work that we do here. There is a DNA to the company; the worldview will change with the next leadership team, but the great storytelling will remain."[24]

IMAGINARY FORCES AT WORK

In its first twenty-five years, Chicago Shakespeare Theater not only has established itself as one of Chicago's premier cultural institutions but has garnered a reputation for excellence and innovation that extends across the world. Like Chicago, CST has gone global. In fact, Chicago Shakespeare Theater was the only American company to participate in the Globe to Globe 2012 festival at Shakespeare's Globe in London, a six-week-long event serving as a precursor to the 2012 London Cultural Olympiad, in which all of Shakespeare's thirty-seven plays will be presented, each by a separate international company and each in a different language. The selection of CST for this honor is an indicator not only of the theater's prestige but that its work is seen, from an international perspective, as representative of Shakespeare on the American stage and as distinguished in the English-speaking world. Twenty-five years after conjuring its first production on the "unworthy scaffold" of a rooftop of a pub in Chicago, Chicago Shakespeare Theater is again bringing its own swelling scene to Shakespeare's "wooden O."

Today, critics from across the globe carefully attend to what is happening on Navy Pier. Theater companies from around the world are eager to collaborate with CST. Celebrated directors and actors of international repute work frequently on its stage. What this volume seeks to do, however, is to look beyond accolades and the fruits of accomplishment, to trace the impact of the theater as a social, cultural, and artistic institution. Perched above the waters of Lake Michigan, the work of CST ripples outward. To follow its trajectories, we have gathered in this collection a variety of voices, from actors and critics to scholars and the public. Our hope is that by providing a broad perspective from which to evaluate and appreciate Chicago Shakespeare Theater, the pages of this collection might turn into an hourglass the accomplishment of many years.

In Part I of this volume, we look at some of the fundamental components that have shaped Chicago Shakespeare Theater. Terry Teachout, the drama

6. Ilotopie's *Water Fools (Fous de Bassin)* (2009). Photo by Klaus Tummers

critic for the *Wall Street Journal*, describes in "Chicago First" his initial encounter with CST, as well as subsequent experiences with the company. Tasked with covering the expansive landscape of American regional theater, Teachout, a New York–based critic, found his encounters with the work of CST transformative: "After my first few visits, I realized that what I was seeing was not just a theater company but a theatrical concept, a modern approach to the classics fully in accord with my own developing sense of what American regional theater at its best is all about."

Regina Buccola in her essay examines the formative influence upon this theatrical concept—Artistic Director, Barbara Gaines. In "Catapulting Shakespeare into the Present: The Artistic Vision of Barbara Gaines," Buccola follows Gaines's career from the founding of the first company in Chicago dedicated to performing the works of Shakespeare to leading the multifaceted theatrical institution that exists today. Gaines's directorial vision, which she describes as "humanist," is imprinted on the company in all its pursuits. In accord with this human-centered focus, Buccola explains, Gaines has always been attracted to Shakespeare's "problem plays"; the reasons she gives are very much in line with her deep sensitivity to the human condition: "I am interested in complexity, problems that can't be solved, the mystery inside of all of us." It is not surprising that as a result of such concerns a robust sense of community has emerged within the company, as well as the commitment to the larger community that is a hallmark of CST.

Jonathan Abarbanel, a critic and educator with an encyclopedic knowledge of theater in Chicago, has known Gaines since they were both teenagers and provides a playful look at Gaines's early years in the theater and beyond, in "Barbara, Shakespeare, and Me." Abarbanel has had a front-row seat to the evolution of CST from its founding days, and he has consistently remained an admirer. Gaines's approach to Shakespeare—pragmatic, down-to-earth—put the "Chicago" in Chicago Shakespeare Theater, Abarbanel notes, by shaking off stale conventions of performance while holding fast to the core integrity of the plays. He describes what was to him, accustomed as he had been to highly stylized "British" Shakespeare, the CST's revelatory approach to the language: "Make sense of the words *first* as expressions of character and intention, and the flow of the language will follow. And speak the speech, I pray you, as well-trained American actors (or Canadian actors, for that matter), not as well-trained American actors trying to sound British."

It is not only the principles and practices of theater artists that have shaped the plays performed by CST, according to Jonathan Walker, but the material theater itself. In "The Spatial Rhetoric of Chicago Shakespeare Theater,"

17

Walker applies the concept of "spatial rhetoric" to CST's main playing space, the Courtyard Theater, which he defines as the capacity to "construct dramatic meaning for their audiences not only through the delivery of dialogue, the blocking of actors, stage and costume design, and so on, but also through a calculated staging of space, which taps into a vocabulary of physical placement and juxtaposition to express both dramatic conflict and harmony, division and alliance, and detachment and intimacy among the characters who populate its stage." Analyzing several productions, Walker shows how the Courtyard's particular spatial configuration—a combined thrust and proscenium stage—has often been used by directors as an active component of productions.

A collection dedicated to Chicago Shakespeare Theater must acknowledge and examine the educational and outreach efforts that are central to its mission. Part II of this volume begins with Alicia Tomasian's account of Josie Rourke's 2009 *Twelfth Night*. Tomasian, a professor at a Chicago-area community college, found this production to be a provocative introduction to Shakespeare for her community-college students, and she reads Rourke's production through their responses to the play.

CST's commitment to its audience extends to nurturing new generations of playgoers through "Short Shakespeare!" a series that adapts Shakespeare's plays with younger viewers in mind. Since this endeavor is as idealistic as it is practical, CST eschews simplifying or popularizing the plays; rather, it insists that each production is a fully realized artistic work, ensuring that it is still Shakespeare that these audiences are getting. Like Tomasian, Jeffrey Gore finds at CST an appealing entrée into Shakespeare, in this case, for his own children. "Short Shakespeare! and the Corruption of the Young" relates Gore's experiences taking his daughters to see the 2008 *Romeo and Juliet*, directed by Amanda Dehnert. Impressed by the vivacity exhibited by the young audience during the Q&A session following, Gore reflected on the impact of CST's efforts to reach out past their subscription base: "This group of schoolchildren, who might normally be playing Nintendo or attending soccer practice on a Saturday morning, get to have an experience with their parents and schoolteachers, devoted actors, and everyone who is normally backstage holding together this messy 'conspiracy' of education, entertainment, and a thriving cultural enterprise. And a few of them just might get hooked and become fans and customers for life." Peter Sagal, National Public Radio personality, also reflects upon the efficacy of Short Shakespeare! in "Doing Things with Words . . . and, Sometimes, Swords." Sagal's experience teaching Shakespeare to seniors has made him realize that Shakespeare's work has at its heart a quality that appeals to young and old alike: "that is, as active, enacted depictions of human beings doing things. Shakespeare's genius, it seemed to me, was not so much his poetry as his sense of motivation, and how people acted upon one another." It is by distilling this essence that Short Shakespeare! manages to be both short and Shakespeare.

While Chicago Shakespeare Theater has been and remains very much an institution grounded in Chicago, a product of the city's rich theatrical tradition, CST frequently hosts guest artists from across the nation and the world. Part III explores the ways in which directors, actors, and playwrights have found this crucible to be a site of particular inspiration. Celebrated British thespian Simon Callow describes in "Chicago Shakespeare" the experience of stepping into the Courtyard: "When I did, I felt what every actor who has ever stood or worked in it must feel—an absolute rightness. The space holds you, it gives you focus and freedom. The energy lines converge with huge dynamic power, but at the same time, you're speaking to the audience as if they're in your front room." This sense of intimacy that fosters the establishment of direct relationships is one of the features often remarked upon by those who come to CST, either as actors or as audience. Such relationships are also cultivated backstage and behind the scenes. In "Chicago Shakespeare Theater and the Canadians," Richard Ouzounian, drama critic for the *Toronto Star*, chronicles the many dynamic alliances between theater artists from "up north" and CST. Such collaborations have proven to be a potent combination; as Ouzounian writes of Terry Hands's 2006 *Hamlet*: "Even though it had a Canadian lead and a British director, I think of it as the archetypal Chicago show: played with power, clarity and emotional honesty like you really don't see in any other city."

Collaboration is the issue at the crux of Gina Marie Di Salvo's essay, "The Framing of the Shrew." For its 2010 production, directed by Josie Rourke, CST commissioned the controversial, often inflammatory, playwright Neil LaBute, to refashion the Induction that frames the action of *Taming of the Shrew*. Di Salvo relates the very complex effect that this had on the production, both during the rehearsal process and once the play opened: "LaBute's script called for depicting the problematic story of Katherina's taming as conventionally as possible and used the frame to move the sexual politics out of the realm of traditional heterosexist hierarchies. Instead of representing the problem of widespread and ongoing societal misogyny, LaBute moved the conversation of *Shrew* into the realm of personal and particular abuses of power." In ways that echo Kate's resistance to Petruchio's efforts to "tame" her, the cast and audience pushed back against LaBute's interpolations, providing particularly apt responses to the provocative choices made by both the playwright and the theater.

Resistance to convention has always been a feature of the work of Michael Bogdanov, including his 2003 CST production of *The Winter's Tale*. While it has been customary for directors (and scholars) to try to find ways to fuse together the radically disparate halves of the play—the world of jealousy, re-crimination, and death that is found in Sicilia with the realm of amity, trust, and fertility found in Bohemia—Bogdanov refused facile compromise, according to Bradley Greenburg: "Bogdanov's approach to the play is to contrast the two sites and times of the drama as dual genre-specific spaces: Sicilia & tragedy, Bohemia & comedy. If he rejects the 'romance' label, he does so by attending to the play's paradox as a productive source for what is a realistic set of conflicts." Greenburg argues, in "Michael Bogdanov: An International Director's *The Winter's Tale* at Chicago Shakespeare Theater," that by allowing the two parts of the play to remain in tension with each other, the possibility for a final reconciliation emerges, not within the action of the play but following it, through the marriage of Perdita and Florizel, and that this choice accords with Bogdnaov's political approach to all of his work, which is ultimately not didactic but dialectical.

Taking chances, bucking conventions—these are also themes explored by Clark Hulse in "Risky Business: *Rose Rage* at Chicago Shakespeare Theater." Edward Hall's 2003 *Rose Rage*, a conflation of *Henry VI, Parts 1, 2*, and *3*, was an immensely ambitious and risky production, a massive, intricate narrative enacted within the confines of a virtual slaughterhouse, running the good part of a day, and featuring a meal during the break. Hulse catalogues the obstacles that Hall and CST were compelled to face:

> Would audiences be willing to commit six hours to the production, plus travel time to and from the theater? Would anybody want to sit down to a meal in the midst of the butchery and mayhem? Could the actors maintain the stamina and focus to put the show on four times a week? Could the set withstand a constant pounding with knives and staves, and would the stage floor—slippery with blood and offal—cause some horrible accident? And above all, would purists and innovators alike recognize and respond to a distinctive style that was a combustive mix of Shakespeare and Chicago?

In his essay, Hulse recounts how risk has been endemic to the *Henry VI* plays from their inception on the Elizabethan stage; but in detailing Hall's effort in the Studio Theater, he illustrates how and why CST has proven willing to embrace such risky endeavors.

When Michael Billington entered Chicago Shakespeare Theater in the summer of 2004, he found that the intimacy of the Courtyard reminded him of the Swan Theater, one of the Royal Shakespeare Company's playing spaces in Stratford. But the aura of familiarity was immediately dispelled by the production he had come to watch:

> what hit me most was the play itself: *King John* directed by Gaines with political urgency so that when Greg Vinkler's king wrapped himself in the flag to justify his military chauvinism, one was reminded less of a medieval English monarch than of George W. Bush. I couldn't quite believe that I was seeing one of Shakespeare's least-loved plays speaking so directly, in the course of a sold-out, ten-week run, to an audience that seemed like a cross-section of Chicago in its mix of middle-class Shakespeare buffs, blue-collar workers, and students.

Building on this experience, Billington, theater critic for *The Guardian*, argues in "In Defense of Ruffled Feathers" for the restoration of the entire Shakespearean canon on contemporary stages and the regular revival of those plays that most directly challenge our modern sensibilities, while noting that this is the standard practice of Chicago Shakespeare Theater, from which, he concludes, the rest of the theatrical world might learn a lesson. The accompanying essays in Part IV of the collection provide examples of these principles at work at CST.

In "'Never did young man fancy': *Troilus and Cressida* and Chicago Shakespeare Theater," Peter Kanelos recalls the three productions of *Troilus and Cressida* that the company has produced in its twenty-five-year history (1987, 1995, and 2007) and recounts how each influenced his own career and work. In fact, the very first play that the company produced in its original home, the Ruth Page Theater, was the very first play of Shakespeare that Kanelos had seen, and the experience proved seminal.

> When the Prologue emerged to introduce the play's action, I was immediately taken with the play. Something was happening in front of me, literally in front of me by a few feet. The drama penetrated the way films never had. This was a singular event, a happening in the here and now. There was something so utterly human, both vulnerable and powerful, that the machine-driven cinema could never replicate. And I was experiencing something quite transformative; not that I knew it then, nor have I ever really considered it until quite recently.

Looking back, Kanelos recounts how a single person, a single theater, and a single play can intersect dynamically over time.

In "At Home with Shakespeare: *Merry Wives* on Stage," Wendy Wall, like Kanelos, demonstrates how scholarship and performance can inform each other. Wall's research focuses on the representation of the domestic sphere on the early modern stage; she found that CST's 2004 production of *Merry Wives of Windsor*, through its design elements and staging, reflected the very themes that were at the center of her own work:

> social tensions come to light—the fraught economics of the marriage market; conflicts over who has the authority to settle local legal matters; class tensions between profligate noblemen and prudent citizens; and concerns about how people of varying national and ethnic backgrounds can unite to form a community. As the play's title insists, these tensions emerge—and are managed—through the lens of domesticity.

After a careful reading of the 2004 production, Wall ultimately concludes that its most profound effect was to make the spectators of the play collaborators in the staging of domesticity.

Michael Shapiro also finds in the productions of CST a prism through which to view subjects central to his own scholarly work. "Two *Merchants*: The Glow of the Roaring Twenties and the Shadow of 9/11" places the two *Merchants of Venice* that the company has staged, in 1997 and 2005, side by side. Shapiro argues that the terror attacks conducted against the United States on September 11, 2001, reverberated in the latter production: "The 1997 production, four years *before* 9/11, encapsulates anti-Semitic 1920s New York, a world characterized by naive frivolity and unaware of the Holocaust to come. The 2005 production, four years *after* the planes hit the Twin Towers and the Pentagon, not only reflects but addresses a world in which ethnic, political, and religious conflicts threaten to engulf us all." Shapiro's essay, in its astute and sensitive comparison of the two *Merchants*, shows us that the boundaries between the stage and the world are porous and ever-shifting.

Yet boundaries *on* stage are also porous and ever-shifting, as Wendy Doniger reminds us in "Gender Blending and Masquerade in *As You Like It* and *Twelfth Night*." Doniger contends, "Gender has a penchant for the theater, and the theater for gender," and, focusing on CST's 2009 *Twelfth Night* and 2011 *As You Like It*, she reads two of Shakespeare's virtuoso gender-contorting performances beside and against each other. Her conclusion is that although gender may be performative, and we can readily recognize its artificiality, we are still subject to its power: "*Twelfth Night* is more fantastic than *As You Like It*, more like *The Tempest*, but both are fantasies, and one should not look too closely at a fantasy. Or, perhaps, we should grant to the characters in the inner frame the same 'double pleasure' and 'conscious illusion' that we grant to ourselves, the right both to see through the trick and to be taken in by it." In the struggle between sober rationality and deeply embedded desires, Doniger suggests, the fantastical, both in life and on the stage, often carries the day.

As is evident from the scope of these collected essays, over its first twenty-five years Chicago Shakespeare Theater has brought new audiences to Shakespeare, invigorated audiences who had become settled in their expectations, provoked reflection, generated debate, and challenged orthodoxies, all while presenting on its stages work that has garnered worldwide acclaim. CST has always remained popular in focus, while insisting that its productions push the edges, aesthetically and conceptually. This compelling combination has served the company well and inspired its artists and its ever-expanding audiences and will most assuredly continue to do so through the next quarter of a century and beyond.

NOTES

1. Sid Smith, "Sounds of the City Fail to Spoil Robust Charm of 'King Henry V,'" *Chicago Tribune*, August 5, 1986.

2. William Shakespeare, *The Life of Henry the Fifth*, ed. Gary Taylor, in *The Oxford Shakespeare*, ed. Stanley Wells and Gary Taylor, 2nd ed. (Oxford: Oxford UP, 2005), Prologue, l.29–31.

3. Gaines won the 1975 Joseph Jefferson Award for best principal actress for her performance in Eugene Ionesco's *The Lesson* for the Orphans Theatre Company and appeared in the world premiere of Marisha Chamberlain's *Scheherazade* at Victory Gardens in 1984 with Aidan Quinn, under the direction of Dennis Zacek. The production earned Victory Gardens its first national honor, the FDG/CBS New Play Award.

4. Qtd. in Richard Christiansen, "'The Prologue and Stage 1, 1986–1990': CST at 20, 1986–2006," *Bill* (Autumn 2005): 17.

5. Barbara Gaines (Artistic Director, Chicago Shakespeare Theater), discussion with the author, July 13, 2011.

6. Ibid.

7. Ibid.

8. Ibid.

9. Ibid.

10. Criss Henderson (Executive Director, Chicago Shakespeare Theater), discussion with the author, December 2, 2011.

11. Gaines, discussion, 2011.

12. Henderson, discussion, 2011. Richard Christiansen is the former chief theater critic at the *Chicago Tribune*.

13. Gaines, discussion, 2011.

14. Henderson, discussion, 2011.

15. Ibid.

16. Gaines, discussion, 2011.

17. See the essays on the "Short Shakespeare!" series by Peter Sagal and Jeffrey Gore in this collection.

18. Beth Charlebois, e-mail message to author, December 7, 2011.

19. Henderson, discussion, 2011.
20. Ibid.; Gaines, discussion, 2011.
21. Henderson, discussion, 2011.
22. Ibid.
23. Ibid.
24. Ibid.

BIBLIOGRAPHY

Christiansen, Richard. "'The Prologue and Stage 1, 1986–1990': CST at 20, 1986–2006." *Bill* (Autumn 2005): 17.

Shakespeare, William. *The Life of Henry the Fifth*. Ed. Gary Taylor. *The Oxford Shakespeare*. Ed. Stanley Wells and Gary Taylor. 2nd ed. Oxford: Oxford UP, 2005.

Smith, Sid. "Sounds of the City Fail to Spoil Robust Charm of 'King Henry V.'" *Chicago Tribune*, August 5, 1986.

PART I

Chicago First

TERRY TEACHOUT

Unlike other Manhattan-based drama critics, I spend almost as much time on the road as I do in New York City. As well as reviewing plays on and off Broadway, I cover regional productions throughout America, and I've learned in the course of my travels that you needn't go to New York, or anywhere near it, to see a first-rate show. Most of this country's theatergoers, alas, don't know that. They reflexively assume that the most important shows are all on Broadway. So did I, until my editor at the *Wall Street Journal* suggested in the winter of 2004 that I might want to see for myself what regional theater was like. Little did I know that I was to become American theater's most frequent flyer, routinely jetting from Massachusetts to Oregon and back again without thinking twice.

It was pure luck that my first stop was Chicago, about whose thriving theater scene I then knew nothing whatsoever. Neither, to be sure, did most New Yorkers: *August: Osage County* had yet to burst upon Broadway in 2004, and my colleagues' awareness of the Chicago stage began and ended with Steppenwolf and the Goodman. The only reason I picked Chicago was that my best friend lived there, and the only reason I picked Chicago Shakespeare Theater was because it was simultaneously mounting a pair of shows—Edward Hall's *Rose Rage* and a revival of *A Little Night Music*—that sounded promising. It never occurred to me when I booked press seats for those two shows that I was about to hit the jackpot, much less that I was destined to return to Chicago's Navy Pier again and again, irresistibly drawn by the work of a company that I have come not merely to esteem but to love.

After my first few visits, I realized that what I was seeing was not just a theater company but a theatrical concept, a modern approach to the classics fully in accord with my own developing sense of what American regional theater at its best is all about. In retrospect, the turning point was Barbara Gaines's 2007 production of *Troilus and Cressida*, to which I responded with the electric enthusiasm that makes a critic's life worth living:

> This is a wartime *Troilus* with a hard political edge—the main set piece is a blood-soaked obelisk reminiscent of the Washington Monument—but Ms. Gaines has taken care not to wear her opinions on her sleeve. Instead, she lets Shakespeare do the talking: "And appetite, an universal wolf, / So doubly seconded with will and power, / Must make perforce an universal prey, / And last eat up himself." You're more than welcome to draw parallels with the war in Iraq if you wish, but it's no less acceptable to approach Ms. Gaines' *Troilus* as a broader parable of man's monstrosity to man. That's where the battle scene comes in. Imagine a dark, empty space filled with mist and lit from below with lurid shafts of light that slice through the fog of war to show us pairs of desperate men locked in mortal combat. You can almost smell the blood—and the fear. . . .
>
> I see a lot of Shakespeare, both in New York and across the country, and the more I see, the more impressed I am by Chicago Shakespeare Theater. Its productions are smart yet accessible, personal yet universal and—above all—consummately theatrical. I can't think of a Shakespeare troupe in America with a higher batting average, and this production of *Troilus and Cressida* will surely be remembered as one of its signal achievements.[1]

That production opened my eyes to the nature of Barbara Gaines's special gift as a director: she is, in the very best sense of the word, a populist, a true believer in the power of the classics to speak directly to contemporary audiences when staged with sharp immediacy and infectious gusto. She is also sure enough of her own talents to make room for equally talented colleagues, and it says much about her generous, enlightened artistic leadership that so many of Chicago Shakespeare's finest productions should be the work of other hands. The best *Follies* I've ever seen, for instance, was the one that Gary Griffin staged there in the fall of 2011 (and how many classical companies, by the way, can claim to do fully as well by Stephen Sondheim as they do by William Shakespeare?).

That said, it is Barbara's shows of which I think first when I think of Chicago Shakespeare, and it is her tough-minded 2005 *Merchant of Venice* that stands out most boldly in my memory.

> Played in modern dress and set in a black-walled rehearsal hall, Ms. Gaines' *Merchant* grapples head-on with the chief problem the play poses for today's audiences, which is that Shakespeare's portrayal of Shylock is widely felt to be openly (if not merely) anti-Semitic. It does so by underlining every reference to Shylock's Jewishness, to the point where the incessant repetition of the word "Jew" shrieks as shrilly as fingernails on a chalkboard. Not that the man himself is spared: Mike Nussbaum plays Shylock as a smug semi-gentleman in a three-piece suit whose elegant cut cannot conceal his raging bloodlust. Yet the more savagely he is treated by the other characters—to the point of being beaten and spat upon in a dark alley—the more intelligible his hateful longings start to seem.[2]

Many Shakespeare productions have moved me, and not a few have thrilled me, but I don't know another one that has *taught* me more about a play I thought I knew well. That, too, is part of Barbara's rich legacy to her fortunate audiences: she is a great teacher whose classroom is the stage. Yet of all the priceless lessons I've learned in the house that Barbara Gaines built, the one I treasure most was the very first one she taught me, which is that great American theater doesn't stop on the banks of the Hudson River. More and more, that's where it starts.

NOTES

1. Terry Teachout, "Tough Nut, Sweet Meat," *Wall Street Journal*, May 18, 2007.
2. Terry Teachout, "Above and Beyond," *Wall Street Journal*, September 30, 2005.

Catapulting Shakespeare into the Present

The Artistic Vision of Barbara Gaines

REGINA BUCCOLA

In 1986, Barbara Gaines made a decision that would prove momentous for her, for the Chicago theater community, and for Shakespearean theater worldwide—she decided that Chicago needed a theater devoted to Shakespearean productions. Chicago had a strong tradition of supporting classical arts through institutions such as the Art Institute, the Lyric Opera, and the Chicago Symphony Orchestra, and a clear appetite for more, evinced by the successful relocation of the Joffrey Ballet to Chicago from New York City in 1995. Gaines, however, noticed shortly after her own relocation to Chicago from New York that few Chicago theaters routinely performed Shakespeare plays. Then, as now, Shakespeare appeared in periodic rotation in the seasons of major theaters, such as the Goodman and the Court, or smaller companies, like the Shattered Globe Theatre. Storefront theaters, such as Stage Left, could strategically anchor adventurous theater seasons with Shakespearean plays, audience draws for which the company did not have to pay royalties. But no theater company focused on staging Shakespeare for the Chicago theatergoing audience.

Shakespeare in Chicago seemed a logical choice for Gaines, who finds Shakespeare a playwright that consistently takes the measure of humanity, and Chicago "a human city"; as Gaines declared in a recent interview,

Chicago "is not a cold place. The flesh and blood and nerve endings of the city are very close to the surface; there is a lot of cement in New York City. There is a lot of sky and water and flowers in Chicago—there is less armor to get through."[1] Gaines had found her niche, and she set about filling it.

HUMANIST SHAKESPEARE

During its formative years, the fledgling company, then known as Shakespeare Repertory, presented exclusively Shakespeare's works at the Ruth Page Theater, home to a dance school. Now that the company has been rechristened and taken up residence in its own theater, non-Shakespearean works are often staged, but directors other than Gaines typically oversee these productions. For the twenty-fifth-anniversary season, Gaines shifted gears to direct a non-Shakespearean play (Timothy Findley's *Elizabeth Rex*) featuring Shakespeare as a character. Even when Gaines ventures into other theatrical forms, in other venues, as she did in 2010 with Verdi's *Macbeth* at the Lyric Opera of Chicago, Shakespeare's work has constituted her jumping-off point.

Despite her career-long devotion to Shakespeare's plays, Gaines is not a purist. Discussing her twenty-fifth-anniversary season production of *Timon of Athens*, Gaines bluntly announced: "I've changed the end—I often make a prologue or an epilogue in my productions—no added words, but it's still very powerful."[2] So, for example, the prologue for Gaines's 2009 production of *Richard III* consisted of the central characters of the House of York posing for a family portrait. As an opening bit of stage business, the family portrait provided the audience a crucial visual introduction to many of the significant characters in the devious plots of the title character, upon whose hunched back the entire plot of the play rests. Significantly too, they posed for their portrait on a staircase, with Richard, the heir-aspirant, perched at the very top. Below Richard were assembled the other claimants to the throne, along with his sundry relatives, most of whom would be dead, many by Richard's own machinations, by the play's end.

Gaines's 2004 production of *King John* concluded with a similar gesture: after the slow death spiral of John's disastrous reign ended along with his life, a janitor sauntered onto the stage to remove a defaced poster of King John, replacing it with an image of Prince Henry designed to the exact same specifications, ruefully suggesting that the new regime would, like its promo pieces, mirror the one that preceded it.[3] Even when directing a non-Shakespearean play, such as Timothy Findley's *Elizabeth Rex*, Gaines uses strategically designed prologues to literally set the stage for her production. Gaines cut Findley's frame, set on the night of Shakespeare's death when he recalls the night-long vigil he kept with Elizabeth I prior to the Ash Wednesday 1601 execution of the Earl of Essex. Instead, Gaines's production began with a bit of the final scene of the play Findley imagines the Lord Chamberlain's Men to have performed before Elizabeth on this grim occasion, *Much Ado About Nothing*. Gaines chose to show the Queen watching the final scene, in which Beatrice and Benedict admit their love for each other. Confessions of love loom large in the plot of Findley's play, so this scene prepared the audience for the politically freighted emotional confessions to follow. Such action-based prologues or epilogues to Gaines's productions typically reinforce her interpretation of the text.

David Brailow's review of the 2004 production of *King John* captures another of Gaines's predominant directorial instincts with respect to the structure of Shakespeare's texts: the opportunities they afford for intercutting scenes. When the theater opened on Navy Pier in 1999, Gaines described what a revelation it was to direct in a thrust-stage space, with opportunities for actors to enter from any position upstage, from above, from below, and through the aisles dividing the seating in the main house into three "wedges," one directly downstage, one stage right, and one stage left.[4] It is possible for one huddle of actors to complete their scene upstage right, as another group sweeps into position downstage left and begins their exchange as the upstage actors silently disappear backstage. The pace of the action increases dramatically under such direction, a distinct asset in the tragedies and histories, with plots that often hinge on building and maintaining suspense.

In the case of the 2004 production of *King John*, Gaines not only intercut scenes but also rearranged and layered lines within scenes to suggest the media frenzy of contemporary sound-bite political culture. As David G. Brailow noted in his review:

> 2.1 was framed as a full-fledged political campaign, with King Philip and King John debating at podiums before a fully lit house, the audience standing in for the citizens of Angiers. The speeches of the two Kings were edited and intercut, so that, for example, when France brought Arthur downstage and offered to go home if Angiers accepted him as king, John quickly returned to his podium to interject "Which trust accordingly" into his microphone. As they grew more strident, they spoke simultaneously, each trying to drown the other out.
>
> The Bastard and Constance acted as a contrasting pair to enliven and deconstruct the elaborate show unfolding before us. . . . . Every twist and

7. *King John* (2004) directed by Barbara Gaines, with scenic design by Alexander Dodge. Photo by Liz Lauren

> turn of the politicians evoked a sarcastic comment from the Bastard and a passionate response from Constance, rooted in her undisguised ambition and love for her son.[5]

The production thus showcased Gaines's persistent attraction to the seamy underbelly of the political world: the feral teeth behind the saccharine smiles, the manipulation inherent in the rhetorical flourish, the corrupt desire for power over others that taints the claims of desire to serve others.

Although she was a theater major at Northwestern University in Evanston, Illinois, Gaines recalls:

> I took some really great political science courses at Northwestern—they were my favorite classes. I am tremendously oversensitive to what happens in the world. It affects me in a way that isn't healthy for me. . . . When I was in Czechoslovakia in 1989, I saw Russian tanks, I saw people—including children—with such sad eyes. I thought of *King John*: "If law can do no right . . .

let it be lawful that law itself is perfect wrong." I did my first *King John* with barbed wire, and Russian words graffitied on the walls.[6]

Gaines's productions thus engage in dialogue with the world around her, representing her impressions of and responses to that world. Asked whether she designs her productions to fit the times or chooses the plays in concert with sociopolitical events from the start, Gaines replies, "Anything can set me off—it can be something in the newspaper, a painting, a dynamic between two people. I am here in the present, and the present catapults me into these shows."[7]

Gaines has tackled with gusto Shakespearean works that are seldom staged, either because they have not been popular with mainstream audiences or because they are perceived as too difficult, complex, or muddled. Gaines's first move, once she decided that Chicago needed a Shakespeare theater, was to mount *Henry V* on the roof of the Red Lion Pub, with rowdy patrons crammed into bleacher seating to watch. A pub-rooftop premiere meant the show was liable to be canceled by the city's notoriously fickle weather, exuberant actors were liable to pitch headlong into a street or alleyway below, and the hard-fought Battle of Agincourt was liable to leave the pub—or Gaines herself—liable for injuries to the patrons, who sometimes witnessed the deaths of soldiers at alarming proximity. *Henry V* is by no means one of Shakespeare's more obscure plays, but neither is it a "standard," like *Hamlet* or *Romeo and Juliet*. In the retrospective conversation that we had about her first quarter century at the helm of Chicago Shakespeare Theater, Gaines recounted going to visit her parents in Florida after *Henry V* closed to wild acclaim. They asked what she planned to do next, recommending "a show that everyone's heard of," instead. Gaines pointed out that she went with "*Troilus and Cressida*, which no one has heard of. One of the reviewers called it 'Toyota and Cressida.' That turned out to be a smart decision, but I didn't do it because it was smart—it's one of my favorite plays. When you're an artist, you follow your soul."[8]

Gaines admits to being a somewhat troubled soul, profoundly moved by the senseless violence, social inequality, and disintegration of community that are fixed features in the modern world. "In many ways I can be a depressive," Gaines muses. "I think the world can be a cruel, dark place, but I think there is warmth in Shakespeare's work, and it can soften us."[9] The operative word in Gaines's assessment is "can." Many of her productions leap directly into the battleground staked out by New Historicist critics of Shakespeare's texts at the end of the twentieth century such as Stephen Greenblatt and Stephen Orgel, who fiercely debated whether the plays—particularly the histories and "problem plays"—offer subversive social commentary, or whether these plays' theatrical depictions of social subversion are meant to serve a cathartic function for viewing audiences.[10] In such formulations, the play's more turbulent moments are smoothed over in the memories of the audience by the changing of the guard; the final speeches of Henry VII in *Richard III* or of Malcolm in *Macbeth* are read as wake-up calls from the nightmarish chaos the play has explored. However, those Gainesian epilogues at Chicago Shakespeare Theater typically serve the function of unsettling the foundations of whatever order has been (re-) established in the final scene.

So, for instance, the war(s) against terror catapulted Gaines into her 2007 production of *Troilus and Cressida*, which was bookended with stunning stage pictures that reminded viewers of the soldiers engaged in battle in Iraq and Afghanistan at the time, as well as soldiers of other times, and other wars. *Shakespeare Bulletin* reviewer Paul Hecht compellingly described the production's haunting prologue and epilogue:

> a huge sheet of gauzy fabric billowed out, hanging from the proscenium and extending to the end of the platform; fog machines were turned on high, eerie music played, and one by one, dead, whitened, stiff warriors strode out of the darkness and through the gauze toward the audience, first a trickle, and by the end a crowd. That these were soldiers not just from the Trojan War was indicated by the occasional American WWII-style helmet—war dead of the ages, then. That seemed a perfectly weighted reminder of our own current slow-burn war, of the ceaseless stream of soldiers sent down into darkness. The play ended with the same motif: this time the dead carried out the billowing fabric themselves, and covered and enveloped the cursing, coughing Pandarus and, as it were, swept the whole play back into oblivion.[11]

Returning to the play with the results of the United States' ill-fated effort to "shock and awe" Iraq into submission still unfolding inexorably with a daily accruing body count, Gaines looked at *Troilus and Cressida* anew and saw even the Greeks' bold siege of Troy, mounted by a vast fleet of a thousand ships, as an ancient attempt to "shock and awe" the Trojans into returning the abducted Helen to her husband, which likewise failed miserably, leading to the appalling destruction of Greeks, of Trojans, of Troy itself. "That's the other reason to do Shakespeare," Gaines explains. "He is constantly evolving as you evolve. I've directed some shows three times, but when I go back to them, I find new things in them, because I'm not the person I was when I directed it before."[12]

Gaines has returned to *Troilus and Cressida* twice since first offering it to Chicago audiences in 1987. The play came back into favor with theater companies in the early part of the twenty-first century in productions clearly influenced by the Crimean War, World Wars I and II, the Vietnam War, and the Persian Gulf War(s), the wartime resonance of the play clearly providing a reason for its more frequent appearance onstage.[13] The recurrence of war in eastern Europe and the Middle East over the course of the twenty-five years that Gaines has been directing Shakespeare in Chicago has repeatedly driven her back to the cold brutality of *Troilus and Cressida*, in which war heroes are murdered by gangs of vengeful thugs, and women are traded and treated like chattel.

Famously, Shakespeare does not show his audience the Trojan horse, but he does show us Helen; it is a challenge to present onstage the "face that launched a thousand ships" as Shakespeare's theatrical rival Christopher Marlowe put it.[14] Therefore, many directors refuse to even suggest that she is worthy of the attention and, like Barbara Gaines in her 2007 production, depict her as appallingly trashy and cheap, heightening the senseless nature of the conflict.[15] Gaines's 2007 Helen, Mary Kay Cook, subtly channeled a slightly drunken Marilyn Monroe.

Michael Merritt collaborated with Gaines on her 1987 production of *Troilus and Cressida*. Gaines recalled her conversation with Merritt about the stage entrance of Helen. She told him:

> "This is a major moment. Thousands of men were dying during the eleven years of this war for this babe. The moment needs to be sensual and unforgettable." It took Michael all of a few seconds to come up with the idea that to this day people still remember. Across the entire upstage wall of the theatre hung a 20 x 30 foot royal blue scrim. From the distance the audience saw someone take up the bottom of the scrim, a follow spot from upstage hits this blond wild head of hair and perfect body dressed in a white satin gown. She holds the cloth over her head and as she walks downstage it floats down behind her as she carries it towards the audience. Erotic, simple and inexpensive. Theatre at its most dynamic.[16]

Though Gaines now has enviable resources at her disposal for realizing dynamic productions, the early days were much leaner. Gaines considers herself "really lucky—the early designers were so dedicated. They made very little money, as did the actors. Everybody sacrificed so that Chicago could have a Shakespeare Theater."[17]

Paradoxically, the designers who worked on Gaines's 2007 production of *Troilus and Cressida* used their expanded resources to create a war-ravaged set and tattered costumes. Shakespeare's play brings us into the action in medias res, seven years into the war, as the Greek army's morale is sinking and various military leaders in both camps are beginning to absent themselves from battle. The set for Gaines's 2007 production, designed by her frequent collaborator Michael Philippi, conveyed this sense of battle fatigue.[18] The stage floor looked weathered, and it tilted at crazy angles upstage; there was a gigantic, phallic tower stage right, surrounded by scaffolding. Clearly, the war had taken a toll on Troy's infrastructure. The costumes for Helen and Cressida, designed by Nan Cibula-Jenkins, were beautiful, but the fabric was distressed, and soiled around the ankle line. A personification of the physical degradations of war, from trench foot to syphilis, Gaines's Thersites, Ross Lehman, was a creature of rags and patches who seemed to be held together by nothing more than his own sense of outrage and the blood and mucus oozing from the open sores all over his body.

The dynamic that seems to compel Gaines the most is the power dynamic, whether that be the conflict between two rival political powers, the conflict inherent in any attempt to resolve a love triangle into a pair, or power dynamics within relationships that have wider implications, such as Paris's cuckolding of Menelaus. Often, Gaines's production choices telegraph the ways in which centuries of Shakespeare audiences have failed to learn from the plays, highlighting the human tendency to keep making the same mistakes over and over again. In her 2007 production of *Troilus and Cressida*, the titular couple consummated their love on the same bedding used by Paris and Helen. Moreover, Stephen Ouimette's Pandarus voyeuristically ogled both couples, underscoring the common thread in these romances, the savage response these men would have to even the threat of losing "their" woman.

THE WOMAN'S PART

As a feminist performance studies scholar, I often find Gaines's casting and directorial choices to contain powerful, pointed, politicized representations of the female characters, their relationships to the male characters, and their place within the world of the play. Her choices with respect to Cressida and Helen of Troy in 2007's *Troilus and Cressida* offered clear examples of this effect.

Cousin battles cousin in *Troilus and Cressida*, in a conflict that can seem almost arbitrary; when the Trojan Paris—whose theft of Helen occasioned the entire fray—escorts the Greek Diomedes to transfer his brother's beloved

Cressida to the Greeks, he dismisses the sacrifice with: "There is no help: / The bitter disposition of the time / Will have it so," then asks Diomedes, "Who in your thoughts deserves fair Helen best, / Myself or Menelaus?"[19] The shameless hypocrisy inherent in Paris's blithe assertion that the "bitter disposition of the time"—occasioned by his theft of Helen and his refusal to relinquish her to her husband—makes it necessary for his own brother Troilus to surrender *his* beloved to the Greeks was brought to harsh life at Chicago Shakespeare Theater. Diomedes acerbically responded to Paris's comparison of himself and Menelaus, refusing to damn with even the faintest praise, as he witheringly responded: "Both merits poised, each weighs nor less nor more, / But he as he, the heavier for a whore" (4.1.67–68).

No sooner did Gaines's Diomedes (Andrew Rothenberg) take custody of Cressida than he set out to render her a whore as well. The leering Greeks passed Cressida (Chaon Cross) around, heaping lascivious compliments on her as they pawed and fondled her; she was, in essence, gang-raped the moment she entered the Greek camp.[20] Cross played Cressida with compelling nuance, however, leaving ambiguous whether she was a victim of circumstance, who turned to Diomedes for protection in a military camp where she was manhandled from the moment she arrived, or if she was, as Ulysses would have it, a perfect match to Helen in whoredom, as "daughters of the game" (4.6.64). Scholars such as Anthony Dawson have noted the deliberate parallels that Shakespeare constructs between the two women in the play: "both are tokens of war; they each change sides, Helen the Greek is given to [or taken by] a Trojan, Cressida the Trojan is traded to the Greeks. Each takes a new lover in her new environment, though exactly how willingly is not clear. Each is an object of desire, and, precisely because of her desirability, each becomes a 'theme of honour and renown'—an incentive to battle."[21]

Gaines's staging emphasized the interconnections between sexualized politics and politicized sex in the play. Gaines set Cressida's meeting with Diomedes, in which she throws over Troilus for the Greek warrior, on the same mat used in the wrestling match between Ajax and Hector, underscoring the extent to which both encounters feature a Trojan grappling with a Greek. Moreover, Gaines concluded both pairs of meetings on the wrestling mat with an embrace. As Dawson notes, the Greek and Trojan men think that they are fighting "for" women, "over" Helen and Cressida, but notably, the women in the play fight against war. Andromache and Cassandra struggle to prevent Hector from engaging in the battle that both know will prove fatal (5.3.1–93). In his review of the production, Paul Hecht noted the stunning sound effect that accompanied Cassandra's maddened grief in Gaines's production: "a scream in reverse that crescendoed up to an actual scream by

Cassandra."[22] And yet, when asked, in the light of her compelling portrayals of Shakespeare's female characters, if she considers herself a feminist, Gaines demurs, self-identifying instead as a "humanist."[23]

That may be, but the plays to which Gaines has been repeatedly drawn over the course of her career and her productions of them offer much with which feminist Shakespeare scholars such as Wendy Wall, Frances Dolan, and I can grapple. Gaines expresses frank delight that one of the first pieces of theater that some of the thousands of Chicago-area students who attend matinee productions at Chicago Shakespeare Theater each year have ever encountered is *Troilus and Cressida*, and that they have been "completely engaged and overwhelmed" by the force of the play's social critique. "That's the play that I'd like to take to every country and to every world leader," Gaines avers, adding, "I am interested in complexity, problems that can't be solved, the mystery inside of all of us. I've been thinking a lot lately about doing *Measure for Measure* again, and *All's Well*."[24] "Problem plays" like *Troilus and Cressida*, and "problem comedies" like *Measure for Measure* and *All's Well That Ends Well*, with their sordid bed-trick entrapments and queasy depictions of headstrong young men champing at the bit to go to war, are problems with which Gaines enjoys grappling, thereby compelling her audience to grapple.

The signature Gaines prologue and epilogue opened and closed her 2000 production of *All's Well That Ends Well*. The production began with the funeral of Bertram's father, the Count of Roussillon, an event that has already occurred when the action of the play proper begins. The somber opening took its cue from the first scene of Shakespeare's play. In it, the widowed Countess is bidding farewell to her son, who is being sent as a ward to the King of France, and Helena is bidding farewell to the companion of her youth, with whom she has fallen in love, having recently lost her own father. Snow fell softly on the scene; the setting altered over the course of the production to suggest the change of the seasons and the passage of a year. In the production's epilogue, snow fell once again outside of the upstage windows, as the assembled courtiers waltzed. In a moment reminiscent of the final wistful scene in *The Graduate*, when Benjamin Braddock (Dustin Hoffman) and Elaine Robinson (Katharine Ross) sit mutely in growing consternation in the rear of a bus after jubilantly fleeing her marriage to another man, the reunited Bertram and Helena whirled through a ballroom full of joyful dancers to a standstill center stage, looking at each other, silently taking the full measure of all that had passed between them already and the long road that stretched ahead of them.

Chicago theater critic Lawrence Bommer described *All's Well That Ends Well*, which rounded out the inaugural season on Navy Pier, as an "alleged comedy" and "a misanthropic fairy tale"; however, he found that Gaines's

8. Cast of *All's Well that Ends Well* (2000), with Bertram (Timothy Gregory) kneeling before a visibly pregnant Helena (Lia D. Mortensen), directed by Barbara Gaines. Photo by Michael Brosilow

"redemptive staging recalls Francois Truffaut's *The Story of Adele H*, another tale of a haunted woman who lost her heart (and mind) to an unregenerate soldier. Somehow this production makes Helena's misery matter."[25] In discussing the play, Gaines conveyed her sense both of the way that the male-dominated world depicted in the play circumscribes the choices of Helena and the other female characters and of the ways in which Helena's choices prove deleterious for her. "Women have no power at all in the world of this play," Gaines noted. "The fact that women take control over the bed trick as a response to male dominance is, for me, not a bad thing. . . . I like the way Shakespeare uses the convention [the bed trick], both in this play and in *Measure for Measure*, because his women find a way to expose the males' duplicity. But to be entirely fair, the women have been duplicitous, too."[26]

Gaines's keen interest in the complexity of the female characters in another of her favorite plays, *Measure for Measure*, was readily apparent to reviewers of her 2005 production. Writing for the *Shakespeare Bulletin*, Harvey Young noted:

Contrary to expectations, the brothel scene helped to maintain the theme of female independence that Gaines consistently developed throughout the play. The onstage prostitutes, who performed a series of simulated sex acts and repeatedly yawned throughout each of them, gave the impression that they did not derive any enjoyment from their job. This was work, nothing more. Mistress Overdone was big and bawdy. In her interactions with assembled audience members, she repeatedly bullied married men—urging them to leave their wives and to select a prostitute of their choosing. Over and over again, the embarrassed spectators, stunned into silence, would wait powerlessly until Mistress Overdone decided to move on to another victim. In the other scenes, this theme of female independence chiefly appeared in Dana Green's characterization of Isabella as a brash, powerful, and self-involved woman.[27]

Emphasizing Isabella's self-possession and verve certainly bolsters the critique of patriarchal hegemony in *Measure for Measure*, which divides its settings among a prison visited by a faux friar, the world of the brothel, and the world of a corrupt court where sexual negotiations worthy of the brothel are falsely promised as a get-out-of-jail-free card.

Significantly, the lone comedy not classed as a "problem play" that keeps Gaines coming back for more is *The Merry Wives of Windsor*, the only Shakespearean comedy that foregrounds and celebrates its female characters from the title straight through to Act 5. Gaines recounts: "One day, Michael Boyd, Artistic Director at the Royal Shakespeare Company, was here and we were talking about shows that we liked, and he asked if I do any comedies. I said that I hoped I matured enough to be able to do the comedies. One of my favorite plays is one that most people like the least—*Merry Wives of Windsor*—because it's about community."[28] Specifically, *The Merry Wives of Windsor* is about a community with women at its heart—the witty and wise merry wives of the title responsible for the maintenance of social and marital order; the gossipy governess of domestic affairs, Mistress Quickly; and the self-actualized Anne Page, who forges her own path into her own future family.[29]

However, it is not only instances in which Gaines depicts female characters as "brash" and "powerful" that call attention to her directorial vision of them; sometimes it is her decision to depict them at all. Consider Gaines's *Richard III*, the first play of the 2009–2010 season. Writing during the reign of a powerful female monarch, Elizabeth I, Shakespeare, significantly, placed a trio of women at the center of his version of a well-known story of bloody civil conflict based in political competition that could just as easily have been a testosterone-fest. These three women are Margaret of

9. Felicia P. Fields and Kevin Gudahl in *Measure for Measure* (2005), directed by Barbara Gaines. Photo by Liz Lauren

Anjou, the widowed queen of Henry VI; Queen Elizabeth, almost immediately widowed herself when King Edward IV dies in the play's second act; and Queen Anne, widowed in the action of *3 Henry VI* before she could become the Lancastrian queen of Henry's son, Edward. Dismissed by Richard as a "foul wrinkled witch" (*Richard III*, 1.3.164), Margaret was played in Gaines's production by Jennifer Harmon as a wild-haired, white-faced embodiment of collateral damage. Costume designer Susan Mickey placed Margaret in tattered clothing that served to remind the audience that the banished former queen was, effectively, a homeless woman. Mickey delivered her first lines standing in the center aisle of the main floor seating in a voice as ragged as her clothes, a monarchal Miss Havisham frozen at the moment she lost king/husband, prince/son, and kingdom.

Margaret serves as a sort of Chorus figure, who keeps reminding the audience of what has happened, and foretelling events to come.[30] The authority with which Margaret delivers horrific prophecies that come inexorably true links her to the spirit world that plays a prominent role in Shakespeare's play, as it did in Gaines's production, which was repeatedly haunted by ghosts of the recently dead.[31] Gaines said of the women in the play:

> Even though not one of them is flawless, the women are, for me, the soul of the play. They are the observers and the witnesses of carnage. Their entire lives have been lived through the lens of this hundred-year war—and it has made them tough. They are articulate and, in some ways, fearless—and they are tied together by their hatred for Richard. Because they have no political power, the women are afforded a wisdom and see things that the men do not. It is the women who witness and acknowledge that violence begets more violence, generation after generation.[32]

And yet, these very women are often cut from productions, a trend that began in the eighteenth century, with the tender revisionary ministrations of the celebrated Shakespearean impresarios David Garrick and Colley Cibber. Cibber cut Margaret entirely, an impulse followed centuries later by Laurence Olivier in a 1944 theatrical production of *Richard III* famously reprised ten years later in his third Shakespearean film.

Predictably, perhaps, Olivier sharply cut the women's roles in order to focus attention on Richard himself, whom he portrayed; thus, he eliminated Margaret entirely, and Anne's and the Duchess of York's lines were severely curtailed. Richard Loncraine took the same course a half century later in his mid-1990s film version of *Richard III*, which envisions Richard as a fascist sporting a Hitler mustache, whose speech accepting the mantle of king is suggestive of the Nuremberg rally. No Margaret once again, though some of her more spectacular curses of Richard were put in the mouth of Annette Bening, as Queen Elizabeth.[33] Historically, Margaret was not present in the Yorkist court of Edward IV and Richard III; Shakespeare's decision to place her anachronistically there in the role of Cursemaster General compellingly complicates the male dominance of the royal line during the Wars of the Roses, a complexity fruitfully explored in Gaines's production.

THE CHICAGO SHAKESPEARE THEATER COMMUNITY

When Gaines says of Shakespeare, "He's the closest thing to life itself that humanity has; most of us spend our lives trying to figure out who we are and what it's all about, and Shakespeare is the greatest single source of human understanding that we have—what your own humanity, personally, can mean to you," one could be forgiven for hearing echoes of Harold Bloom. In the prologue to his book that made the audacious titular claim that Shakespeare invented the human, Bloom opined, "Bardolatry, the worship of Shakespeare, ought to be even more a secular religion than it already is. The plays remain the outward limit of human achievement: aesthetically, cognitively, in certain ways morally, even spiritually. . . . Shakespeare will go on explaining us, in part because he invented us."[34] While Gaines may not agree that Shakespeare invented the species in all of its existential, introspective glory, she certainly sees the plays as explorations of what it means to be human.

However, Gaines's long relationship with Shakespeare has not rendered her a Bardolator. Speaking of Timothy Findley's depiction of Shakespeare in *Elizabeth Rex*, Gaines said, "I love what he [Findley] did with Shakespeare. He's just a cranky, annoyed writer and producer. He's so real; in some ways, so ordinary, and I like that because Shakespeare was a man."[35] Sounding her common theme, Gaines is drawn to the humanity of Shakespeare, as she is drawn to the humanity of the characters he created.

Economic imperatives might drive a Shakespeare theater situated next to a Ferris wheel on a former naval installation that is currently one of the Second City's major tourist attractions to steer a steady course for popular, palatable Shakespeare in the main house, where ticket sales are the stuff of life: a superabundance of Ariels and Pucks and Romeos and Juliets. Criss Henderson and Barbara Gaines have eschewed such an approach. As David G. Brailow noted of the 2004 season:

> Patrons of Chicago Shakespeare Theater had a unique opportunity in the
> 2003–04 season to see four of the least often performed history plays—the

three parts of *Henry VI* in *Rose Rage* and *King John*. They were also treated to widely divergent presentational and interpretive styles. *Rose Rage* depicted the English political world as a meat locker trapping its denizens in a gory cycle of brief triumph and death. But *King John*, despite its caustic treatment of power politics, became an intensely emotional portrayal of deeply flawed human beings trying as best they could to find their way "among the thorns and dangers of this world." The tightly focused, lucid direction and performances laid bare the characters' struggles between self-interest and conscience.[36]

The 2004 season's offering of *King John* on the main stage, and *Rose Rage* in the upstairs "black box" studio space, offers a prime example of the dialogic dynamic among the productions onstage at Chicago Shakespeare Theater over the course of a season, enabled by the upstairs/downstairs structure of the theater.

Like Shakespeare himself, Gaines began her career in theater as an actor but has had her greatest success as a stakeholder in a theater company. Also like Shakespeare, she has a cohort of loyal actors around whom she can build her concepts for shows, many of whom have appeared in numerous productions, progressing from youthful roles to mature ones. Chicago Shakespeare Theater stalwart Larry Yando began his career with the theater as Hortensio in the 1993–1994 production of *Shrew*, took on the role of Henry IV in 1999, and has recently played Malvolio (in Rourke's production of *Twelfth Night* in 2009), among numerous other roles. Like many actors who have portrayed Celia in *As You Like It* only to "graduate" to the role of Rosalind, Kate Fry, who garnered rave reviews for her performance as Rosalind/Ganymede in Gary Griffin's 2011 production, cut her teeth in the play as David Bell's Celia in his 2001 production for Chicago Shakespeare Theater. Kevin Gudahl has appeared in numerous Chicago Shakespeare Theater productions over the years, including as William Shakespeare himself in the 2011 production of *Elizabeth Rex*, and like many of the theater's "regulars," he is also a familiar face in Shakespearean productions at other prestigious Chicago theaters; he appeared in *Othello* at the Writers' Theatre and in *Titus Andronicus* at the Court Theatre and served as the loyal Albany to Stacy Keach's *King Lear* at the Goodman.

"Chicago is a city a talented actor can make a life in and work regularly in," Executive Director Criss Henderson noted. "Our actors were excellent to begin with, but now many of them have twenty-five years of experience—they can get their heads and mouths around the language regularly. That is certainly part of the muscularity with which we are able to stage these plays."[37]

Without actors, there is no theater. In recognition of the fact that the new theater belonged to them, the lone time that the thrust stage at Chicago

Shakespeare Theater has been used in a conventional proscenium manner was the first day that the actors got to see it. They were ushered into the backstage area where they assembled, champagne in hand, before a vast fire curtain. Once all were present and accounted for, the curtain rose to unveil the thrust stage, the gallery seating, the theater. Their theater.

Some members of the Chicago Shakespeare Theater community have completed an apprenticeship with the theater before going on to pursue other endeavors. They have a tendency, however, to return "home" to the theater. Sean Graney, for example, worked as Chicago Shakespeare Theater's house manager when they were based at the Ruth Page Theater, shortly after he finished college. He went on to start the wildly successful Hypocrites Theater Company. A wunderkind director, Graney made a triumphant return to Chicago Shakespeare Theater in 2008 to direct Christopher Marlowe's *Edward II* in a promenade staging for the upstairs studio theater, which Andrea Stevens characterized as "simply put, one of the most exciting performances I've recently seen" in her review for *Shakespeare Bulletin*.[38]

When asked what has surprised her the most over the course of her twenty-five years building and nurturing Chicago Shakespeare Theater, Gaines replies, "How beloved the theater has become has been the most surprising,"[39] referring not only to the theater's loyal audience and patron base but also to the small army of creative and administrative staff that has signed up to serve under Gaines's command:

> We have an amazing staff that is just so dedicated. People are passionate about their work—it's inspiring; I understand why I'm inspired, but it's touching to see the eighty other people who work here that passionate, every day. And the level of the talent grows every year. Just when you think it can't get any better, it takes a huge step forward; Gary Griffin, Rick Boynton, Bob Mason—they are great collaborators; trust me, we would never have gotten as far without them.[40]
>
> Deb Acker—our Stage Manager since 1990; Lisa Stec—one of the greatest drapers; Dan Hess, who started out as House Manager and now he's Company Manager; Chris Plevin has just turned thirty and he's Director of Productions; it's a job for a fifty-year-old—he's astounding. They are really proud of the work that we do—their hearts are in it. I couldn't have imagined that. I didn't know anything, other than that Shakespeare needed to be done. We've created a community, Gaines marvels; I had no idea that I would be creating a community.[41]

Marilyn Halperin, Director of Education and Communications, points out that a community is precisely what is created at the end of Gaines's favorite comedy, *The Merry Wives of Windsor*. The cuckold-phobe, Ford, makes amends with his long-suffering loyal wife; the Pages reconcile for their abortive efforts to outwit one another as matchmakers for their daughter and resign themselves to her own choice of husband; Falstaff is punished for his treble efforts to disrupt marital harmony with his lecherous, adulterous advances and is then reintegrated into the Windsor community. All of this is accomplished under the wise and witty leadership of the Windsor wives, Mistress Ford and Mistress Page, who script, direct, and stage manage the play's increasingly elaborate metatheatrical deceptions. Little wonder that Barbara Gaines has been repeatedly drawn to this play—like the Windsor wives, she is in the business of making theater that is equal parts myth, magic, and moral message.

NOTES

1. Barbara Gaines (Artistic Director, Chicago Shakespeare Theater), discussion with the author, July 13, 2011.

2. Ibid.

3. For a full discussion of this production, see David G. Brailow, "*King John*," *Shakespeare Bulletin* 22.2 (2004): 90–95, accessed August 8, 2011, *Academic OneFile*.

4. Barbara Gaines, discussion with the author, Chicago Shakespeare Theater, October 1999. While the stage at the Ruth Page Theater offered a shallow thrust design, the stage at Chicago Shakespeare Theater extends much farther into the audience. For more on the relationship between the theater's design and the productions mounted within it, see Jonathan Walker's essay in this volume.

5. Brailow, "*King John*," 92.

6. Gaines, discussion, 2011.

7. Ibid.

8. Ibid. While Chicago audiences (and reviewers) may have thought "Toyota" when they heard "Cressida" in 1987, Anthony B. Dawson notes that, since the 1960s and 1970s, when *Troilus and Cressida* "came into its own as an anti-war play . . . it has become a standard in the repertoire, performed almost as often as *Hamlet* or *As You Like It* in theatres in England and North America." See Anthony B. Dawson, ed., introduction to *Troilus and Cressida*, by William Shakespeare, *The New Cambridge Shakespeare*, ed. Brian Gibbons (Cambridge: Cambridge UP, 2003), 50. Nevertheless, Gretchen Minton was still able to recall in 2008 that "as an undergraduate student, I was part of a ten-person performance group within my Shakespeare class; our daunting task was to produce a portion of the strangest and most difficult play we had read all year: *Troilus and Cressida*," ultimately referring to it as "this odd play that none of us had even heard of before." Minton later mused over Toyota's injudicious choice of "Cressida" as a car model name: "Why would anyone buy a car that is destined to be unfaithful?" See Gretchen E. Minton, "'Discharging less than the tenth part of one': Performance Anxiety and/in *Troilus and Cressida*," in *Shakespeare and the Cultures of Performance*, ed. Paul Yachnin and Patricia Badir (Burlington, VT: Ashgate, 2008), 101 and 114, n. 32.

9. Gaines, discussion, 2011.

10. For one of the clearest articulations of the subversion/containment model, see Stephen Greenblatt, *Shakespearean Negotiations* (Berkeley and Los Angeles: U of California P, 1988). For a few foundational articulations of New Historicist theoretical constructs, see Catherine Gallagher and Stephen Greenblatt, "Introduction," in *Practicing New Historicism* (Chicago: U of Chicago P, 2000), 1–19; Lisa Jardine, "Introduction," *Reading Shakespeare Historically* (New York: Routledge, 1996), 1–18; David Scott Kastan, *Shakespeare after Theory* (New York: Routledge, 1999); and *New Historicism and Renaissance Drama*, ed. and intro. Richard Wilson and Richard Dutton, Longman Critical Readers, ed. Raman Selden and Stan Smith (New York: Longman, 1992). For more recent critical response to the formulations of New Historicism, see Jürgen Pieters, "Critical Self-Fashioning: Stephen Greenblatt and the New Historicism: General Introduction," in *Critical Self-Fashioning: Stephen Greenblatt and The New Historicism* (New York: Peter Lang, 1999), 11–20; and Douglas Bruster, *Shakespeare and the Question of Culture: Early Modern Literature and the Cultural Turn*, Early Modern Cultural Series, ed. Ivo Kamps (New York: Palgrave Macmillan, 2003), particularly the preface, xv–xxi.

11. Paul Hecht, "Shakespeare in Chicagoland," *Shakespeare Bulletin* 26.2 (2008): 201–11, accessed August 8, 2011, *Academic OneFile*; the quoted passage appears on page 205. As Peter Holland notes, such an approach must be carefully calibrated, to avoid

> the lure of the analogue, the precise historical analogy that would serve to illuminate the whole, relying on our knowledge of more recent history to explicate the Shakespearian text as if the play had no function in relation to its own time and, more significantly, could only be made popular by the recreation of the play as modern parable . . . at its worst . . . trying to make Shakespeare popular makes the productions weakly populist, offering simple answers where the text is complex, failing to follow through the implications of analogy.

See Peter Holland, "Shakespeare Performances in England, 1990–1," *Shakespeare Survey: An Annual Survey of Studies and Production* 45 (1993): 115–44; the quoted passage appears on page 130.

12. Gaines, discussion, 2011.

13. See Dawson's overview of this trend in *Troilus and Cressida*, 50–52.

14. Christopher Marlowe, *Doctor Faustus*, in *The Complete Plays*, ed. J. B. Steane (London: Penguin Books, 1986), 5.1.97–98.

15. Sam Mendes took a similar approach with his Helen (Sally Dexter) at the Royal Shakespeare Company in 1990. Helen made her initial stage entrance on a plinth draped with gold lamé; the drape covered her entirely, making her resemble, curiously, a pyramid. When the drape was whipped away to reveal her to the Greeks and to the theater audience, they were treated to a garish vision in heavy make-up, with particular emphasis on her pouty, shiny, cherry-red lips.

16. "About Michael Merritt," The Merritt Award for Excellence in Design and Collaboration, accessed August 8, 2011.

17. Gaines, discussion, 2011.

18. Philippi died suddenly in Chicago in 2009, while working with another of his frequent collaborators, the Goodman Theatre's Robert Falls, on *High Holidays*. Chris Jones, "Michael Philippi, Major Chicago Lighting Designer, Dies," *Chicago Tribune*, The Theater Loop, October 27, 2009.

19. William Shakespeare, *Troilus and Cressida*, ed. Gary Taylor, in *The Oxford Shakespeare: The Complete Works*, 2nd ed., ed. Stanley Wells and Gary Taylor (Oxford UP, 2005), 4.1.48–50 and 55–56. Subsequent references to the plays will be to this edition and will be parenthetically cited in the text. Anthony Dawson notes "the intermingled blood and desire that underpin the whole conflict, which is in many respects a civil war." See Dawson, ed., *Troilus and Cressida*, 15 and also 63.

20. As Dawson notes in offering a production history of *Troilus and Cressida*, such an interpretation of Cressida's arrival in the Greek camp is not uncommon. See Dawson, ed., *Troilus and Cressida*, 55–59 and 62. Minton notes that Cressida's reception in the Greek camp is of a piece with her treatment elsewhere in the play, since Pandarus and Troilus collude to "tease Cressida the morning after [her sexual liaison with Troilus], making jokes about her anatomy—a sort of locker-room banter with her present. The near gang rape that she experiences at the hands of the Greek soldiers is a horrific extension of how she has already been treated by her lover and uncle." See Minton, "'Discharging less than the tenth part of one,'" 106.

21. Dawson, ed., *Troilus and Cressida*, 15.

22. Hecht, "Shakespeare in Chicagoland," 205.

23. Gaines, discussion, 2011.

24. Ibid.

25. Lawrence Bommer, "*All's Well That Ends Well*," *Chicago Reader*, May 4, 2000.

26. Marilyn Halperin and Gina Buccola, "A Conversation with Director Barbara Gaines," All's Well That Ends Well *Teacher Handbook*, Chicago Shakespeare Theater, 2000.

27. Harvey Young, "*Measure for Measure*," *Shakespeare Bulletin* 23.3 (2005): 115–17, accessed August 8, 2011, *Academic OneFile*; the quoted passage appears on page 116.

28. Gaines, discussion, 2011.

29. For feminist analyses of *Merry Wives*, see Sandra Clark, "'Wives may be merry and yet honest too': Women and Wit in *The Merry Wives of Windsor* and Some Other Plays," in *"Fanned and Winnowed Opinions": Shakespearean Essays Presented to Harold Jenkins*, ed. John W. Mahon and Thomas A. Pendleton (New York: Methuen, 1987), 249–67; Carol Thomas Neely, "Constructing Female Sexuality in the Renaissance: Stratford, London, Windsor, Vienna," in *Feminism and Psychoanalysis*, ed. Richard Feldstein and Judith Roof (Ithaca, NY: Cornell UP, 1989), 209–29; and Wendy Wall, "Why Does Puck Sweep? Fairylore, Merry Wives, and Social Struggle," *Shakespeare Quarterly* 52.1 (2001): 67–106.

30. See also Marie-Hélène Besnault and Michel Bitot, "Historical Legacy and Fiction: The Poetical Reinvention of King Richard III," in *The Cambridge Companion to Shakespeare's History Plays*, ed. Michael Hattaway (Cambridge: Cambridge UP, 2002), 119.

31. In her interview for the play's program, Barbara Gaines told Director of Education and Communication, Marilyn Halperin: "Peter Brook once said that if you don't believe in the spirit world, then you really needn't bother to open these plays, because for Shakespeare the spirits are real and palpable. For me, the spirit world is connected to our collective unconscious and, like our dreams, is truthful. It is a world that we are inclined to push away, that we wish not to deal with. Shared by all humankind, past and present, I see it as a great undertow that connects us to one another." Barbara Gaines and Marilyn Halperin, "The Undertow of *Richard III*: Director Q&A," *Richard III Playbill* (Autumn 2009): 12.

32. Ibid., 11.

33. *King Richard III*, dir. Laurence Olivier, perf. Laurence Olivier, John Gielgud, and Claire Bloom (London Film Productions, 1955) and *Richard III,* dir. Richard Loncraine, perf. Ian McKellen, Annette Bening, Kristin Scott Thomas, John Wood, and Maggie Smith (Mayfair Entertainment International, 1995).

34. Harold Bloom, "To the Reader," in *Shakespeare: The Invention of the Human* (New York: Riverhead Books, 1998), xix–xx.

35. Gaines, discussion, 2011.

36. Brailow, "*King John,*" 90–91.

37. Criss Henderson (Executive Director, Chicago Shakespeare Theater), discussion with the author, December 2, 2011.

38. Andrea Stevens, "Edward II," *Shakespeare Bulletin* 27.1 (2009): 117–22, accessed August 8, 2011, *Academic OneFile*; the quoted passage appears on page 117.

39. Gaines, discussion, 2011.

40. Gary Griffin is the Associate Artistic Director, Rick Boynton is the Creative Producer, and Bob Mason is Artistic Associate/Casting Director.

41. Gaines, discussion, 2011.

BIBLIOGRAPHY

"About Michael Merritt." The Merritt Award for Excellence in Design and Collaboration. Accessed August 8, 2011.

Besnault, Marie-Hélène, and Michel Bitot. "Historical Legacy and Fiction: The Poetical Re-invention of King Richard III." *The Cambridge Companion to Shakespeare's History Plays.* Ed. Michael Hattaway, 106–25. Cambridge: Cambridge UP, 2002.

Bloom, Harold. *Shakespeare: The Invention of the Human.* New York: Riverhead Books, 1998.

Bommer, Lawrence. "*All's Well That Ends Well.*" *Chicago Reader.* May 4, 2000.

Brailow, David G. "*King John.*" *Shakespeare Bulletin* 22.2 (2004): 90–95. Accessed August 8, 2011. *Academic OneFile.*

Bruster, Douglas. *Shakespeare and the Question of Culture: Early Modern Literature and the Cultural Turn.* Early Modern Cultural Series. Ed. Ivo Kamps. New York: Palgrave Macmillan, 2003.

Clark, Sandra. "'Wives may be merry and yet honest too': Women and Wit in *The Merry Wives of Windsor* and Some Other Plays." *"Fanned and Winnowed Opinions": Shakespearean Essays Presented to Harold Jenkins.* Ed. John W. Mahon and Thomas A. Pendleton, 249–67. New York: Methuen, 1987.

Dawson, Anthony B., ed. "Introduction." *Troilus and Cressida.* By William Shakespeare. The New Cambridge Shakespeare. Ed. Brian Gibbons. Cambridge: Cambridge UP, 2003.

Gaines, Barbara, and Marilyn Halperin. "The Undertow of *Richard III*: Director Q&A." *Richard III* (Chicago Shakespeare Theater, Autumn 2009): 10–12.

Gallagher, Catherine, and Stephen Greenblatt. *Practicing New Historicism.* Chicago: U of Chicago P, 2000.

Greenblatt, Stephen. *Shakespearean Negotiations.* Berkeley and Los Angeles: U of California P, 1988.

Halperin, Marilyn, and Gina Buccola. "A Conversation with Director Barbara Gaines." All's

Well That Ends Well *Teacher Handbook*. Chicago: Chicago Shakespeare Theater, 2000.

Hecht, Paul. "Shakespeare in Chicagoland." *Shakespeare Bulletin* 26.2 (2008): 201–11. Accessed August 8, 2011. *Academic OneFile*.

Holland, Peter. "Shakespeare Performances in England, 1990–1." *Shakespeare Survey: An Annual Survey of Studies and Production* 45 (1993): 115–44.

Jardine, Lisa. "Introduction." *Reading Shakespeare Historically*. New York: Routledge, 1996. 1–18.

Jones, Chris. "Michael Philippi, Major Chicago Lighting Designer, Dies." *Chicago Tribune*. The Theater Loop. October 27 2009.

Kastan, David Scott. *Shakespeare after Theory*. New York: Routledge, 1999.

King Richard III. Dir. Laurence Olivier. Perf. Laurence Olivier, John Gielgud, and Claire Bloom. London Film Productions, 1955.

Marlowe, Christopher. *Doctor Faustus*. *The Complete Plays*. Ed. J. B. Steane. London: Penguin Books, 1986.

Minton, Gretchen E. "'Discharging less than the tenth part of one': Performance Anxiety and/in *Troilus and Cressida*." *Shakespeare and the Cultures of Performance*. Ed. Paul Yachnin and Patricia Badir, 101–19. Burlington, VT: Ashgate, 2008.

Neely, Carol Thomas. "Constructing Female Sexuality in the Renaissance: Stratford, London, Windsor, Vienna." *Feminism and Psychoanalysis*. Ed. Richard Feldstein and Judith Roof, 209–29. Ithaca, NY: Cornell UP, 1989.

New Historicism and Renaissance Drama. Ed. and introduced by Richard Wilson and Richard Dutton. Longman Critical Readers. Ed. Raman Selden and Stan Smith. New York: Longman, 1992.

Pieters, Jürgen. *Critical Self-Fashioning: Stephen Greenblatt and The New Historicism*. New York: Peter Lang, 1999.

Richard III. Dir. Richard Loncraine. Perf. Ian McKellen, Annette Bening, Kristin Scott Thomas, John Wood, and Maggie Smith. Mayfair Entertainment International, 1995.

Shakespeare, William. *Troilus and Cressida*. Ed. Gary Taylor. *The Oxford Shakespeare: The Complete Works*. Ed. Stanley Wells and Gary Taylor. 2nd ed. Oxford UP, 2005.

Stevens, Andrea. "*Edward II*." *Shakespeare Bulletin* 27.1 (2009): 117–22. Accessed August 8, 2011. *Academic OneFile*.

Wall, Wendy. "Why Does Puck Sweep? Fairylore, Merry Wives, and Social Struggle." *Shakespeare Quarterly* 52.1 (2001): 67–106.

Young, Harvey. "*Measure for Measure*." *Shakespeare Bulletin* 23.3 (2005): 115–17. Accessed August 8, 2011. *Academic OneFile*.

Barbara, Shakespeare, and Me

JONATHAN ABARBANEL

Chicago Shakespeare Theater? Sure, I can tell you how I started that. Have a seat.

Barbara Gaines and I met as Cherubs the summer we were seventeen. We were attending the National High School Institute at Northwestern University in Evanston, Illinois, a program for precocious high-schoolers between their junior and senior years, nicknamed "The Cherubs" since Time Immemorial. We weren't the only Cherubs that summer to become rich and famous: the successful actors Joe Bratcher and Davis Hall were among our number, as well as little Bobby Reich, a charismatic overachiever who went on to pursue a doctorate in economics and become Secretary of Labor under President Bill Clinton.

The times being what they were—this was about forty-five years ago—the concept of in loco parentis was in full force, which meant that boys and girls were housed in separate dormitories at the extreme opposite ends of the campus, about a mile apart. There would be no casual familiarity in this happy camp (and it *was* a happy camp because we knew we were the brightest and the best, and we were having a wonderful time) and no private intimacies on the nearby beaches of the Lake Michigan shoreline. To hammer the nail into the coffin of adolescent libido, our dormitory cafeteria food was liberally laced with saltpeter—no disguising that unsavory taste—leading to much-discussed frustration among the boys. You'll have to ask Barbara how the girls reacted to it. Or maybe they thought only boys needed to be dosed.

In addition to classes in acting, costume design, and scenic design, each acting Cherub was in an end-of-summer show, fully mounted in the then splendid (and now sadly outdated) Cahn Auditorium, at that time the main theater venue on the Northwestern campus. There were four or five shows, as I recall, each one running between forty and ninety minutes. One of the staff directors did *The Apollo of Belloc,* and there also were productions of act 1 of the musical *Archy and Mehitabel,* a condensed *Romeo and Juliet,* and then the project that Barbara and I were in, a condensed staging of Turgenev's *A Month in the Country.* We must'a been the brightest and the best, because our directors were throwing some serious stuff at us. At seventeen, I barely knew who Chekhov was and had not yet read any of his plays, let alone his less-famous, heavy-duty precursor Turgenev. Hey, I'd never even acted in a classical play of any kind, unless you count a drama club reading of *The Importance of Being Earnest.* And here Barbara and I were in made-to-measure period costumes (another first for me as an actor), performing on scenery created just for us and receiving a crash course in Russian tea drinking, samovar protocol, and mid-nineteenth-century Slavic society.

More to the point, Barbara and I played opposite each other in *A Month in the Country,* I as Dr. Shpigelsky and Barbara as Lizaveta, the governess-companion in the wealthy household in which the play is set. Both were supporting roles, but not insubstantial ones, and we had a flirtatious scene together that included dancing. Somewhere, in someone's trunk (perhaps mine), there is a photo of us *en scène.* At the final celebratory dinner, which ended our intense five weeks as Cherubs, Barbara and I vowed to reunite "in ten years on Broadway together."

I went on to attend Tufts University and then, sponsored by Tufts, lived in London where I studied with playwright James Forsyth, eminent directors E. Martin Brown and Anthony Cornish, theater architect Victor Glasstone, and poet George Macbeth, among others. Curiously, in all my studies at home and abroad, I never performed Shakespeare. My classical acting efforts included Jacobean revenge tragedy, Restoration comedy, Molière, and medieval mystery cycle plays. But I saw—live, and more than once—the great actors of the older generation such as Laurence Olivier, John Gielgud, Ian Richardson, and Edith Evans, and those of the mid-generation such as Paul Scofield, Alec Guinness, Flora Robson, and Donald Sinden, and those of the new generation such as Derek Jacobi, Jeremy Brett, Judi Dench, and Frances de la Tour. I inhaled the work of directors such as Peter Brook, Peter Hall, Clifford Williams, and Trevor Nunn, as well as then-new playwrights such as Tom Stoppard and Simon Gray. I also bought a peacock's wardrobe of mod clothes on the King's Road, but that's another story.

Barbara enrolled at Northwestern (which used the Cherubs as a recruitment tool), where she came under the life-altering professorship and mentorship of Dr. Wallace Bacon. She then went on to New York, where she spent a decade or so doing I-don't-know-what before returning to Chicago, where she had theater friends, Northwestern friends, and —obviously—ambitions.

Barbara and I had our roughly ten-year reunion in 1975, but it wasn't on Broadway; it was at Orphans Pub on Lincoln Avenue in Chicago, in a then-radical-chic neighborhood that was the epicenter of the Off-Loop Theater Movement in its first flower. Just down the street from Orphans were The Body Politic (home to Paul Sills's Story Theatre and Stuart Gordon's Organic Theater Company) and Kingston Mines Theater Company (where *Grease* was created). I worked as an actor and a director at both houses for little to no pay at a time when few Off-Loop venues were under Equity contracts. Barbara, who had earned her Equity card in New York, received a tiny bit more at Orphans, where the owner had turned the back room into a pub theater. Barbara was there performing in Ionesco's *The Lesson*. It ran just a few weeks but was a surprising Off-Loop hit for which Barbara received the first of many Joseph Jefferson Awards, her only Jeff Award for acting (although she was nominated one other time).

We saw each other at widely spaced intervals over the next several years, usually briefly backstage when I saw her in a show or at the odd party or two. I gradually moved out of acting and into theater criticism (initially for underground papers) and then literary management at the Goodman, St. Nicholas, and Milwaukee Repertory Theaters, and for the Midwest Playwrights Program and the Chicago Theater Project. Barbara continued to act and, initiating her true life's work, began to teach Shakespeare classes for Chicago actors.

How audacious! How dare she teach Shakespeare? What did she have to offer? She had her Northwestern degree and her Wallace Bacon pedigree, but certainly she wasn't recognized as a Shakespeare scholar or a deeply experienced Shakespearean actor or even as a director of record (whether of Shakespeare or anything else). Here was chutzpah! But ya know what? She was right. Because of teachers and mentors like Wallace Bacon, *something was going on* with Shakespeare in America, and Barbara was among the first-generation recipients of new thinking that proved to be wise thinking. I don't know whether she knew this empirically when she began teaching Shakespeare or merely understood it intuitively. Either way, because of Barbara and others of like mind across the country, there was a sea change in American classical theater of which even I became aware, but it took a few years, so allow me to backpedal.

Here's the deal: when Barbara and I were coming of age, every American actor approaching Shakespeare wanted to sound as British as he or she possibly could. It was the influence of the greats (already named above) who had The Voices and could follow a line of Shakespearean poetry forever and ever. Shakespeare seemed to sail, to take wing, on the music of the vocalization. The passion of the voice conveyed the emotion of the moment *even when the words didn't make sense to us.* NO one ever said to us, "Darling, you know you don't *have* to sound British," not even my British instructors in London.

After returning to the United States, I supported my evening theater work with a daytime job as an advertising copywriter ("America spells cheese K-R-A-F-T" is mine, I kid you not). I vacationed in London every year or eighteen months to take in theater: Peter Hall's *Hamlet* with Albert Finney at the National Theatre at the Old Vic, Peter Brook's Royal Shakespeare Company white-gymnasium *A Midsummer Night's Dream*, an astonishing *Edward II* at the National (still at the Old Vic). To this day, I'm the only American theater critic I know—and I ask my colleagues about this—who has seen six different productions of *Edward II*, among them one in the upstairs black box at Chicago Shakespeare Theater in 2008 (directed by Sean Graney).

And then there came a period of nine or ten years during which I didn't return to London at all. It was during this time that Barbara launched Shakespeare Repertory Theater, as it was called until it moved to Navy Pier, with her now-legendary $3,000 production of *Henry V* in the beer garden of the Red Lion Pub, on Lincoln Avenue just a block down from Orphans. Her Henry was young Si Osborne, very much in the blond-haired-blue-eyed tradition of the role, who had been one of Barbara's Shakespeare students, as were so many of the actors she has used repeatedly over the years. It wasn't just the charm and delight of the physical production that made it a hit, with battles happening between and in the beer garden trees, but the vigor and clarity of the acting. Barbara never looked back from this modest launching pad. When it comes to Shakespeare, it was Chicago's own beer hall putsch.

During this same period of years, I twice visited the Oregon Shakespeare Festival where some of my old Tufts friends—Peter Silbert, Megan Cole, William Hurt—were in the company. I was aware there, too, that there was a new clarity to the presentation of Shakespeare. At this time (and for many years afterward), I was a site reporter for the National Endowment for the Arts, visiting nonprofit theaters large and small across the country, and encountering Shakespeare (although not exclusively Shakespeare) good, bad, and indifferent. The best of it matched what I was seeing and hearing in Barbara's productions, and what I'd found at the Oregon Shakespeare Festival.

What I was seeing and hearing was *American* Shakespeare. Our actors coming of age in the 1970s and 1980s finally were moving beyond the compulsion to sound British. Once you discarded a put-on accent or dialect, and the line of the verse for its own sake, a new world opened up, and that was the world of Wallace Bacon: don't worry about the poetry. Make sense of the words *first* as expressions of character and intention, and the flow of the language will follow. And speak the speech, I pray you, as well-trained American actors (or Canadian actors, for that matter), not as well-trained American actors trying to sound British.

Every time I went to see a Chicago Shakespeare Theater show, I heard things—I *understood* things—that previously had passed me by in even the most familiar plays. Sometimes they were profound understandings, sometimes they were simple ideas or jokes or ironies of the moment. Every production, therefore, was refreshing, as if I were seeing and hearing the play for the first time. Dear God, I was a virgin again and again! And that sense of freshness remains today when I visit Navy Pier.

The upshot—or at least one upshot—is that when I finally returned to London, I rushed to the wonderful Cottesloe Theatre at the new Royal National Theatre complex to see Fiona Shaw in the title role of *Richard II*. The physical intimacy of the Cottesloe was wonderful, and every actor was first-rate . . . and it all sounded so absolutely phony to me! Every actor, it seemed to my ears and altered sensitivities, was playing the language and not the character, playing the words but not the sense. I understood that evening what Barbara Gaines had achieved back in my own home town, and how she and her work had helped me mature and grow as a theater lover, as an astute (presumably) member of the audience and as a theater critic, too. I continue to treasure every trip I make to the CST precincts at Navy Pier, never mind that it has the best damn views of the city skyline and lakescape in the whole damn city!

I remember so well, too, those words I had with Barbara back when we were seventeen and cherubic at Northwestern, sharing a Coke after rehearsing *A Month in the Country*. "But, Babs," I said, "what about Shakespeare?"

"Shakespeare?" she said. "Gosh, I've never thought about Shakespeare."

And so you see, I was the one. Nice to talk to you. Have a good day.

4

The Spatial Rhetoric of
Chicago Shakespeare Theater

JONATHAN WALKER

Chicago Shakespeare's Courtyard Theater combines the expansive scenic area of a deep-set, unframed proscenium stage with the intimacy
and versatility of a central, often bare, thrust stage, which reaches out to
touch the very heart of its auditorium. Occupying three vertical levels, the
Courtyard's auditorium embraces the thrust stage on three sides, arranging
as many playgoers to the stage's flanks as it does in front of the thrust. Such
a configuration between performance and spectatorial spaces is not entirely
novel among large-scale and high-budget theaters—the company's website,
for instance, states explicitly that its architects drew inspiration from the
Royal Shakespeare Company's Swan Theatre in Stratford-upon-Avon.[1] And
yet the hybrid nature of the Courtyard's design formulates spatial relationships between the action and the audience that are paralleled by very few
professional theaters. Of course not all of the theater's productions utilize
its proscenium and thrust spaces in the same ways, though the auditorium
space is always fixed. The specific relationships that the interior architecture fosters between performances and playgoers comprise what I will be
calling the Courtyard's spatial rhetoric, within which different productions
and directors make various scenic or dramatic statements. The playgoers'
proximity to and physical points of view onto the stage offer opportunities

for highlighting thematic and characterological tensions in the dramatic action by capitalizing on the space itself. Some productions in the Courtyard Theater, in other words, construct dramatic meaning for their audiences not only through the delivery of dialogue, the blocking of actors, stage and costume design, and so on but also through a calculated staging of space, which taps into a vocabulary of physical placement and juxtaposition to express both dramatic conflict and harmony, division and alliance, and detachment and intimacy among the characters who populate its stage.

A few of the Courtyard's productions that have actively deployed space in these ways are the inaugural *Antony and Cleopatra* (1999), *The Tempest* (2002), *Julius Caesar* (2002–2003), and *Romeo and Juliet* (2010). Before discussing specific scenes, however, I should like to detail certain technical features of this theater, which will help to illuminate the spatial context in which these plays have been performed. First of all, the thrust portion of the stage measures 20' wide x 27' 8" deep (553.4 sf), stopping just shy of the auditorium's midpoint. One of the features that distinguishes this open stage from many others is its contiguous proscenium stage, which measures 42' wide x 28' deep (1,176 sf); see Figure 10. Incidentally, this proscenium is mere inches smaller than the apron stage that the master carpenter Peter Street built for Philip Henslowe's Fortune Theater in 1600, which was to measure 43' wide x 27' 5" deep.[2] From the front edge of the Courtyard's thrust to the extreme upstage of its proscenium, where overhead doors open onto a backstage area, the stage's total depth stretches over 61', and, in several productions, the playing space was extended yet farther into the backstage for a depth of nearly 88'. Both segments of the stage regularly make use of traps, though the height of the thrust is only two feet above the main floor surrounding it. In addition to the great depth and appreciable width of the theater's solid playing area, productions often press the vertical space above the stage into the service of performance, using a single fly system over the proscenium stage and independent rigging (but no built-in line sets) over the thrust. Characters' ascents into the fly space can have vastly different effects, as we shall see, but they all naturally tend toward the spectacular as bodies mount or hover at the eye-level of gallery patrons and, on occasion, even swing out above the audience on the main floor.

Turning to the space of the auditorium, we find that both galleries are rather shallow and steep, with the topmost providing only a single row of seating, and the Dress Circle below it furnishing two rows. Although the Courtyard Theater offers vantage points with greater and lesser visibility, no member of the audience sits more than thirty-eight feet from the stage, while not a few sit within only a couple feet of it. Figure 10 shows

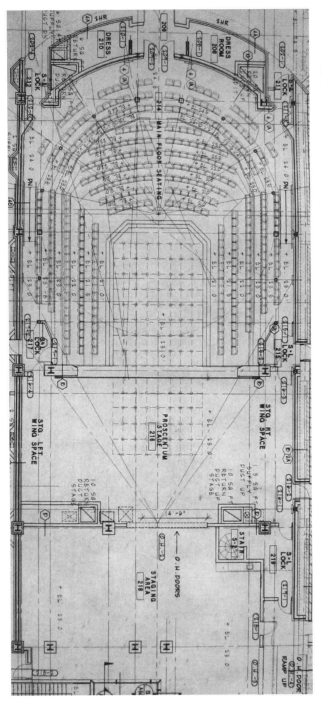

10. Architectural plans for the Courtyard Theater by VOA Associates Inc., version AR-7, sheet A2.06 (detail).

how seating on the main floor, like that in the galleries, follows the U-shaped perimeter of the auditorium, while also adding nearly two-fifths of the house's seats in the area forward of the thrust. The outer perimeter of the Courtyard's auditorium is particularly interesting with an eye to early modern theater history, insofar as the interior design emulates the same geometrical pattern by which amphitheaters like the Rose and the Globe were constructed in the late sixteenth century. As excavations and evaluations of the Rose and the Globe sites have shown, these two London amphitheaters—and probably most of the period's other open-air theaters—were built on polygonal designs, which oriented seated playgoers toward a central apron stage. Each of the polygon's bays that was devoted to spectatorial space contained raked seating and housed two galleries above a ground floor. In Figure 11, for example, a yard-level plan for the new Globe in London shows how the structure's polygonal shape distributes playgoers 270° around the stage, which, like the Courtyard's, extends to the center of the auditorium. By comparison, in Figure 12 we see that half of the Courtyard's auditorium is modeled on a sixteen-sided polygon, with seating governed by the centripetal orientation of each bay.[3]

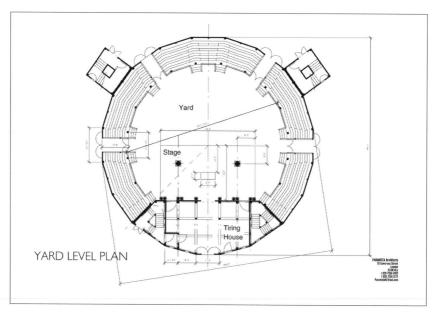

11. Yard-level plan of Shakespeare's Globe, London. Courtesy of Jon Greenfield, Globe Architect

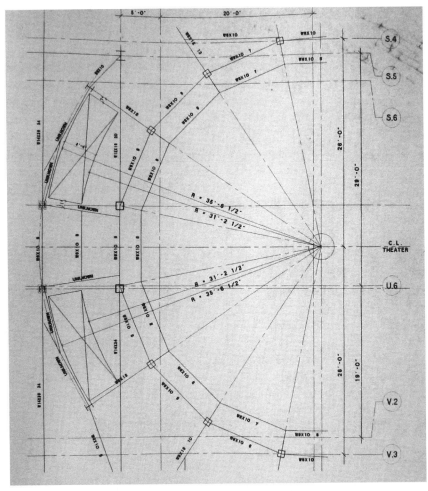

12. Architectural plans for the Courtyard Theater by VOA Associates Inc., version AR-10, sheet A4.03 (detail).

As suggested above, Courtyard spectators occupy positions both parallel and perpendicular to the thrust stage, which radically dehomogenizes the playgoing experience; see Figure 13. Theaters that utilize thrust, apron, transverse, and other open stages seek "to bring auditorium and acting area into the same architectural space and to get as close as possible a relation between the action of the play and the spectators watching it. The focus of the audience's attention is on the centre of the drama and members of that audience tend to group themselves round this focus."[4] In such theaters, this "close . . . relation between the action of the play and the spectators watching it" usually makes the dramatic tensions and conflicts represented in performance more physically immediate, and thus more powerful, to the audience. The Courtyard attains such immediacy partly by staging hundreds of its entrances and exits through the auditorium, which does not privilege any one spectatorial angle or viewpoint but instead multiplies the directionality of the performance up to at least 180° around the thrust stage. In contrast, traditional proscenium-arch theaters tend to compress their audiences' sightlines into narrower corridors that idealize the angle at which spectators observe the performance, thereby exercising more control over how playgoers perceive dramatic action. On the other hand, early modern amphitheaters offered spectators a degree of encirclement around the stage and, concomitantly, a freedom of perspective as well as physical mobility vastly greater than those of the Courtyard's. It is by mixing various components of these two designs that Chicago Shakespeare Theater achieves certain rhetorical effects through its staging of space.[5]

If the configuration between performance and spectatorial spaces in the Courtyard is fixed but also visually heterogeneous, giving playgoers a consistently broad array of physical positions and sightlines onto the dramatic action, then the primary way that the theater produces new spatial formations is through its manipulation of perspective on the thrust and proscenium stages. Although productions like Peter Brook's adaptation *The Tragedy of Hamlet* (2001) have been staged almost entirely on the thrust and others have dominated the proscenium, the size and the perpendicular arrangement of the two distinct but contiguous spaces enable directors to block characters and locate dramatic action either in very close quarters near the audience or at considerable distances upstage.[6] The manipulation of space is of course what all good directors do, and even the simplest stages of whatever size can craft a sense of both nearness and distance during performance. Yet, without being integrated into the thematic and characterological tensions of a dramatic fiction (those social conflicts and interpersonal strains around which the dramatic agon turns), physical nearness and distance on the stage are simply relative qualities with neutral values. Proximity does not really signify on its own. But when a production deploys space and physical juxtapositions in ways that both emphasize and interpret these dramatic tensions, then the space itself acquires significant meaning for playgoers.

For example, in representations of either demure or intense emotional intimacy, such as those involving lovers like Romeo and Juliet or Antony and Cleopatra, the downstaging of action tends to reproduce those feelings of intimacy—sometimes coupled with voyeurism—within individual audi-

13. Chicago Shakespeare's Courtyard Theater. Photograph by Steinkamp-Ballogg Photography, Chicago

ence members, who observe characters touching, kissing, and embracing while they themselves sit very near to these gestures of closeness. On the other hand, if *Richard II*'s Northumberland, Willoughby, and Ross gather at the edge of the stage to lament Henry Bolingbroke's exile and to insist that "The King's grown bankrupt like a broken man,"[7] then their physical proximity to the audience activates a different kind of intimacy, one involving treasonous secrets and plots that transform the downstage space they occupy into a site of anxious or cloying conspiracy. The strategic upstaging of scenes often produces similar correlations between playing space and dramatic action. At the conclusion of *Richard III*, for instance, the new King Henry VII declares victory over the dead king and prays to his God:

> Enrich the time to come with smooth-faced peace,
> With smiling plenty, and fair prosperous days.
> Abate the edge of traitors, gracious Lord,
> That would reduce these bloody days again
> And make poor England weep forth streams of blood.[8]

Just prior to this speech in the Courtyard's 2009 production, the eleven ghosts who had earlier blessed Henry and cursed Richard were standing in a line across the upstage area, invoking a visual impression of the devastation caused by the Wars of the Roses. Yet, after the new king speaks the play's concluding lines and exits, the ghosts back up in succession and recede into the darkness, suggesting that under Henry's rule this devastation would now be moving into the past instead of haunting the present.[9] Conversely, Julius Caesar's triumphal entry at the opening of the 2002–2003 production began inside a small corridor that issued from the backstage area onto the proscenium. As the emperor's entourage filed out of the passageway, which was initially lit only from within, it engulfed the stage and proceeded onto the thrust, where light likewise flooded the scene. Reminiscent of entering a coliseum, the procession communicated an image of grandeur through the vast distance it covered and the throngs of followers celebrating Caesar's rule.[10]

The contrast produced by upstage and downstage character-groupings is also a potent means for exposing divisions and proclaiming alliances within the social fabric of a play, especially in a space like the Courtyard's. In the same production of *Julius Caesar*, Cassius and the other conspirators visited Brutus at home early in act 2. The thrust was lit dimly with blue light, signifying nighttime, and the proscenium was largely in darkness. After Brutus's servant Lucius announced their unexpected visit, saying "half their faces [are] buried in their cloaks, / That by no means I may discover them / By any mark of favour,"[11] the conspirators entered slowly through the same upstage passageway that Caesar had used in the opening scene, and they then assembled into two single-file lines, suggesting their tight militaristic discipline. Meanwhile, Brutus moved down and sat on the steps at the corner of stage left, meditating on the threat of conspiracy while glancing back toward the entering group. He said:

> They are the faction. O conspiracy,
> Sham'st thou to show thy dang'rous brow by night,
> When evils are most free? O then by day
> Where wilt thou find a cavern dark enough
> To mask thy monstrous visage? Seek none, conspiracy. (2.1.77–81)[12]

From any seat in the auditorium, Brutus appeared separate, even isolated, from the men on the proscenium, creating a great spatial gulf that bespoke his distance from the others' political positions. That the conspirators were visible but shrouded in darkness corresponded vividly with Brutus's lines above, but the fact that he was himself in near-darkness and in a marginal

location during this scene suggested that he may not be as politically re-
mote as his words and physical distance from the others implied. Eventually,
they would all mingle and bathe their hands together in the blue light of
the thrust. By spatializing and lighting them in these ways, the production
staged the initial political divide between these characters. But it also staged
Brutus's humanity and his own self-division, making it difficult for playgoers simply to vilify him.[13]

The 2001 production of *Richard II* used a similar spatializing technique
to differentiate political positions, though instead of manipulating the horizontal planes of foreground and background as *Julius Caesar* would do the
following year, the confrontation scene between Richard and Bolingbroke at
Flint Castle employed a visual vocabulary of physical height and lowliness.[14]
The earliest printed text of *Richard II*, a 1597 quarto, offers the stage direction: "*Richard appeareth on the Walls*,"[15] which is to say that he enters with his
men in an elevated position, probably in a gallery above the stage (originally
at The Theater in Shoreditch), while Bolingbroke and his men remain below
on the stage. After Bolingbroke learned that Flint Castle lodged the king, in
the Courtyard production he and his men began to exit through the auditorium, when suddenly Richard appeared brightly lit on a very high platform
in the space above where the proscenium and thrust meet. He stood tall, he
was crowned, he wore regal accoutrements, and he was surrounded by his
loyal advisors, as light beamed down from above as if bestowing a divine
blessing. Moreover, Richard was commanding and emphatic in his speeches
to Bolingbroke's envoy Northumberland, controlling the scene both aurally
and visually. When Northumberland returned to the darkened aisle of the
auditorium to confer with Bolingbroke, however, Richard weakened and
collapsed to his knees, saying to Aumerle: "We do debase ourself, cousin, do
we not, / To look so poorly and to speak so fair?" (3.3.126–27), which put
the visual splendor that playgoers had just witnessed into tension with Richard's own degraded self-perception. To be sure, the king had already given
up before the fight—had given up to avoid the fight—so when Northumberland returned and said of Bolingbroke, "My lord, in the base court he doth
attend / To speak with you. May it please you to come down?" (3.3.175–76),
Richard replied, "In the base court: base court where kings grow base / To
come at traitors' calls, and do them grace" (3.3.179–80).[16]

The differential between the king's height and his subjects' lower status
is a conventional social figure that also expresses their political relationship. The text activates this figure through its language—"debase," "poorly,"
"base court," "come down," and so forth—and, as already suggested, the 1597
quarto's stage direction for Richard's entry aloft makes the sociopolitical

relationship between the king and his subjects more intelligible and poignant. The production's physical elevation of Richard above other characters and audience members alike is an obvious enough image of the king's superior standing, but the positioning of Bolingbroke and his allies in an aisle of the auditorium introduces fascinating convulsions both to the audience's subordinate relationship with Richard and to its lateral relationship with Bolingbroke. If we are all subject to Richard's visual and rhetorical dominance in this scene, then Bolingbroke's invasion and occupation of spectatorial space reenacts his invasion and occupation of English soil, from which the king had earlier banished him for six years. In both the dramatic fiction and in the theater, in other words, Bolingbroke audaciously strides through places where he doesn't belong. And since he so readily shares the audience's territory in this and other scenes, Bolingbroke literally associates himself and his sedition with playgoers, who certainly hold different attitudes and degrees of sympathy toward him as well as toward the king, but who are also obliged to tolerate his occupation of their space—a political predicament not unlike Richard's own. By taking advantage of the Courtyard's substantial fly space as well as the permeable barrier between the thrust and the auditorium, the staging of this scene drew spectators' own physical positions into the meaning of the play, making them participants in, and not just passive observers of, Richard II's downfall.

Whatever playgoers might think about the legitimacy or the corruption of Richard's reign, on the one hand, or about the treason or the justification of Bolingbroke's deposition of the king, on the other, the Courtyard's staging of this scene demonstrated how the very notions of majesty and authority are both constructed and efficacious. That is, although majesty and authority were here fashioned out of spectacular symbolic materials such as Richard's crown and regalia, his visually dominant position, and his imposing voice, they also exercised real power through their awe-inspiring display, in spite of their constructedness. Playgoers were made to feel this power during his long, commanding speech to Northumberland denouncing Bolingbroke's impudence, which is why the evacuation of that power was so startling a sight when he fell to his knees on the elevated platform. The 2002 production of *The Tempest* likewise inspired a sense of great power through dazzling and lofty spectacle, but when the scene's artifice revealed itself to the audience it did not diminish Prospero's authority, as Richard's collapse diminished his, but enhanced it. Act 4, scene 1 opened on the thrust stage with Prospero lecturing Ferdinand about the "rich gift" of his daughter Miranda, whose "virgin-knot" he must not untie "before / All sanctimonious ceremonies may / With full and holy rite be ministered."[17] The two lovers sat together on a large swing as Prospero spoke. He then set the swing in motion, and it rose into the air, mounting above the audience seated in front of the stage on the main floor.

Thus began the play's masque scene, wherein the goddesses Iris, Juno, and Ceres sang a marriage blessing to the lovers. Clad in long white dresses and masks, the three figures seemed to float sideways onto the proscenium from the wings as the stage lighting shifted to a numinous dark blue and as Prospero took a seat on the edge of the stage. Halfway through their serenade, Iris, Juno, and Ceres began to ascend together, creating a visual harmony to match their melodic one. Even as they rose to the very top of the proscenium opening, the thick gatherings in their skirts continued to unfurl, extending many yards to the stage below. The goddesses hovered there singing, when Prospero abruptly roused himself and said:

> I had forgot that foul conspiracy
> Of the beast Caliban and his confederates
> Against my life. The minute of their plot
> Is almost come. (4.1.139–42)

The urgency of this matter demanded that Prospero end the masque and call on Ariel for assistance, and so he said to the goddesses, "Well done! Avoid; no more!" (4.1.142).[18] At this point in the action, the first printed text of *The Tempest* in the 1623 folio supplies the stage direction: "*Prospero starts sodainly and speakes, after which to a / strange hollow and confused noyse, they heauily vanish.*"[19] What "*a / strange hollow and confused noyse*" sounded like in the early modern theater is difficult to say, but when Prospero shouted: "Well done! Avoid; no more!" in the Courtyard's production, bright light immediately flooded the scene, exposing a rather stagey set in the background as the floating goddesses ungracefully drifted back to the wings. Further, playgoers could distinctly hear mechanical sounds from the fly-rigging as it wheeled the three figures out of sight, which was accompanied by the kind of jarring motions one would expect from suspended bodies being trailed by wires: "*they heauily vanish.*"

At one moment Prospero orchestrates a spectacular vision in the airspace over the proscenium stage, and in the next he dispossesses it of its brilliance. While the *Richard II* and *The Tempest* productions each put magnificent power on display and then suddenly exposed their theatrical artifice, there was an important difference between them. The supremacy that Richard projected from his elevated position at first appeared as natural as can be, which is but one mythology of kingship, yet his collapse undercut that appearance precisely because it was involuntary and therefore beyond his sovereign control. The high platform that would seem merely to be a symbol of Richard's innate majesty he revealed, in fact, to be its prop. On the other hand, Prospero never lost control over his masque as he commenced and concluded it at will. That he could ostensibly call on, conduct, and dismiss three goddesses as he pleased only reinforced his power; and, in exercising it, he did not need to exalt himself to a superior position, since he remained just as potent from below. In his review of the Courtyard production, David G. Brailow wrote of this scene:

> Prospero breaks off the masque with disproportionate rage, modulating into bitter sadness through the speech on the insubstantiality of life. [Larry] Yando makes it clear that, while Caliban is no real threat, the thought of Prospero's failure to control and civilize him fills him with a deep sense of futility and loss. The limits of his power remind him of the limits of mortality itself.[20]

Both the *Richard II* and *The Tempest* productions, then, drew on a spatial rhetoric in which the physical elevation of characters—along with the trappings of royalty on one side and the aura of the supernatural on the other—persuaded spectators that they were witnessing exhibitions of great power. The calculated use of the theater's substantial vertical space in these scenes affected far more than the staging of pure spectacle, however. The spectacle first convinced playgoers of the power it represents, making that power real, but the revelation of its artifice showed playgoers both the efficacy and the credibility of spectacle, making the power of theater the more real.

While such contrasts between high and low make the theater space signify in conjunction with political distinctions already embedded in the dramatic action, the oppositional staging of characters and sets evokes other kinds of social configurations and conflicts. The Courtyard's 2010 production of *Romeo and Juliet*, for example, featured building façades gazing at one another from opposite sides of the proscenium, with the playing space in between functioning as a street; in some scenes, the middle ground represented indoor space with the façades resembling an Italian villa's interior walls.[21] The buildings were necessarily angled upstage to increase playgoers' visibility, but this angling also had the advantageous effect of causing the set to recede from view, creating an implied vanishing point in the distance; see Figure 14. As with the deep entry corridor used in *Julius Caesar* (along with similar uses in other productions like *Antony and Cleopatra* [1999] and *The Merchant of Venice* [2005]), *Romeo and Juliet* extended its playing space into the backstage area beyond the overhead doors, which enhanced this

14. The set for Chicago Shakespeare Theater's 2010 production of *Romeo and Juliet*. Directed by Gale Edwards with scenic design by Brian Sidney Bembridge. Photograph by Liz Lauren

implied vanishing point during performance. Contributing to the sense of recession in space were three slightly trapezoidal grates built into the central floor of the proscenium, with another two on the thrust. Elongated and tapered toward the upstage, these metal grates allowed for indirect lighting from beneath as well as opportunities for trap use. Thus, the symmetrical positioning of the facades conveyed an impression of likeness as well as confrontation, which is precisely how the play's Prologue describes the Capulets and the Montagues:

> Two households, both alike in dignity
> In fair Verona, where we lay our scene,
> From ancient grudge break to new mutiny,
> Where civil blood makes civil hands unclean.[22]

When the action of the play began, A-frame construction barricades with flashing amber lights lined the middle of the street, sitting atop the central grates. Immediately, several metal garage doors in each of the façades flew open in unison, out of which stepped two groups of servants from the "two households." The swaggering and exchanging of insults between the Capulets and the Montagues inevitably resulted in a physical confrontation as the men threw and kicked down the barricades while attacking one another. The use of construction barricades, in particular, suggested that some Veronese authority had placed them there in the first place, but they did not provide any actual barrier, relying instead on law-abiding citizens to heed their silent warning. Dividing the households as they divided the street, the barricades were but a temporary and insubstantial solution to an already fragile peace, which the servingmen managed to destroy with ease. A complement to the street barricades, moreover, the scaffolding that covered much of the façade at stage right gave the appearance that the building was undergoing construction, which hinted that the household may also harbor disorder within its doors.[23] During the Capulets' masquerade ball a short while later, the audience observed just such disorder when Tybalt spied Romeo in the crowd and went "to strike him dead" (1.5.56). But the Capulet patriarch intervened, telling his nephew: "I would not for the wealth of all this town / Here in my house do him disparagement. / Therefore be patient, take no note of him" (1.5.66–68).[24] When Tybalt tried to disobey, Capulet threw him to the ground—the very ground, not coincidentally, where the opening brawl had occurred—and made his nephew submit. For the moment, Capulet had restored order to his household, but like the barricades it was precarious and subject to the volatility of youth.

The opening tableau's confrontation between two opposing building façades, which were in states of disrepair and were divided by construction barricades, offered playgoers a scenic metonym for the "ancient grudge" between "two households." Whenever the central playing area represented a street, then that space too acquired symbolic value in relation to the feuding families. Because the houses never managed to contain the conflict between the Capulets and the Montagues, the fighting routinely spilled out into the street, a common space where the inhabitants of Verona should be cultivating civil relationships instead of shedding "civil blood." The visual perspective created by the production's scenery, finally, and the implied vanishing point far upstage are familiar theatrical effects, which were popularized in the sixteenth century by Sebastiano Serlio, whose second book of *Tutte l'opere d'architettura* (1584) supplied early set designers with elaborate woodcuts for fashioning perspective scenery appropriate to comic, tragic, and satiric plays.[25] In the Courtyard's *Romeo and Juliet*, the visual perspective created by its receding set emphasized an uncertain but ominous conclusion to the play's action, since the vanishing point was obscured and the upstage was often cloaked in darkness. If streets are made for travel, then the destination toward which the dramatic fiction drives as it moves into the middle distance looks woeful indeed. For Romeo and Juliet, the street itself became "the fearful passage of their death-marked love," through which playgoers would likewise journey during "the two-hours' traffic of our stage" (Prologue 9, 12).

Chicago Shakespeare Theater's website showcases the configuration between performance and spectatorial spaces in the Courtyard, noting specifically the relationships that their arrangement fosters: "The design celebrates the importance of the audience in performance by surrounding the actors with the audience and the audience with fellow audience members. The intimacy of the 500-seat house serves to energize the work on the stage and the excitement in the seats."[26] Such physical intimacy can certainly help to make the playgoing experience less mediated by incorporating the audience into private, sometimes quite clandestine encounters between characters. But it can also alienate audience members—a valuable theatrical effect— by bringing conspiratorial, disconcerting, or even violent action a bit too close for comfort. Conversely, the depth of the proscenium gives the theater the flexibility to forgo the intimacy associated with the thrust in order to stage either more grandiose or more desolate scenes from a distance, which downstage space is less effective at conveying persuasively. The sizable fly space, too, can put great power on display through stunning spectacle, just as it can reveal emptied-out power consisting of little more than its faltering exhibition. With the capacity to position scenes either very near to or very far from the audience, both on, around, and high above the stage, and also in several of these locations at once, the theater is able to exploit a wide vocabulary of space. Productions in the Courtyard frequently draw on this vocabulary to make visual assertions about the social divisions and alliances that are fundamental to dramatic action.

The central aim of rhetoric is to persuade an audience either to adopt or abandon a particular intellectual position, one that is based on a speaker's argumentative discourse. If the theater positions playgoers in seats that orient them toward a stage, and furthermore, if the stage delivers to them a dramatic discourse that is itself a narrative of conflicting intellectual or characterological positions, then live performance is at core a rhetorical enterprise that convinces spectators not to adopt a specific perspective—at least not in worthwhile theater—but to observe and adjudicate between the multiple perspectives that its characters espouse. The size, shape, and design of the Courtyard's stage and auditorium maximize the potential for staging the physical space playgoers see, so that its nearness and distance, its height and lowness, and the juxtaposition between these locations might all signify in conjunction with the characters' relationships and the social conflicts that bring dramatic space into being.

NOTES

Acknowledgments: My thanks to Gina Buccola and Peter Kanelos for their invitation to contribute to this volume. I am also grateful to Jon Greenfield for the use of one of his drawings of the new Globe. At Chicago Shakespeare Theater, I would like to thank Susan Knill, Theater and Facility Manager, who gave me access to architectural documents and answered innumerable questions; to Marilyn J. Halperin, Director of Education and Communications, who is always as delightful as she is helpful; to Edward Leahy, Technical Director, who kindly provided me with essential technical information about the theater; to Elizabeth Neukirch, Public Relations Manager, for assistance acquiring several images; and to Ellen Shipitalo for furnishing me with crucial details about the *Richard III* production.

1. "Facility and Virtual Tour," Chicago Shakespeare Theater, accessed September 21, 2011.

2. The building contract for the Fortune Theater states that its "Stadge shall conteine in length ffortie and Three foote of lawfull assize and in breadth to extende to the middle of the yarde," which was to be fifty-five feet square. For a transcription of the contract, see R. A. Foakes and R. T. Rickert, eds., *Henslowe's Diary* (Cambridge: Cambridge UP, 1961), 308. The contract is housed at Dulwich College, Muniment 22.

3. For recent theater historical work on early modern playhouses and their archeology, see, for instance, Julian Bowsher and Pat Miller, *The Rose and the Globe—Playhouses of Shakespeare's Bankside, Southwark: Excavations 1988–91* (London: Museum of London Archaeology, 2009); and J. R. Mulryne and Margaret Shewring, eds., *Shakespeare's Globe Rebuilt* (Cambridge: Cambridge UP, 1997), especially John Orrell, "Designing the Globe: Reading the Documents," 51–65, and Jon Greenfield, "Design as Reconstruction: Reconstruction as Design," 81–96.

4. Roderick Ham, ed., *Theatre Planning* (Toronto: U of Toronto P, 1972), 17.

5. Although the Courtyard Theater's acoustical properties are beyond the scope of this essay, I will note that the space achieves a rich auditory environment through a mixture of both absorbent and highly reflective surfaces, including not only wood (mainly white ash) but also several rows of 45°-angled brick in the walls of the auditorium and air pockets built under the galleries, which effectively distribute sound without the booming reverberation associated with more rigid materials. For the acoustical properties of early modern theaters, see Bruce R. Smith, *The Acoustic World of Early Modern England: Attending to the O-Factor* (Chicago: U of Chicago P, 1999), especially chapter 8.

6. Adapted and directed by Peter Brook, *The Tragedy of Hamlet* ran from May 10 to June 2, 2001.

7. William Shakespeare, *Richard II*, in *The Norton Shakespeare: Based on the Oxford Edition*, ed. Stephen Greenblatt et al. (New York: W. W. Norton, 1997), 2.1.258.

8. William Shakespeare, *Richard III*, in *Norton Shakespeare*, 5.8.33–37.

9. Directed by Barbara Gaines, *Richard III* ran from September 23 to November 22, 2009. Gloucester/Richard III was played by Wallace Acton and Richmond/Henry VII by Brendan Marshall-Rashid.

10. Such staging decisions employ a parallel early modern practice wherein the performance aims to create a sense of immense crowding, usually indicated by permissive stage directions during mass entries like "*and others as many as can be*," a phrase that appears toward the opening of the first quarto of *The Most Lamentable Romaine Tragedie of Titus Andronicus* (London: Printed by Iohn Danter for Edward White and Thomas Millington, 1594), sig. A4^v. See "permissive stage directions" in Alan C. Dessen and Leslie Thomson, *A Dictionary of Stage Directions in English Drama, 1580–1642* (Cambridge: Cambridge UP, 1999), 161–62. Running from December 7, 2002, to February 23, 2003, *Julius Caesar* was directed by Barbara Gaines.

11. William Shakespeare, *Julius Caesar*, in *Norton Shakespeare*, 2.1.74–76.

12. In the Courtyard production, Brutus was played by Kevin Gudahl, Cassius by Scott Parkinson, and Lucius by James McKay.

13. In his review of *Julius Caesar*, directed by Barbara Gaines, Chicago Shakespeare Theater, Justin Shaltz wrote that "Gaines contrasts Brutus's role in the murderous conspiracy with his acts of compassion: he kneels before Portia to attend to her self-inflicted thigh wound, welcomes the aged Ligarius into his home, and finally shows tenderness toward the servant Lucius." *Shakespeare Bulletin* 21.2 (2003): 37–38, at 37.

14. Barbara Gaines directed *Richard II*, which ran from September 7 to November 18, 2001.

15. *The Tragedie of King Richard the Second* (London: Printed by Valentine Simmes for Androw Wise, 1597), sig. F4^v.

16. Richard II was played by Scott Parkinson, Bolingbroke by Scott Jaeck, Northumberland by Fredric Stone, and Aumerle by Reginald Nelson.

17. William Shakespeare, *The Tempest*, in *Norton Shakespeare*, 4.1.8, 4.1.15–17.

18. Directed by Barbara Gaines, *The Tempest* ran from March 29 to June 16, 2002. Prospero was played by Larry Yando, Miranda by Cassandra Bissell, Ferdinand by Timothy Edward Kane, Iris by McKinley Carter, Juno by Ariane Dolan, Ceres by Deborah Monson, and Caliban by Scott Jaeck.

19. William Shakespeare, *The Tempest*, in *Mr. William Shakespeares Comedies, Histories, & Tragedies* (London: by Isaac Iaggard and Ed. Blount, 1623), sig. B2^r.

20. David G. Brailow, review of *The Tempest*, directed by Barbara Gaines, Chicago Shakespeare Theater, *Shakespeare Bulletin* 20.2 (2002): 18–19, at 19.

21. Directed by Gale Edwards with set design by Brian Sidney Bembridge, *Romeo and Juliet* ran from September 15 to November 21, 2010.

22. William Shakespeare, *Romeo and Juliet*, in *Norton Shakespeare*, Prologue 1–4.

23. I am grateful to Gina Buccola for reminding me of the scaffolding and suggesting this reading.

24. Capulet was played by John Judd, Tybalt by Zach Appelman, and Romeo by Jeff Lillico.

25. Sebastiano Serlio, *Tutte l'opere d'architettura* (Venetia: Presso Francesco de' Franceschi, 1584), "Della scena comica," sigs. G1^v–G2^r; "Della scena tragica," sigs. G2$^{r–v}$;

"Della scena satirica," sigs. G3^{r-v}. Books I and II were first printed in Paris in 1545, and an English translation appeared in London in 1611. For reproductions of the three Serlian scenes, see Stephen Orgel, "Shakespeare Imagines a Theater," *Poetics Today* 5 (1984): 549–61, at 550–52.

    26. "Virtual Tour."

BIBLIOGRAPHY

Bowsher, Julian, and Pat Miller. *The Rose and the Globe—Playhouses of Shakespeare's Bank-side, Southwark: Excavations 1988–91*. London: Museum of London Archaeology, 2009.

Brailow, David G. Review of *The Tempest*, directed by Barbara Gaines. *Shakespeare Bulletin* 20.2 (2002): 18–19.

Chicago Shakespeare Theater. "Facility and Virtual Tour." Accessed September 21, 2011.

Dessen, Alan C., and Leslie Thomson. *A Dictionary of Stage Directions in English Drama, 1580–1642*. Cambridge: Cambridge UP, 1999.

Foakes, R. A., and R. T. Rickert, eds. *Henslowe's Diary*. Cambridge: Cambridge UP, 1961.

Ham, Roderick, ed. *Theatre Planning*. Toronto: U of Toronto P, 1972.

Mulryne, J. R., and Margaret Shewring, eds. *Shakespeare's Globe Rebuilt*. Cambridge: Cambridge UP, 1997.

Orgel, Stephen. "Shakespeare Imagines a Theater." *Poetics Today* 5 (1984): 549–61.

Serlio, Sebastiano. *Tutte l'opere d'architettura*. Venetia: Presso Francesco de' Franceschi, 1584.

Shakespeare, William. *The Most Lamentable Romaine Tragedie of Titus Andronicus*. London: Printed by Iohn Danter for Edward White and Thomas Millington, 1594.

———. *The Norton Shakespeare: Based on the Oxford Edition*. Ed. Stephen Greenblatt et al. New York: W. W. Norton, 1997.

———. *The Tempest*. In *Mr. William Shakespeares Comedies, Histories, & Tragedies*. London: Printed by Isaac Iaggard and Ed. Blount, 1623.

———. *The Tragedie of King Richard the Second*. London: Printed by Valentine Simmes for Androw Wise, 1597.

Shaltz, Justin. Review of *Julius Caesar*, directed by Barbara Gaines. *Shakespeare Bulletin* 21.2 (2003): 37–38.

Smith, Bruce R. *The Acoustic World of Early Modern England: Attending to the O-Factor*. Chicago: U of Chicago P, 1999.

PART II

This One's for the Girls
Millennial Ladies in Josie Rourke's Twelfth Night

ALICIA TOMASIAN

By 2007 Chicago's new millennium had hosted two highly praised all-male productions of *Twelfth Night*, both at Chicago Shakespeare Theater. Until Josie Rourke's 2009 mixed-sex cast, CST fans might have begun to assume that the play's cross-dressing heroine, Viola, only made sense played by a man. These nods to Elizabethan casting perhaps gave new meaning to the character's plaint, "Disguise, I see, thou art a wickedness / Wherein the pregnant enemy does much."[1] For a time, the play's gender bending provided a platform for agendas precluding a female Viola. By contrast, the theater's third *Twelfth Night* of the millennium promised a more feminist approach, even in the choice of Rourke as director. Her 2005 *Much Ado About Nothing* had switched a number of the play's male roles (including Dogberry's watch) to female characters in what theater critic Charles Spencer bemoaned as the young director "making a feminist point" about women's intuition.[2] If Rourke was hired to reinstate a feminist gaze through Viola and Olivia, she certainly delivered. For my community-college students, most of whom saw the production in conjunction with a Shakespeare course they were taking with me, she did more than that. Drawing on Shakespeare's 400-year-old gender bending, she incorporated fresh young heroines to address a new generation of young women—straight, gay, or bisexual—convincing them that Shakespeare's androgynous erotics were all about them: their generation, their city, their desires, and their theatrical pleasure. While the all-male productions had been hugely popular, Rourke's *Twelfth Night* exemplified CST's specific appeal to a new audience, one bolstered by sales targeted at college groups, such as my own students at Harper College. Transforming CST's thrust stage into a 7,000-gallon pool splashing onto those groups, Rourke's production literally connected with the audience through the water some saw as representing personal freedom.[3] She invited young viewers to identify powerfully with Shakespeare's characters, almost as millennial peers.

In so doing, Rourke went back to the drawing board in the play's celebration of youth and, arguably, female strength, but with enough of a modern twist in the form of athleticism, racial ambiguity, and girly sass to aim directly at a fresh generation of female theater novices. Further, she invited the entire audience to participate in their gaze, one that defines itself through personal freedoms and various female subjectivities. I hesitate to label Rourke's production as feminist; the term *feminism* itself is something many of my current students disavow, including those who consistently promote feminist agendas in class discussion, as a term invoking overly political and sometimes anti-male sentiment. Even when I read in class the O.E.D.'s comparatively sterile definition of feminism—"advocacy of the rights of women (based on the theory of equality of the sexes)"[4]—I usually get no more than half of a given class to claim the title of feminist. In this respect, my students actually most closely embody what Jenny Coleman identifies as third-wave feminism, dedicated to personal freedom and personal narratives. My students, like the third wave Coleman describes, typically reject earlier generations' feminism as too political, stymieing individuality, complexity, and diversity.[5] Coleman also references a number of critics who see women of the new millennium rejecting feminism as "anti-men, anti-feminine; anti-family; over-prescriptive; interfering in private lives."[6] I recognize these attitudes in my students, which may explain their pleasure in Rourke's distinctly feminine Viola. Third-wave feminism most closely captures how many first-generation college women see themselves: strong yet feminine, sexually ambiguous but pro-men, progressive but not aggressive. Thus, although they usually reject the label of feminist, I read Rourke's approach and their enthusiasm for it as third-wave feminist.

Rourke's third-wave gaze introduced the play to a broad audience, more diverse, young, and less culturally and educationally elite than a second-wave feminist or a distinctly male homoerotic gaze might. In fact, to many of my students attending the production with me, Rourke's joyful, watery romp felt mostly like a teen "chick flick" (perhaps one of the recent Shakespearean adaptations, such as *Ten Things I Hate about You* or *She's the Man*). In his review for *Shakespeare Bulletin*, Samuel Park agreed, arguing Michelle Beck as Viola "played up the character's tomboy-ish quality, giving Cesario a convincing teenage swagger."[7] For Park, an adolescent Viola relating to a more authoritative Olivia made these characters "more contemporary in psychology,"[8] because it emphasized Olivia's attraction to a younger man and Viola's fascination with an older woman's power. While I would argue that neither of these phenomena is unique to the twenty-first century, my students did identify with two exuberant, aggressive, but girly leading ladies. *New City* saw Rourke's vision as "actually quite traditional,"[9] and the *Tribune*'s Chris Jones praised it as "a happily organic homage both to traditional Shakespearean comedy, pretty much as the old fellow wrote it for land-locked London, as well as to those warm-weather pleasures of the water,"[10] but my students felt that the production made a splash in more ways than one. Rourke seemed to be targeting a new generation of women who believe they can be both totally feminine and assertive.

CST'S GROUNDLINGS

I took a group of about fifteen students to Rourke's production of *Twelfth Night* in 2009. It should be noted that my group, as is often the case with college groups, sat directly to the side of the stage, alongside Rourke's pool. CST's Group Sales department has always made a point of placing us in the first rows on either side of the thrust stage, even though college groups pay just $30 a student. Jonathan Baude, Group Sales Coordinator, explained, "Those seats on the right and left sides, those are fun seats. If those are open, that's one of our favorite places to put groups."[11] According to Chicago Shakespeare Theater's website, the thrust stage "necessitates an intimate, immediate relationship between actors and their audience."[12] My students' comments about the production during and just after the trip asserted their feeling of connection to the performers. This was especially the case with the women in my group. One young woman, who had been on several CST trips before, asserted that she thought this one the "Best! Play! Ever!"[13] She insisted to her classmates who had not attended that the lead actresses spoke right to her. "They were looking at us and talking to us!" she exclaimed. Several other women agreed with her. I asked if the men felt the same direct address. None said they did, although they agreed with their female classmates that the production intensely engaged the audience. According to Baude, this effect was deliberate: "The performances are designed with our [thrust] stage in mind, so I think it is really cool to sit on one of the sides." He described such an experience as "immersive," providing a "slightly unconventional view," and explained that it often adds to the spectacle when the most intimate relationships between actors and audience involve college groups. "You'll see people gasping, hooting, and hollering," he said.[14] Baude estimated that college groups, often with fifty or sixty people, attend an average of three nights a week.[15] Thus, they can radically shape the audience experience.[16] While I cannot recall whether any of my students hooted or hollered, we certainly gasped as characters fell into the pool, splashing us. I occasionally hear our happy, newly minted theater enthusiasts boast of being close enough to feel the spit and to look the actors in the eye, but *Twelfth Night* took this feeling of identification to a whole new level.

In class discussion after the trip both men and women agreed that, despite the Elizabethan dress, the performance felt contemporary to them; they saw the characters as their peers. All of the attendees had read *Twelfth Night* before the show. We had discussed it in class, even performing scenes, and indeed most of these students had loved the text. In particular, they loved the homoerotic aspects of attraction between Olivia and Viola as well as Orsino and Viola. In discussion after attending the production, they all talked about how relatable Rourke's production was to them, and they raved to their classmates about the pool as well as Michelle Beck's Viola. In class, several students described Beck in great detail, commenting on how attractive, feminine, and funny she was. While they had all enjoyed Shakespeare's challenge to traditional gender roles when we read the play, most felt that the production made this element more real for them. In other words, they agreed with Charles Spencer that Rourke had a thoroughly modern (feminist) agenda. Of course, my students were not theater critics or Shakespeareans (although one is now in the process of becoming the latter, and two have just completed certification to teach high school English). What I found to be important in their comments was the relationship they developed with the stage, their belief that the production catered to them, CST's groundlings.

With class discussion in mind, I was curious to see what they would remember two years later when I interviewed them about their impressions. I wanted to know whether, after seeing other productions and after transferring to four-year universities, they still felt as they had two years ago. I also wanted to know if their impressions would be different beyond the context of class. Most students on the trip were in one particularly vocal and lively section of Introduction to Shakespeare. They had all bonded quickly, and in fact, on the night of the trip, dinner conversation lingered on issues of romantic relationships. Although both men and women were vocal in class, very vocal women outnumbered men. Thus, I also wondered if men would reflect on the performance differently once out of the group. Using my notes from class discussion, I developed interview questions. I was not surprised that many of them remembered our general class discussions about gender, but I was shocked that so many of my former students remembered intricate details, such as the wooden heart-shaped frame of the set, the bare feet of the actors, and specific moments, such as falls and leaps into the pool. More than that, I was amazed by how many told me that Rourke's production made them want to return to CST whenever possible, how this show made them feel like CST was their chosen indulgence, their place.

In interviews two years later, many female students still felt that Rourke's production and leading ladies aimed squarely at them. However, even separated from the group, most of the men I interviewed continued to speak highly of the production. (Only one man from Introduction to Shakespeare, who seemed to enjoy the show at the time, criticized it two years later.) One of the men who loved the show told me, "The women made more of an impression." They were, he thought, "gesturing to the audience," giving him "the idea that they're who we are supposed to be relating to." Another student, a woman in her late twenties, brought two friends with her. All three were recent immigrants to the United States from South America, still struggling to learn English. The student, in fact, called me simply "teacher." Her group arrived late, as they came right from work, sporting jeans and carrying large cups of pop. Although the student I knew was hardworking, smart, enthusiastic, and intellectual (she is majoring in engineering), I was worried that she and her friends might find Elizabethan English an insurmountable barrier. It had, in fact, been an obstacle in class. Instead, they all experienced Rourke's production as a celebration—their girls' night out—and worth every penny. In the lobby afterward, they raved about the show, going on and on about how much fun it was. Two years later, my student, who had never before attended a play in English, told me, "Going to the show was actually the best way to understand the book. For me, English is a second language, but the play made it understandable. It was great!" She also related to Viola: "I found it appealing that the main character was a girl. It was like Shakespeare's play, but there was something different, something a bit more, a twist." One of her friends also said she felt immersed in the production due to our seats. "I had never had an opportunity to attend a play like that before," she said. "I have only been to theaters where you sit in front of the stage. We were a little more incorporated, so I felt like a part of the play." She added, "I loved when one of the characters jumped in the pool!" Over the next two years, the student made an effort to participate in a number of trips to CST. She was clearly won over to Shakespearean theater.

According to my students, even the first image of the show, the set, cued them to expect a female perspective. One young woman remembered the excitement of walking in and seeing designer Lucy Osborne's heart-shaped frame, recalling that she instantly thought, "It was pretty. . . . I guess it could be seen as more feminine. I thought it was cute!" The first few minutes of the production provided another strikingly "girly" image. Rourke made quick use of the set's most surprising feature, the large pool, dropping Michelle Beck (Viola) from the ceiling with a shocking splash. After an alarming pause, Beck surfaced, gasping for air and pulling herself out of the pool in wet, thin clothes revealing her curvy, womanly body as well as her very feminine facial features. To my students, this image of Beck endured, even though Osborne's Elizabethan costuming provided some impressive cover. (As Osborne explained in an interview, "The sexual ambiguity of clothes at that time is . . . really interesting, which is so helpful when Viola dresses as Cesario."[17]) Most of my students, however, never forgot the youthful, pretty, voluptuous Viola of her first appearance. Most said the costuming never really hid Beck's true gender (an effect perhaps amplified by the fact that Viola looked up to a taller Olivia), but that seems not to have been a problem. To the young women I interviewed, Beck's body *mattered*; it felt preferable to the more boyish Viola (Imogen Stubbs) we had watched in clips from Trevor Nunn's film. Said one young woman in her interview, "I liked it. It would have been a more distant thing if she was a woman who looked like a man, because I don't relate to that. It made her a more romantic figure." Incidentally, Beck's body seemed to matter to the young men in our crowd as well. One man described her as "feminine" and "elegant." Another commented that he felt it would have been hard to hide Beck's curvy, attractive figure.

Both the women and the men who attended agreed, to some degree, with Jean E. Howard's view of Viola's "'feminine' subjectivity,"[18] and, for the most part, with Nancy Lindheim's reading of Viola: "She is always female for us, regardless of what she wears; constant asides and speeches remind us that her fears or desires are those conventionally ascribed to women and girls."[19] Did this kill the play's homoeroticism? The woman who saw Viola as a romantic heroine argued, "I think it is more believable if she [Viola] is pretty and more womanly. If she just looked like another man, then why wouldn't she [Olivia] just fall in love with another man?" Asked if she thought this Olivia was gay, the student answered, "bi-curious." She also thought this element of the production might seem scandalous to older generations. Her grandmother would have hated it, she told me, because her grandmother would be offended by the homoeroticism already present in Shakespeare's play but accentuated in Rourke's production. For this student, the disguise never really hid the truth of the play, Viola's womanhood. This same woman, however, asserted that she felt the women of the production were girly *and* physically assertive. She saw the female leads as "stronger than the men. Their posture was always straighter, more aggressive, more powerful." In fact, she said, she barely remembers the men. "I focused more on the women. I think the production did that." Said another woman of Viola, Olivia, and Maria, "They weren't so much masculine, but just leaders."

Karen Aldridge as Olivia and Michelle Beck as Viola also offered my students another point of bodily identification as African American or mixed race. Most of my students felt this made them more relatable to a younger and more diverse audience. In interviews, one woman, a returning student in her forties, identified herself as mixed race and said she related to light-skinned Beck. Being mixed, she mused, pushes people to "put you in a box." (This student said she is almost always assumed to be African American, even though she is a quarter white.) Regarding the racial diversity of the cast, she said, "I think it has got to be purposeful . . . more people can connect to the characters." This student had previously attended performances with racially diverse casts. While she always appreciated such choices, she had never before read it as purposeful the way she read a mixed-race Viola and Sebastian. She said she also felt that the seemingly "mixed" appearance of Viola and Sebastian might have been playing on ideas of "mixed" gender, or indefinite identity. Rourke's interpretation of *Twelfth Night*, she said, asked, "Who am I? What am I supposed to be? Who am I expected to be?" Also notable was African American Ora Jones as Maria, of whom the returning student asked, "Did she do a neck roll?" She seemed to be indicating that Maria not only *appeared* to be African American, but also that she gestured like a black woman. For most of my students, Rourke's diverse cast defied the trap Lisa M. Anderson describes as a well-meaning attempt at overcoming racism. For Anderson, despite the good intentions of mixed-race casts, the results often range from "merely distracting to quite discomforting."[20] Anderson describes some mixed-race casting as "colorblind casting,"[21] but my students did not perceive Rourke's choices as "blind," even though some of them had perceived previous casts in this light. To my students, the bodies of the actors, black, white, mixed, men and—most important—women, were not to be ignored. They were invitations to a new generation of Windy City Shakespeare fans willing to dive in. They were also tools used by Rourke and her cast to express a generational shift, a subtle new approach to the breaking of boundaries or the growing insignificance of them.

"THAT 'YOU KNOW WHAT I MEAN' LOOK"

Key to the youthful exuberance of the production was what the *Chicago Reader* called "a giddy cast,"[22] dressed as Elizabethans but moving as millennials. One young woman told me that she loved the traditional dress with the twist of bare feet, which she says she noticed right away. It looked, she said, "Shakespearean but a little different." Of course, the bare feet made splashing in the pool possible, but it also gave the characters a more contemporary look and freedom of movement, if only because we rarely see actors in doublets, bodices, and ruffs but without shoes. For this student, that connection between Shakespeare's material and her contemporary world (including Chicago) also came through in Lucy Osborne's waterside setting. "It looked inspired by Navy Pier," she said, and then continued, "It made you more aware that they are by the beach." For her, the production felt at once traditional but also current. (The watery location of the theater was particularly immediate to a few of my students, who had taken the water taxi to Navy Pier.)

For a young audience, it would seem, the key to that contemporary access was mostly the female bodies and the way those bodies moved, addressing the audience. Contemporary gestures and the dynamics they created invited the women in my class to relate to the women of the play, cued by the playful splashing of water. As the *New City* review observed, "water, after all, can reveal gender and desire. . . . Meanwhile, a good portion of the audience, especially the younger end, mostly likes getting splashed."[23] Indeed, my group got multiple splashings, much to their amusement. Some said they felt the water was a reminder of gender bending or sensuality. Tellingly, the young woman who loved the bare feet described Illyria as "by the beach," not the sea, perhaps evoking the same sense of freedom a generation of spring breakers would associate with a beach. In fact, we attended the production just after our break, as the show ran from March 29 to June 7. Whether or not Osborne was considering spring break, she said she wanted "to give a sense of being on a really beautiful, hot summer holiday. . . . It's a very comfortable, hot place to lounge around."[24]

Splashes, sprinkles, and dunks often punctuated moments of confused gender identity as well as erotic excitement. As Orsino observed of his new favorite, "Diana's lip / Is not more smooth and rubious; thy small pipe / as the maiden's organ, shrill and sound, / And all is semblative a woman's part" (1.4.31–34), he sprinkled her with water.[25] Later, as the two listened to music, Orsino grabbed Cesario and threatened to throw her in as she struggled to free herself. Tellingly, Cesario did not jump in until the final scene, when

15. Michelle Beck (center) with cast of *Twelfth Night* (2009), directed by Josie Rourke. Photo by Liz Lauren

she revealed her identity to Sebastian. Both then plunged in at the same time, leaping from either side of the stage and meeting in the middle. Thinking of this moment, the returning student explained that she thought the pool equaled truth. "Water seems to add an element of freedom and clarity," she said. Of Viola's exuberant leap into the water, she gushed, "The joy she felt, you could feel it. She could release the masquerade and rinse off all that stuff." The pool also provided the opportunity to show Orsino in a relative state of undress, without his ruff. Osborne clearly seized on Elizabethan attitudes regarding dress, opting to have Orsino at times forgo a ruff, which, by the time of the original performance of the play, was an androgynous accessory. Meanwhile, both Olivia and Viola (as well as Cesario) wore one. "It's an age where the men are trying to emulate Elizabeth I and become more feminine, and the women, also because of Elizabeth I, are becoming masculine," Osborne observed.[26] Contemporary audiences most often associate a ruff with Elizabeth, so it would make sense that this gender-neutral accessory would be an important part of costuming in this production. Yet Orsino's many dips into the pool allowed for a bare chest and neck, revealing an obviously masculine physical trait (chest hair).

Indeed, Orsino's more casual bare neck contrasted with Olivia's ruff in the promotional poster, although in her first appearance as Olivia, Aldridge clearly expressed sassy, girly, uncontained excitement over Cesario. As she became increasingly interested in her disguised visitor, she looked out to spectators audibly responding to her. After Cesario left, she rehashed their conversation—"What is your parentage?" (1.4.284), she repeated, then pounded her fists against her skirt and groaned in embarrassment. Calming herself, she continued, "'Above my fortunes, yet my state is well; I am a gentleman,' I'll be sworn thou art! / Thy tongue, thy face, thy limbs, actions and spirit do give thee fivefold blazon" (1.5.285–88). She punctuated this thought with a loud "woooo!" of passionate sexual attraction. Then, seemingly having worked herself into a frenzy, she slapped her chest a few times, as if catching her breath while she exclaimed, "Not too fast! Soft, soft" (1.5.288). (One of my students remembered this moment as Olivia fanning herself because Cesario was so "hot.") This received a big laugh, clearly inspired by her "giddy" excitement. Still breathless, she threw her arms in the air and yelled, "Well, let it be" (1.5.293). The more excited she got, the more contemporary seemed her side utterances and gestures. The returning student remembered a moment when "she came right to the edge of the stage and gave that 'You know what I mean' look right at the audience." Another of the women described her behavior as "like a high school girl," adding, "The gestures . . . were all more modern, but they really did seem timeless." One of the men, asked about Olivia, exclaimed, "I thought she was great! She seemed modern." (Her youthful demeanor also seemed in stark contrast to Mark L. Montgomery's slightly balding Orsino.) Aldridge's Olivia seemed to bounce and bound about in erotic excitement; her essence was far more girlfriend than countess. As she ordered Malvolio, "hie thee," she actually galloped to send the message home. Forfeiting all control, she called out, "I do I know not what, and fear to find / Mine eye too great a flatterer for my mind. / Fate, show thy force" (1.5.303–5). With that, she fell backward in joyful abandon, skirt, ruff, veil, and all, into the pool. As she willingly threw herself into the deep end, the audience applauded, wiping themselves dry. Aldridge's Olivia washed away all facade, literally and figuratively, in a gesture of youthful exuberance. While it was surprising to see her voluminous clothes immersed, her hair and makeup were clearly natural enough that she looked herself as she emerged, dripping.

Telling us, "You know what I mean," with her "look," she demanded of us to share her gaze. Her third-wave feminism invited even my self-identified straight female students to feel and understand Olivia's attraction to pretty, womanly Cesario/Viola. When the two women met for a second time, Olivia began the scene with composure but finally could not contain herself. Hilariously trotting up to Cesario as she waved her hands, she fawned, "Cesaaaari-oooo," then confessing, "by the roses of the spring, / By maidenhood, honor, truth, and everything, I love thee so that, maugre all thy pride, / Nor wit nor reason can my passion hide" (3.2. 148–52). Clearly, many of my students felt complicit in this adolescent adoration, and many enjoyed the homoerotic tension. There were several moments during Olivia and Cesario's first meeting when Olivia nearly kissed Cesario, and during their second encounter, Olivia grabbed a squirming Cesario around the chest from behind, palming her disguised breasts. Aldridge's confused look won increasing laughter as she then fondled her own breasts for a point of comparison.

All of my students noted the sexual tension between women. Many also felt that Sebastian's more feminine features invited a certain pleasurable androgyny. I asked the woman in her forties about the appeal of a more feminine Cesario and Sebastian that we had discussed in class two years before. She thought for a moment, then began with the disclaimer, "I'm not gay." Contemplating Sebastian, who she thought "looked a little feminine," and Viola, she confessed, "I was attracted to him [Sebastian], but I couldn't help but be attracted to her too!" Struggling to describe her response to Beck, she said, "I'm trying to think of another word for 'masculine.' She didn't act butch. She was assertive without being aggressive." Tellingly, this student rejected traditional terms for her gaze and attraction, much the way third-wave feminists challenge traditional sex- and gender-based identifications. While her response to androgyny was no doubt largely the result of Shakespeare's original play, her reaction also clearly resulted from her twenty-first-century understanding of female sexuality as well as her response to Beck's person and performance. Finally, this student came to the conclusion that Beck's feminine beauty and presence as well as masculine disguise sparked her erotic gaze. "When she first came out [of the water] and she was so stunning, my admiration for the beauty was there," she recalled. "Then I was attracted to an assertive, attractive, intelligent woman." Animated, she continued, "I remember Viola came right to the corner of the stage and looked right at me, right through me. She was talking about how she felt as a woman, but looking at her as a man was sexually confusing because she was so cute!" This student experienced her interpretation as enjoyment of both hetero- and homoeroticism, but all within the context of appreciating traits she saw as feminine. The traditionally aged college women had similar responses; besides the woman who identified Olivia as "bi-curious," another, who attended with her fiancé, complained that Sebastian was "not feminine enough!" Initially, it seemed Olivia agreed. Perhaps because of Sebastian's submission to the lady's request, "Would thou'dst be ruled by me!" (4.2.63), the male version seemed unable to arouse Olivia's erotic excitement as had Cesario. The couple began walking off stage, arm in arm, quiet and composed, until Olivia turned back to face the audience (her girlfriend confidantes) and released a loud squeal of infatuation and triumph.

It was Beck's Viola, however, who obviously cultivated the closest relationship with young female patrons, using eye contact and body language to assert a strong female physicality. As she came to the awkward realization of Olivia's devotion—"She loves me, sure!" (2.3.22)—she looked squarely out at the first rows. To Orsino's misogynist observations, "Women are as roses, whose fair flower / Being once displayed, doth fall that very hour" (2.4.38–39), she once again looked out at the audience, reminding them of the woman beneath the doublet. She then responded wistfully, "Alas that they are so" (2.4.40). While none of the men I spoke to commented on these moments, all of the women did. Said one, "It definitely felt like the women were looking at the audience more than the men. . . . There were at least three different times when Viola and Olivia made eye contact with *me.*" These moments were often accompanied by modern gestures of familiarity and sarcasm. Some of the most obvious sarcasm involved interactions with Orsino. Draping his arm around Cesario, the duke invited her to sit by the pool and listen to Feste's odd love song, which in class many of my students identified as "emo" (emotional). As explained to me in class discussion be-

fore the trip, "emo" most often refers specifically to music but also sometimes to those who listen to emo music, as in the term "emo boy." This term
also implies effeminacy. According to Urbandictionary.com, "the emo boy
is a xy [*sic*] chromosome-based apology for the sinful excess of patriarchal
society, achieved chiefly through the adoption of more stereotypically feminine traits," and as a group, emo boys "gather much of their inspiration from
the more nihilistic aspects of 1980s rock/punk bands, typically due to it's
[*sic*] prolifically morose tones and androgynous fashion."[27] Orsino's choice
of song, then, helps to define him as an "emo boy," and in this production,
so did Orsino's response to the music. As Feste sang, "Come away, come
away death, / And in sad cypress let me be laid. / Fly away, fly away breath; /
I am slain by a fair cruel maid" (2.4.51–54), the duke nodded to the music,
then he covered his face in dramatic, exaggerated emotion. Viola watched
his reaction and rolled her eyes. (One of the men in our group specifically
recalled this gesture two years later.) Beck then looked away, seemingly stifling a chuckle. As the morbid love anthem continued, "My shroud of white,
stuck all with yew; / Oh prepare it! / My part of death, no one so true / did
share it" (2.4.51–56), Orsino threw himself onto his back, freeing Viola, who
used the moment to stretch her arms. Looking back at his pathetic display,
she shook her head. No longer able to lie still, "emo" Orsino got up to pace
as Feste sang, "Not a friend, not a friend greet / My poor corpse, where my
bones shall be thrown" (2.4.61–63). At this point, Viola turned away again,
fighting to contain her laughter.

My students had been looking forward to this scene, and they were not
disappointed. Beck's mocking gestures made a big impression on them. A
few said how surprised they were and how much they enjoyed it that she
seemed to be making fun of Orsino's lovesickness. "The men were more
ridiculous than the women, because they just seemed like they didn't know
what to do with themselves," one woman said. "You could totally see there
was a power shift." In Jean Howard's reading, the play celebrates "a cross-
dressed woman who does not aspire to the positions of power assigned to
men,"[28] but Rourke took this idea and turned it upside down. For Howard,
Viola's heterosexual desires render her unthreatening, but in Rourke's new
vision, Viola's heterosexual desire underscored the ridiculousness of men,
particularly Orsino.[29] While it is true that my students never forgot Viola's
heterosexual desires, as Howard suggests, a millennial Viola used her disguise to mock and critique the very man to whom she was attracted. In
response to Feste's jest, "The Lady Olivia has no folly. She'll keep no fool, sir,
till she be married" (3.2.33), Viola laughed and nodded, clearly thinking of
Orsino. That being said, one of the men told me, "It was not the mockery of

men I expected it to be. They made it more fun." He clearly felt complicit in playful female subjectivity.

On a number of other occasions, Beck adopted certain gestures and movements that the world of the play presented as masculine, but contemporary young women saw as just confident and sporty. In her first appearance as a boy, she slapped the backs and arms of Orsino's men as they came out of the pool. Later, intermission concluded with a few musicians performing as Cesario watched and danced a bit in the form of some stiff knee bends, applauding with us as the piece ended and the house lights came down. Bantering with Feste, she joked about how she was "almost sick" for a beard, assuring the audience "though I would not have it grow on my chin" (3.1.46–47). Then, in response to a few laughs from the first rows, Beck pointed to the spectators, seemingly crediting them for getting the joke. This in turn won a big laugh from the crowd, during which she continued to stare down the front row, tsk-tsking them with her fingers. She seemed to be implying that we might be having too much fun at her expense or risking exposing her identity. Still, it was clear we were laughing with her, not at her. She was also complicit in the bawdry of the play, obviously pulling at the crotch of her pantaloons as she punned, "A little thing / would make me tell them how much I lack of a man" (3.4.302–3). Preparing to fight, her small, feminine frame seemed athletic, even as she flexed her muscles and gave herself a little slap to bring herself to attention. Like Aldridge, she used her bare feet to spring about the stage in movement neither graceful nor quite androgynous, but nimble, silly, and powerfully communicative: a new kind of woman. She obviously did not want to fight. (In fact, she briefly fainted at the thought, coming to with a slap on the arm from Fabian, which she returned. The two then exchanged two more slaps, with hers hard enough to push him.) Yet she was agile enough that she probably wouldn't have been half bad. Warming up, she shook out her hands and ran in place like a boxer. She took a few practice swings, one of which was forceful enough that Fabian jumped back in alarm.

While her heterosexual desire may, as Howard suggests, naturalize her in a potentially unstable world,[30] her final affirmation of that desire in the production rewrote traditional rules of women in courtship. In the text, Orsino initiates physical contact, asking Viola, "Give me thy hand, / And let me see thee in thy woman's weeds" (5.1.272–73), but in Rourke's production, Viola initiated true physical intimacy. Montgomery's Orsino kept an obvious, uncomfortable distance, holding his arm between himself and Beck as he delivered the lines, "Cesario, come— / For so you shall be, while you are a man; / But when in other habits you are seen, / Orsino's mistress, and his fancy's queen" (5.1.385–88). This moment seemed like an overt attempt to kill any male homoeroticism. He turned to walk away, while Beck looked out at the audience, as if for confirmation or guidance, then looked back at him. Suddenly, she grabbed him and pulled his face down to hers for a passionate kiss. In a complete reversal of stereotypically gendered seductions, he resisted briefly before wrapping his arms around her in a tight embrace.

"NOT THE HELPLESS FEMALE"

The final effect of Josie Rourke's third-wave feminism was one of empowerment, access, and freedom. The youthful, exuberant gesturing of the women no doubt assisted viewers unfamiliar with the play, unfamiliar with theater, and unfamiliar even with English. My community-college students are working hard to afford and excel in college, trying to lift themselves out of difficult economic situations. Rourke's production reminded them of themselves. They saw in both Viola and Olivia a self-determination, a powerful struggle to better one's circumstances. They also saw no threat in these traits. Rather, it seemed, most believed that such ambition made women more attractive to millennial men, both on stage and off. While all the women I spoke to said they felt the show was aimed primarily at women, they all said they would recommend it to male friends. Tellingly, nearly all the men I spoke to really enjoyed it, also saying they would recommend it to male friends, although one specified that he would recommend it only to his more sensitive male friends. Perhaps they related to Orsino, who was essentially rescued from his folly by Viola.

Just as Viola's heterosexual desire became an opportunity to take control of Orsino, her distress, as experienced by my students, became an opportunity for her to show strength. One of the young women wistfully remarked, "Seeing her in distress, drowning in the first scene—you actually see her all wet—it made her seem like more of a romantic heroine." But then the student quickly added, "She helped herself instead of having anybody else help her. That appeals to me more than having a man rescue her." Another young woman echoed this message of empowerment: "She wasn't the helpless female. She was more modern." Although this student had previously said that Viola was always speaking to her "as a woman," she was also impressed by Viola's convincing performance of a man. "I think Viola could pull off being a guy," she stated. Of Sebastian's abilities, she said, "I don't think he could pull off what she did. I don't think men can pull off what women can anyways." Despite the fact that she seemed to read Rourke's production as an assertion of female superiority, however, this same woman reported to me that her fiancé loved the production. Even though he had not read the play and never before attended theater, she said he felt he could "still totally understand what was going on."

The nearly universal appeal of this production for my students spanned an age range of more than twenty years, as well as different backgrounds, races, and countries of origin. My returning student, who said that she felt the production asked, "Who am I? What am I supposed to be? Who am I expected to be?" seemed to feel a profound connection to the show. Perhaps these questions of identity resonated with her because they reflected her own evolution. She was, at the time, in the process of remaking her life. After raising two children and getting divorced, she was returning to college in her forties with the goal of becoming a teacher. For her, even attending the theater felt like a reclaiming of her destiny, an assertion of her future. *Twelfth Night* was her second CST trip. During intermission, I found her in the lobby. "This is my new life!" she exclaimed.

For this student, a new life, engaged with theater, engaged with Shakespeare, leaves room for many different kinds of viewing. In arguing for Rourke's new millennial feminist gaze, I do not wish to discredit the infinite varieties of spectatorship available at any given time in the Windy City. However, I think my students identified in Rourke's production a specific appeal to a new generation, one appreciative of Elizabethan language, costume, music, and humor but also anxious to feel an intimate connection to the stage. They wanted to see versions of themselves onstage, to look in the eyes of actors standing onstage, and even to feel the splash of action from the stage. They wanted to believe that Shakespeare may have considered the experiences of real women, even if his Viola and Olivia had been played by boys. Most important, they wanted to look on female characters with a contemporary understanding of gender. They welcomed a connection with Olivia and Viola, whose sporty, flirty, bubbly, sexually aggressive, and even bi-curious natures seemed as fitting to our century as their own.

NOTES

1. William Shakespeare, *Twelfth Night*, ed. David Bevington and David Scott Kastan (New York: Bantam Dell, 2005), 2.3.2–28. This is the edition with which I teach. All further references appear parenthetically in the text.

2. Charles Spencer, review of *Much Ado About Nothing*, by William Shakespeare, directed by Josie Rourke, Crucible Theatre, Sheffield, *Telegraph*, September 30, 2005.

3. For more on the idea and production of the pool, see "*Twelfth Night*: Designer Lucy Osborne: Preparing for Water," Chicago Shakespeare Theater, accessed November 20, 2011. The website also includes a link to a time-lapse video of the construction.

4. *Oxford English Dictionary*, 2nd ed. (online version, September 2011) s.v. "feminism," accessed November 17, 2011.

5. Jenny Coleman, "An Introduction to Feminism in a Postfeminist Age," *Women's Studies Journal* 23.2 (2009): 10–11, accessed November 15, 2011, *Academic Search Complete*. Coleman also discusses the total rejection of the term *feminist* as associated with anti-male, anti-family agendas (11).

6. Ibid., 11.

7. Samuel Park, Review of *The Tempest*, and *Twelfth Night*, directed by Josie Rourke, *Shakespeare Bulletin* 27.4 (2009): 598, *Project Muse*, DOI:10.1353/shb.0.0117.

8. Ibid., 598.

9. Dennis Polkow, Review of *Twelfth Night*, directed by Josie Rourke, Chicago Shakespeare Theater, New City Stage, *New City*, April 6, 2009.

10. Chris Jones, "Unsinkable Shakespeare; 'Twelfth Night' Makes a Splash at Navy Pier," *Chicago Tribune*, April 6, 2009.

11. Jonathan Baude (Lead Guest Service Associate, Chicago Shakespeare Theater), discussion with the author, November 18, 2011.

12. "Facility and Virtual Tour," Chicago Shakespeare Theater, accessed November 17, 2011. For further discussion of the dynamics of the Chicago Shakespeare Theater space, see Jonathan Walker's essay in this volume.

13. This comment came from class discussion in the first weeks of April 2009, as do some of the other student comments referenced. However, I also interviewed seven former students and one student's friend regarding their memories of the production. Those interviewed included two male students in their mid-twenties; a male student around thirty at the time of the production; one woman in her forties; one woman in her late twenties at the time of the production; her friend, also in her late twenties at the time of the production; and two women of traditional college age, both now twenty-one. All interviews were conducted between June and November of 2011, two years after our trip. I have provided necessary information about each speaker in my prose, but I have refrained from citing individual interviews in order to provide anonymity.

14. Baude, discussion, 2011.

15. The Jentes Family Auditorium seats five hundred. "Facility and Virtual Tour."

16. According to Baude, CST further courts young patrons with $20 tickets for patrons under thirty-five.

17. "*Twelfth Night*: A Conversation with Designer Lucy Osborne," Chicago Shakespeare Theater, accessed September 30, 2011.

18. Jean E. Howard, "Crossdressing, the Theatre, and Gender Struggle in Early Modern England," *Shakespeare Quarterly* 39.4 (1988): 432.

19. Nancy Lindheim, "Rethinking Sex and Class in *Twelfth Night*," *University of Toronto Quarterly* 76.2 (2007): 682.

20. Lisa M. Anderson, "When Race Matters: Reading Race in *Richard III* and *Macbeth*," in *Colorblind Shakespeare: New Perspective on Race and Performance*, ed. Ayanna Thompson (New York: Routledge, 2006), 92.

21. Ibid.

22. Zac Thompson, Review of *Twelfth Night*, directed by Josie Rourke, Chicago Shakespeare Theater, *chicagoreader.com*.

23. Polkow, Review of *Twelfth Night*, *New City*.

24. "*Twelfth Night*: A Conversation with Designer Lucy Osborne."

25. While some of my observations regarding the performance are from memory, most are the result of viewing the DVD from the Chicago Shakespeare Theater Archive.

26. "*Twelfth Night*: A Conversation with Designer Lucy Osborne."

27. *Urbandictionary.com*, s.v. "emo boy," accessed December 29, 2011.

28. Howard, "Crossdressing," 431.

29. Ibid., 430–33.

30. Ibid., 431–33.

BIBLIOGRAPHY

Anderson, Lisa M. "When Race Matters: Reading Race in *Richard III* and *Macbeth*." *Colorblind Shakespeare: New Perspective on Race and Performance*. Ed. Ayanna Thompson. New York: Routledge, 2006. 89–102.

Coleman, Jenny. "An Introduction to Feminism in a Postfeminist Age." *Women's Studies Journal* 23.2 (2009): 10–11. Accessed November 15, 2011, *Academic Search Complete*.

Howard, Jean E. "Crossdressing, the Theatre, and Gender Struggle in Early Modern England." *Shakespeare Quarterly* 39.4 (1988): 418–40.

Jones, Chris. "Unsinkable Shakespeare; 'Twelfth Night' Makes a Splash at Navy Pier." *Chicago Tribune*, April 6, 2009.

Lindheim, Nancy. "Rethinking Sex and Class in *Twelfth Night*." *University of Toronto Quarterly* 76.2 (2007): 679–713.

Park, Samuel. Review of *The Tempest*, and *Twelfth Night*. Directed by Josie Rourke. *Shakespeare Bulletin* 27.4 (2009): 598. *Project Muse*. DOI:10.1353/shb.0.0117.

Polkow, Dennis. Review of *Twelfth Night*. Directed by Josie Rourke. Chicago Shakespeare Theater. New City Stage. *New City*, April 6, 2009.

Shakespeare, William. *Twelfth Night*. Ed. David Bevington and David Scott Kastan. New York: Bantam Dell, 2005.

Thompson, Zac. Review of *Twelfth Night*. Directed by Josie Rourke. Chicago Shakespeare Theater. chicagoreader.com.

"*Twelfth Night*: A Conversation with Designer Lucy Osborne." Chicago Shakespeare Theater. Accessed September 30, 2011.

"*Twelfth Night*: Designer Lucy Osborne: Preparing for Water." Chicago Shakespeare Theater. Accessed November 20, 2011.

6

Short Shakespeare! and the Corruption of the Young

JEFFREY GORE

B ecause I teach early modern literature, my kids experience it as a farmer's kids experience life on a farm. Since they've been young, they've known the Newberry Library as the place their father goes on Saturdays, and they knew the actress who would become Bellatrix Lestrange in the *Harry Potter* films as "the one who played Olivia in *Twelfth Night*." In the same way that running a farm can be an all-consuming activity for a farm family—where the adults care for children while they anxiously watch weather reports or fix the tire of a combine—the fact that my wife and I teach literature and conduct research at home as much as in the library creates for us a domestic environment where social studies textbooks, the Lemony Snicket series, and works by Borges and Renaissance playwrights seem to cover every horizontal surface by the end of any given week. I sometimes worry that I might be accused, as Socrates was, of "corrupting the young" for bringing up my children in a round-the-clock study hall. It is within this domestic milieu—and having usually just received our tax refund check—that my family becomes an obvious target market every spring for the "Short Shakespeare!" series.

As part of its educational efforts, each year Chicago Shakespeare Theater stages a seventy-five-minute version of one of the playwright's works. Set to begin at eleven o'clock in the morning, the "Short Shakespeare!"

performances give our family just enough time after the show to buy our children a Shakespeare pencil in the gift store before rushing them through the chain restaurants and souvenir kiosks on our way to a post-show lunch on the other side of Navy Pier. The performances regularly emphasize physical comedy and often truncate the longer speeches to a comprehensible length for an audience of attentive schoolchildren. But what impresses me most is the Q&A session that follows. It is clear that many of the younger members of the audience have gone through their own "corrupting" experience with an accompanying teacher who has organized the last month of classes around the hard work of digesting one of the plays and a Saturday field trip that just might change them forever. The fifteen minutes for Q&A after the show never seem like enough: there are questions about costumes, about how a favorite line was performed and what could have possibly motivated the "real Juliet" to have fallen in love with someone who wasn't even invited to the party. It's at this moment that I always feel we've actually gotten something right. This group of schoolchildren, who might normally be playing Nintendo or attending soccer practice on a Saturday morning, get to have an experience with their parents and schoolteachers, devoted actors, and everyone who is normally backstage holding together this messy "conspiracy" of education, entertainment, and a thriving cultural enterprise. And a few of them just might get hooked and become fans and customers for life.

In spring 2008, I was teaching *Romeo and Juliet*, and without a budget that semester for taking my students to the play, the stage at least seemed set for our family to see the Short Shakespeare performance of the play. My paternal strategies kicked into gear. I reasoned, the girls are too young to read the whole play on their own, but they'll likely enjoy watching the performance of it if they already know the story. So two family movie nights were devoted to films of the play: Franco Zeffirelli's version, to romance them with Renaissance dress, and Baz Luhrmann's *Romeo + Juliet*, to win "cool points" with our preteen, Lucía. As every teacher knows, however, it's a balancing act to show filmed versions of the plays: what if our students get caught up in various director's "tricks" but don't really listen to the lines or stop to think about what from the text might have motivated a particular performance decision? My daughters were fairly unimpressed with my assertion that Leonardo DiCaprio didn't really "carry the lines." And I had to admit that I was thoroughly captivated by Luhrmann's "fair Verona" set in a deconstructed Mexico City and by the sight of Claire Danes discovering the eyes of her Romeo through an aquarium. What if I had so stacked the deck that my children might feel let down when we actually went to see the play in the theater, with its relatively sparse scenery and no point-of-view shots?

As I would discover from the moment we entered the theater, this production had every bit as much of a "story behind the story" as did Luhrmann's Verona. The male actors in Amanda Dehnert's production were all marked with the Moko tattoos of the Maori people of New Zealand, and the illustrated playbills sought to educate us about both this Maori custom and about how different sets of markings served to distinguish the "two households, both alike in dignity." Every bit as captivating was the single item making up Tom Burch's set: an immense wrought-iron structure that could easily be adapted to form a city wall, a family tomb, a ballroom from which two "holy palmers" escape to share a first kiss, or a balcony for an ever-famous speech to be performed.

I'm always a little uncomfortable when the best-known lines from Shakespeare's plays are about to be spoken, even though I recognize this is genuinely unfair to the actors onstage. With the echoes of college freshmen anxiously repeating lines from soliloquies outside my office door (and of being that very freshman myself anxiously repeating the lines years before), each new performance runs the risk of being upstaged in my mind by the repetition of forced appreciation. Those lines such as "Friends, Romans, countrymen" from *Julius Caesar* have the advantage of being actual speeches within the plays. They don't sound so bad when they come off as deliberated, but by the time the words of a supposedly spontaneous soliloquy such as "to be, or not to be" roll off of Hamlet's lips, I often find it hard in most performances to believe that this truly "is the question."

When the wrought-iron ballroom twisted into a balcony, I braced myself as Romeo asked "what light through yonder window breaks?" The pressure to be genuine seems so much greater to the actor playing Juliet than it does for him playing Romeo, who has just been ridiculed by Mercutio for his forced rhymes—of "love" and "dove"—with the object of yesterday's desire, Rosaline. But when Lee Stark's Juliet looked out from the balcony to ask "Wherefore art thou Romeo?" on this March Saturday, the poetry merged with genuine spontaneity. She sounded thoroughly natural articulating the question, posed in simple syntax, about the very nature of what it means to be an individual and a part of a family. For the rest of the seventy-five-minute play, I completely forgot my role as father and educator. I was captivated by the scenery and the actors' command of the lines, and it was not until the lights came back on and the Q&A began that I stepped back into character. After the play we enjoyed mingling with the actors still in costume in the hallway, and I approached Lee Stark to ask her how she delivered such an oft-heard line without sounding overwrought. "Repetition," she told me. "I just repeat the lines over and over again and think about what they mean until they become my only way of saying it." She had totally gotten it right that day, and her strategy was not so far away from the pedagogical strategy of any old classroom I inhabited, either in the chairs or in front of the room.

As one of my daughters begins working on her first high school play, and the other fills her journals with the lives of countless characters, it is still impossible to know what will become of them as adults. I'm no more in command of their future than Juliet's father was of hers, and my daughters may very well become writers or actors or medical doctors or lawyers or dolphin trainers. And even so much as I proudly recall that my youngest daughter recognized over lunch at Navy Pier that Lee Stark's Juliet "spoke more beautifully" than did Clarie Danes's onscreen Juliet, it is admittedly I who was "schooled" on that March Saturday morning.

7

Doing Things with Words . . . and, Sometimes, Swords

PETER SAGAL

Like a lot of middle-aged people with cushy jobs, I profess nostalgia for my starving artist days; but in my case, at least, I remember vividly hating it at the time. I wouldn't have minded the starving part if I hadn't been so hungry.

But of the many odd jobs I took to support myself until Hollywood or Broadway or somebody, somewhere, came knocking to save me from my obscurity, the one I enjoyed most was teaching Shakespeare to a group of retirees in midtown Los Angeles. My employer was a nonprofit senior center operating out of the former lunchroom at the top of the old May Department Store building on Wilshire Boulevard, a landmark of Modernist architecture that was almost abandoned when I walked inside in 1991. I had gotten the job from somebody I knew who gave it up for a better job; as I remember, his new gig was editing for a magazine for two hundred bucks a week. I could only dream of such riches and hoped that by jumping on his old rung of the ladder I could start my climb to glory as well.

My class was entirely female, as is common among seniors: men die sooner, of course, and those that remain were probably too busy watching sports or their stocks to bother learning about Shakespeare from a twenty-five-year-old aspiring playwright. I remember them as uniform in appearance and background—they were mostly Jewish women who had spent their lives in the surrounding neighborhood of Fairfax, and they all looked at me with the eager expectation of imminent learning.

I was afraid I'd disappoint them, of course. I had studied Shakespeare as a formal academic subject for only one semester in college, in a lecture course taught by the eminent English professor Marjorie Garber, and although just a few years had passed I couldn't remember a single idea she had intoned from the lectern. But I had acted Shakespeare a few times in college—I was a decent Bottom, so I was told, in *Midsummer Night's Dream*, and an overactive Antonio in *The Tempest*, but mostly and most importantly I was an aspiring playwright, and I wanted to teach and discuss Shakespeare's plays as plays: that is, as active, enacted depictions of human beings doing things. Shakespeare's genius, it seemed to me, was not so much his poetry as his sense of motivation, and how people acted upon one another.

So, facing the dozen or so deeply lined and eager faces, I talked about the great scenes of action in the great plays: not the battles, per se, but the scenes of characters acting on each other. I showed them act 1, scene 2 of *Richard III*, in which Gloucester encounters Anne escorting the corpse of her husband, whom Gloucester has killed, and ends the scene by seducing her into marriage. I broke down the scene, talked about Gloucester's stratagems, Anne's resistance, how he overcomes it. I talked about Gloucester's own amazement at his success—"Was ever woman in this humour woo'd? / Was ever woman in this humour won?"[1] and joked it might reflect Shakespeare's own joke about his own daring in attempting to write and sell that scene.

We did it again with five more plays, covering histories, tragedies, comedies, and romances. My appreciation of the playwright was not entirely without quibble. I might even have criticized Shakespeare for giving no final speech or action to Antonio in *The Tempest*, which drove me nuts when I acted the part. But we also talked about the great moments, the St. Crispin's Day Speech from *Henry V*, the brilliant act 3, scene 2 from *Othello*—"Honest, my lord?"[2]—in which Iago plants the seed of jealousy and destruction in Othello's mind by refusing to say anything, making Othello guess and guess more out of his darkest imaginings. And we discussed my favorite line in all of Shakespeare, meaning (because it's me) my favorite joke. It's from *Macbeth*, act 2, scene 2. Macbeth has killed King Duncan during the night and is loitering about the castle the next morning, waiting for the crime to be discovered:

LENNOX: The night has been unruly: where we lay,
Our chimneys were blown down; and, as they say,
Lamentings heard i' the air; strange screams of death,
And prophesying with accents terrible
Of dire combustion and confused events
New hatch'd to the woeful time: the obscure bird
Clamour'd the livelong night: some say, the earth
Was feverous and did shake.
MACBETH: 'Twas a rough night.[3]

Sure 'twas, Mac! I've seen dozens of productions of *Macbeth*, and not a single one of those has played that line for the mordant joke I believe it to be.

By the end of the six-week course, the ladies were excited and eager for each class, and so was I. Many of the women had been theatergoers their whole lives and told me of great productions they had seen twenty or thirty or even fifty years ago. Their enthusiasm for what I had to say, as personal and quirky as it was, made me even more enthusiastic to say it. They had never heard Shakespeare discussed in exactly this way, I think—as a writer for the stage, writing for actors, trying to move his story forward as convincingly and interestingly as he could.

This was years ago, and it makes me sad to think that all of those lovely, wonderful, curious women must now be gone. But Shakespeare endures, and these days I don't teach it anymore, but I watch it, and I take my kids to see it, including a few of the great "Short Shakespeare!" productions at Chicago Shakespeare Theater. I like them especially because when you cut Shakespeare skillfully you end up with the essence of the action, the people doing things to each other with words and, sometimes, swords (my kids like the word parts more, I'm happy to say).

Shakespeare, for all the reams of scholarly books and concordances written about his work, was meant to be acted. He was a playwright who made his living by putting doublets in seats, as it were, so his plays are all—more than anything—incredibly exciting, if done right and done well. (This, by the way, is what makes me angry about the Oxfordians and the Baconiams and all the snotty experts who are sure somebody "educated" must have written Shakespeare's plays. The Earl of Oxford might have been a true Renaissance man, but what the hell did he know about holding an audience's attention? You learn that by trying and doing and failing, in the theater.)

I don't take my family to Chicago Shakespeare Theater because it's good for them. I take them because Shakespeare, done well, is great theater, and great fun. Or so I was able to convince a roomful of nice Jewish ladies, two decades ago.

NOTES

1. William Shakespeare, *Richard III*, ed. Gary Taylor, in *The Oxford Shakespeare: The Complete Works*, 2nd ed., ed. Stanley Wells and Gary Taylor (Oxford: Oxford UP, 2005), 1.2.215–16.

2. William Shakespeare, *Othello*, ed. Stanley Wells, in *The Oxford Shakespeare: The Complete Works*, 2nd ed., ed. Stanley Wells and Gary Taylor (Oxford: Oxford UP, 2005), 3.1.106.

3. William Shakespeare, *Macbeth*, ed. Stanley Wells, in *The Oxford Shakespeare: The Complete Works*, 2nd ed., ed. Stanley Wells and Gary Taylor (Oxford: Oxford UP, 2005), 2.3.53–60.

16. Adrian Lester in Peter Brook's *The Tragedy of Hamlet* (2001), directed by Peter Brooke. Photo by Pascal Victor (Maxppp)

17. Cast of the National Theatre of Scotland's *Black Watch* (2011), by Gregory Burke, directed by John Tiffany. Photography by Manuel Harlan

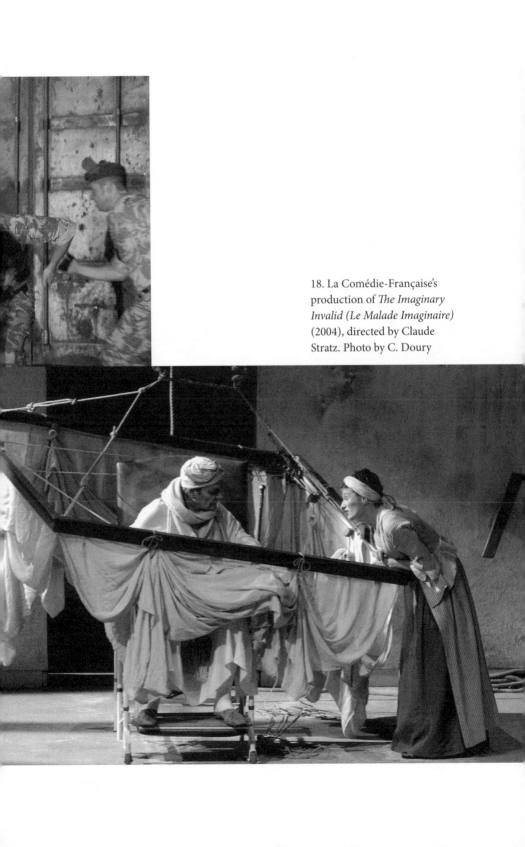

18. La Comédie-Française's production of *The Imaginary Invalid (Le Malade Imaginaire)* (2004), directed by Claude Stratz. Photo by C. Doury

19. Chicago Shakespeare Theater and Carlo Colla e Figli's production of *Marionette Macbeth*, puppetry directed by Eugenio Monti Colla, actors and spoken word directed by Kate Buckley (2007). Photo by Michael Brosilow

20. Kevin Gudahl and Anthony Hite in *Pacific Overtures*, by Stephen Sondheim, directed by Gary Griffin (2002 Chicago Shakespeare Theater; 2003 London's Donmar Warehouse). Photo by Michael Brosilow

PART III

Chicago Shakespeare

SIMON CALLOW

I know Chicago pretty well, because of having written about Orson Welles and having spent some time seeking out his old haunts. And I once played Al Capone and became familiar with *his*, slightly different, old haunts. And I admire the Chicago Symphony to distraction, likewise Chicago's Music of the Baroque; I've spent many happy nights at the Lyric Opera. I've had excellent times at the Goodman, of course, and in the Art Institute. But for the last fifteen years, when I hear the word *Chicago* I think of Shakespeare. That wonderful Elizabethan playhouse at the end of a pier has for me become the absolute magnet in a city that offers many, many seductions. I had heard admiring comments about its work—the beautiful theater and the dazzling and true productions—for years, but it became a reality for me when I met its director, the human dynamo Barbara Gaines. Where and when we met for the first time I can't recall. It's like that with important relationships in one's life—once they start, it's impossible to imagine a time when you didn't know each other. But there was such a time, and however or wherever we met, it led to an invitation to come and do something at CST. Than which, nothing could have pleased me more.

When she said "something," she undoubtedly meant something by William Shakespeare, but at that moment, and for the foreseeable future, I was doing a one-man play about Charles Dickens. Details of that sort never bother Barbara, so an invitation was extended, and in December 2001, I found myself wading through the snow as I made my way down Navy Pier to that wonderful theater. I had arrived just a day or two ahead of the three-week run, after a fairly strenuous tour of the show. It was—well—cold, and I should have been cross and tired, but there is something so quintessentially theatrical about the prospect of that playhouse at the end of a pier that the falling flakes and the strings of colored lights and the flashing neon made me stop and gasp. There are some theaters in which wonderful work is done that are dull buildings, ugly, uninspiring; and then there are theaters like CST. I fancy a tear might have started to my eye, but if it did, it immediately turned into an icicle, so I trudged on till I found the way into the theater, where, in properly Dickensian fashion, I was overwhelmed by a blaze of warmth and goodwill. And it wasn't just the staff, it was the audience, too. The place was simply heaving with excitement and anticipation and good cheer.

When I got backstage, no one could do too much for me. There was a kind of competition as to who could help me most. It was a one-man show, and soon they ran out of options. But when I idly remarked that I liked to eat a bit of fruit before the show, an entire basket overflowing with fruits I had never seen before, from countries with unspellable names, appeared, and it appeared every night. My costume was washed and ironed and refurbished to within an inch of its life. All this before I got into the auditorium. When I did, I felt what every actor who has ever stood or worked in it must feel—an absolute rightness. The space holds you, it gives you focus and freedom. The energy lines converge with huge dynamic power, but at the same time, you're speaking to the audience as if they're in your front room. This much was clear before the audience even arrived. When they did, I experienced something I don't believe I've ever experienced in a theater before—it's what Shakespeare's actors knew, and the masked players in their *kothornoi* in Athens knew: you're talking to the whole city. When I did *The Mystery of Charles Dickens*, there was the mayor and there were students and there were businessmen and women and there were pianists and there were cleaners and there were soldiers and lawyers and athletes. I know, because so many of them stayed behind after to talk. But I knew while I was doing the show, because they reacted like citizens: they picked up on everything. I knew they were going to talk about it after, to argue about it, to feel they needed to see it again. There was nothing passive about them: they had come to see a story about our life. I loved the applause: not sycophantic or cattle-prodded—it was a proper appreciation, a real acknowledgment of a shared experience.

The theater is as alive and well on the end of Navy Pier as it is anywhere in the world. It has found a way to make the citizens come together to celebrate the ancient novelties of this most endurable of art forms, with passion and anarchy and wit. It's twenty-five—but it behaves as if it was at once 2,500 years old and two and a half. Long may it do so, and please may I come back again soon.

9

Chicago Shakespeare Theater and the Canadians

RICHARD OUZOUNIAN

When Shakespeare has Coriolanus say "there is a world elsewhere," he is speaking of an alternative reality where his hero feels he's more appreciated.

When Barbara Gaines first visited the Stratford Shakespeare Festival, she may have uttered the same phrase, but she was speaking of an alternative reality that she wanted to re-create at home.

"From the first time I sat in that magical theater and saw the power of Shakespeare in that space, I knew that's what I wanted to have happen in my own city."[1]

As we now all know, it wasn't that long before she made her dream a reality, starting small, then growing by leaps and bounds until Chicago Shakespeare Theater is one of the most prestigious theaters in North America.

But for Gaines, she felt there had to be some payback.

"As soon as I knew we would be moving into our new home on Navy Pier, I wanted to invite a production from Stratford down to show everyone how our dream had begun."

When Stratford's *The School for Scandal* came down to visit in 2000, it not only marked an important occasion in both theaters' histories, but it began a relationship with Brian Bedford that would continue when he returned, along with fellow company member Graham Abbey, to direct and star in *The Molière Comedies* in early 2004. But between those two dates, I made my first trip to CST, drawn by another Stratford connection.

Chicago's Kevin Gudahl had been in the Stratford company when I directed him as Oberon in a 1989 production of *A Midsummer Night's Dream* (which also starred Eric McCormack as Demetrius), and I remember how fondly he had spoken of his work in Chicago. Consequently, when I visited late in 2001, I couldn't pass up a chance to see Gudahl in *Pacific Overtures*, a production that introduced me not only to CST but to the brilliant work of director Gary Griffin. I rhapsodized about the entire organization in the *Toronto Star*, and Gaines always reminds me that "you were the first journalist outside of Chicago to tell the world about us." Since then, of course, there have been many, many more writers from around the world to join in the chorus of praise.

When I returned to see Bedford and Abbey in 2004, I also thrilled to another Griffin Sondheim, the superb *A Little Night Music*. I don't imagine my continued approbation had anything to do with it, but that was around the time that Gaines began importing Stratford actors to CST with a pleasing regularity that ensured I would get to cover many of the events!

In 2005, Stratford regular Marti Maraden came down to direct *Much Ado About Nothing*, bringing along two Shaw Festival colleagues, Jim Mezon and Kelli Fox, to appear as Beatrice and Benedick. (Fox has since emigrated to Stratford, but Mezon remains one of the Shaw faithful.)

The following year, three Stratford stalwarts (Juan Chioran, Blythe Wilson, and Steve Ross) lit up the stage in the musical of *The Three Musketeers*. Chioran and Ross are still playing leading roles in Stratford, but Wilson is now on Broadway as Mrs. Banks in *Mary Poppins*. That was the first of three roles the protean Chioran would play for CST over the next two years, also including Odysseus in Euripides's *Hecuba* (where he was joined by fellow Canadian Victor Ertmanis) and Iachimo in Gaines's 2007 production of *Cymbeline*.

"I truly loved working with Juan," Gaines recalls. "He's an actor of such enormous vitality, yet clarity. He knew how to enter in the world of the play perfectly."

I too remember that performance with particular fondness, because not only did I get to savor Chioran's work in the wonderfully adult fairy tale that Gaines made out of Shakespeare's late romance, but the next night at CST, I got to see yet another occasion where Griffin made magic with Sondheim.

Passion is one of the master's most difficult works, and yet Griffin found a way to make sense of this story of a romantic triangle that is not at all what it first seems to be. New York's Ana Gasteyer and Kathy Voytko were brilliant as the two women, but I felt a particular twinge of national pride to see Toronto's Adam Brazier in the difficult central role of Giorgio. Brazier began his career at Stratford, went on to the Toronto company of *Mamma Mia!*, played the title role in *Pal Joey* at Shaw, and then went on to Broadway in the juvenile lead of *The Woman in White*. He's now the Artistic Director of Theatre 20, Toronto's newest professional musical theater company. But to see him that night in Chicago, reaching new heights of maturity as an actor thanks to Griffin and his costars, was a real thrill, demonstrating that Gaines's love of Canadian talent is a two-way street, with our northern stars often learning as much as they give.

Stepping back in time a year comes another case where CST helped catch lightning in a bottle.

Ben Carlson was at that point one of the stars of the Shaw Festival, where he had knocked us all out with his John Tanner in an uncut production of *Man and Superman*. His verbal dexterity and physical stamina made me sense he would be a great Hamlet, but even I wasn't prepared for the power of Terry Hands's lightning-fast, virtually uncut production. Even though it had a Canadian lead and a British director, I think of it as the archetypal Chicago show: played with power, clarity, and emotional honesty like you really don't see in any other city.

Another great Canadian came to join up with Gaines in 2007 for *Troilus and Cressida* when Stephen Ouimette crossed the border. One of Canada's most versatile actors, Ouimette also acquired a kind of cult celebrity on both sides of the border once the TV series *Slings and Arrows* became popular, since he was the living spirit of the fictional "New Burbage Festival," bringing both comfort and dismay to people as the ghostly former Artistic Director, Oliver Welles.

"Stephen immediately became one of my favorite actors," says Gaines. "He had such a wicked sense of humor, but a deep, underlying humanity which made him just perfect as Pandarus."

He came back to the company as Grumio in *The Taming of the Shrew* in 2010 and was supposed to stay on as Friar Laurence in *Romeo and Juliet*, but London and Broadway called, with Matthew Warchus wanting him to appear in *La Bête*, and Gaines said, "I just had to let him go. I know he'll be back again with us soon."

The 2007 season also brought Marti Maraden back to direct *Othello*, with an all-Canadian creative team of Patrick Clark (scenery), Christina Poddubiuk (costumes), Melissa Veal (wigs and makeup), and Marc Desormeaux (composer). And in 2008, the entire Shaw Festival company (including Carlson) paid a visit with Artistic Director Jackie Maxwell's production of Shaw's *Saint Joan*. A double whammy of Canadian vitality hit the stage in 2009, when Carlson returned to play the title role in Gaines's nightmarish and diabolically inventive production of *Macbeth* and was joined by Evan Buliung as Macduff, another colleague who had played with distinction at both Shaw and Stratford.

"I felt incredibly fortunate to have them both in the show together," recalls Gaines, "because they gave the production the strength it needed to really fly."

Shaw Festival and Soulpepper Theatre company member Jeff Lillico appeared in the 2010 production of *Romeo and Juliet*, and then, for the twenty-fifth anniversary of CST, Gaines honored Canada (and Stratford) in a complex way. She decided to program (and direct) Canadian Timothy Findlay's 2000 play *Elizabeth Rex*, originally presented at the Stratford Festival. She cast Diane D'Aquila in the title role, re-creating the role she had originated eleven years earlier, and brought in a new Canadian talent, Steven Sutcliffe, who has spent numerous seasons at Shaw and Stratford in the other leading role of Ned.

"I've been thrilled beyond imagining with the relationship that the Canadian theater community has had with all of us here at Chicago Shakespeare Theater," says Gaines, "and I hope it continues for the next twenty-five years."

Speaking purely selfishly, as someone who loves great theater and frequent trips to Chicago to see it, I have the selfsame hopes and dreams.

NOTE

1. All quotes from Barbara Gaines are from an interview conducted by the author on September 29, 2011.

The Framing of the *Shrew*

GINA M. DI SALVO

In the late nineteenth century, playwright George Bernard Shaw became one of the earliest critics to voice his opposition to *The Taming of the Shrew* and question the decisions of theater personnel to continue producing it. Shaw pronounced the play "altogether disgusting to modern sensibility," and a British reviewer in the 1970s echoed Shaw's narrative of progressing beyond *Shrew* when he questioned why we continue "to revive a play that seems totally offensive to our age and society."[1] *Chicago Tribune* critic Chris Jones summed up the difficulty in his review of the 2010 production at Chicago Shakespeare Theater:

> Many otherwise loyal Shakespeareans despise *The Taming of the Shrew*, a comedy that, however it gets shaded or framed, has a persistent narrative trajectory involving the subjugation of a strong woman . . . few relish that notorious moment when she sticks her spirited hand under her oafish husband's foot. Yes, it can be done with irony, but there's the female hand. And there's the male foot.[2]

In April 2010 *The Taming of the Shrew* opened at Chicago Shakespeare Theater and featured a new frame written by playwright Neil LaBute that replaced Shakespeare's original Induction scene with a cast and crew struggling through a problematic technical rehearsal. The choice to commission

LaBute to solve the problem of the *Shrew* is an odd one, considering that his theatrical and cinematic reputation often draws accusations of misogyny, that problematic source of the play's humor that feminist directors since the 1970s have aimed to condemn. However, LaBute's frame departed from the theatrical efforts of directors such as Charles Marowitz, Michael Bogdanov, and Gale Edwards, all of whom adapted the play's original Induction or created alternative framing devices in order to interrogate the main action of Katherina and Petruchio's rough wooing and wedding. LaBute's script called for depicting the problematic story of Katherina's taming as conventionally as possible and used the frame to move the sexual politics out of the realm of traditional heterosexist hierarchies. Instead of representing the problem of widespread and ongoing societal misogyny, LaBute moved the conversation of *Shrew* into the realm of personal and particular abuses of power.

LaBute's frame depicts a cast at odds with one another during a rehearsal of *Shrew*, and these conflicts are born out of the theatrical interpretation of the play. At its center are the Director (Mary Beth Fisher) and the actress playing Katherina (Bianca Amato), two women who are romantic and professional partners. They fight throughout the first half of the show, and their disagreements over their relationship and the staging of the *Shrew* remain unresolved at intermission. Although the second half of the show begins with the Director offering an awkward soliloquy on her dissolving relationship, acts 4 and 5 occur with little interruption and Katherina's taming at Petruchio's house occurs in farcical style, intending its theatricality to be comical rather than abusive. Everything appears to be going smoothly, and Katherina's final speech is delivered with impeccable precision. In LaBute's original frame the story of the actress and her partner mirrored that of Katherina and Petruchio, and their eventual romantic reconciliation occurred as a by-product of the actress's embodiment of Katherina. But after receiving suggestions from the *Shrew*'s actual director, Josie Rourke, and Amato, the actress who played Kate, LaBute revised his frame and offered a stark alternative to a *Kiss Me Kate*-type ending. The revised Kate refuses to finish the final scene as Katherina and responds viscerally to her partner and to a play that required her to be mocked, sold off, abused, and humiliated. The major source of the conflict between Kate and the Director centered on the staging of Katherina's fictional taming, which, in this frame story, became a method of actual manipulation and humiliation. The production proved difficult for critics who could not understand how Shakespeare's classically staged comedy and LaBute's contemporary frame interacted cohesively because they focused on the playwrights instead of the challenges of theatrical practice. Through this examination of the 2010 CST *Shrew*, I address the problems of interpretation presented by this play and bring visibility to rehearsal and revision processes. The major departure from previous feminist *Shrew*s is in LaBute's depiction of particular manipulation rather than general misogyny, but this interpretation is possible only if the frame's context of theatrical rehearsal is put into focus.

PAST *SHREWS*

Shakespeare's original text of *The Taming of the Shrew* begins with an Induction. In this scene, a drunken tinker named Christopher Sly speaks abusively to the tavern mistress and falls asleep. An aristocratic man enters and decides, along with his men, that they will play a trick on him: they will dress him in elegant clothing and treat him as the lord of a great house when he wakes. Sly believes this ploy and takes on his new social role. The ruse continues with a playing troupe that comes to entertain him as lord of the house. He is told that the play will be "a kind of history," and then the main action of *Shrew* begins immediately.[3] Noticeably, Sly never returns to the stage in Shakespeare's *Shrew*. In the anonymous *Taming of a Shrew*, a play published in 1594 that shares the plot and themes of Shakespeare's play, the metadramatic frame extends beyond the Induction. In *A Shrew* Sly interrupts the action of the play multiple times and appears a final time on stage after the taming story has concluded, pronouncing:

> I know now how to tame a shrew,
> I dreamt vpon it all this night till now,
> And thou hast wakt me out of the best dreame
> That euer I had in my life, but Ile to my
> Wife presently and tame her too.[4]

For *A Shrew*'s Sly, the taming play serves as a dramatic manual for enacting a program of violent subjugation of his own wife. It can be argued that Shakespeare's Induction, especially when compared to *A Shrew*'s complete frame, can be understood as a condemnation of the violent misogyny of the Petruchio-taming-Katherina plot, the very thing that the revisionist directors aimed to do with their framing adjustments. This interpretation allows us to read the sexual politics of the play as the sexual fantasy of a low-class drunkard and to interpret the misogyny of the comedy as Sly's ideal entertainment, not Shakespeare's. Unlike a play that successfully markets a program of spousal abuse to a drunken tinker, Shakespeare's story of Katherina's forced marriage, violent taming, and final hand-under-foot monologue is a tinker's grotesque fantasy of female subjugation. *Shrew*, as director Michael

Bogdanov saw it, can therefore be understood as a protofeminist play, because the inclusion of Sly condemns the main action of the play as his idea of a good story, one that is misogynist, crude, and violent. The Induction that had been dropped out of the theatrical repertory by the Restoration period did not return to the stage until the mid-nineteenth century and was not performed with any regularity until the mid-twentieth century.[5]

Beginning with Charles Marowitz's "recycled" *The Shrew* in 1973, feminist directors began to solve the problem of staging the play by offering framing devices that condemned the heterosexist subjugation of Katherina. Marowitz committed an outright act of Bardicide on Shakespeare's *Taming of the Shrew* by stripping the script down to focus on Katherina's courting, marriage, taming, and final scene of feminine submission and interspersing those scenes with a dysfunctional contemporary couple.[6] In Marowitz's "90-minute cut-up version," Shakespeare's comedy became "a black Artaudian fable virtually identifying marriage with a police state dungeon."[7] Marowitz created a sadistic Petruchio who gained pleasure through claiming Katherina as his property and violently abusing her, which, problematically, was depicted as a result of a symbiotic misogynist homosexuality. The most disturbing part of Marowitz's *The Shrew* occurs when Katherina returns to Padua for her sister's wedding and is anally raped by Petruchio with the help of her father and her own servants to punish her for asking for "a night or two" of reprieve.[8] Marowitz found the play despicable

> because no matter how much irony one gets into that last speech of Katherine's to the assembled wives, it always smacks of male chauvinism and a contemptible, contemptuous, attitude towards women. The play itself, shorn of the highjinks and slapstick that usually embroider it, is a detestable story about a woman who is brainwashed by a scheming adventurer as cruel as he is avaricious.[9]

For Marowitz, there was no redeeming *Shrew*, and his method worked to expose "the strenuous mental calisthenics that enable us to separate our contemporary consciousness from that of Shakespeare's."[10] Therefore, Marowitz constructed a version of *Shrew* that viscerally represented the violent enforcement of the original play's patriarchal hierarchy. Nowhere in Shakespeare is Katherina explicitly tortured or raped, but the recycled version took the *implications* of *Shrew*'s original script, staging, and culture and staged them in the extreme.

Other feminist *Shrew*s succeeded Marowitz in the decades following his version, but none of them cut up, rearranged, or committed Bardicide in a similar manner. Both Michael Bogdanov's (1978) and Gale Edwards's (1993) notable productions for the Royal Shakespeare Company left most of the text of the play proper intact. Instead of revising Katherina's and Petruchio's lines, these directors concentrated on the frame to affect the depiction and interpretation of the romance. Bogdanov "substituted an altercation be- tween" a "female usher" and "an intoxicated spectator" who then passed out, in a contemporary version of the tavern mistress and Christopher Sly.[11] The actors playing these roles then doubled as Katherina and Petruchio in a ver- sion that, as with Marowitz, removed the humor from the taming, a tactic that, according to Michael Friedman, risks "failure by potentially disheart- ening viewers instead of inspiring them to seek changes in the way society treats women."[12] In other words, feminist *Shrews* that engage a *via negativa* strategy are theatrical killjoys. Edwards, the first woman to direct *Shrew* at the RSC, played up the comedy, romance, and violence in order to balance "a comic tone and a feminist perspective."[13] To achieve this equilibrium, she looked to the original Induction scene for inspiration. The same actor played both Sly and Petruchio to depict Katherina's taming as the sexist fantasy of an angry drunk, rather than Shakespeare's vision of misogynist comedy. Although Shakespeare's original Induction was lopsided and contained no bookend to follow Katherina's speech of submission, Edwards created one for the production in which "Petruchio falls forward, clutching his brow, the sets vanish and the dream of power abruptly ends, leaving Christopher Sly kneeling before his wife, humbly begging pardon."[14] Lacking Sly's return and sorrowful repentance, Edwards's *Shrew* would have left the audiences without a means to interpret the juxtaposition of violence, romance, and Katherina's submission.[15]

The recent history of these three notable feminist *Shrews* demonstrates a wide diversity in the aims and strategies of directors who used framing to paint parallels between Katherina and Petruchio's relationship and the sexual politics of their audiences. In doing so, they attempted to bring Shakespeare's text, and the perceived inherent problems with it, into dialogue with view- ers. The framing of these *Shrews* sought to use the story of the taming and subjugation of a resistant woman to challenge patriarchal attitudes in con- temporary societies. The LaBute-Rourke *Shrew* departed from these produc- tions, first and foremost in its depiction of power relations that are indeed gendered but do not operate according to the hierarchies of patriarchal het- erosexuality. LaBute's frame shows the workings of sexual manipulation and humiliation, but they are not the mechanisms of men. Instead, the major abuses of power occur at the hands of a woman, because, as the Director, she is in the position to wield her power over her cast, crew, and partner.

The frame showed how the Director "grapples with power" and control while also working to interpret *The Taming of the Shrew*, "a play about power and manipulation and . . . abuse."[16] Whereas Petruchio takes Katherina to his home and uses the means of his household and domesticity to tame her, the Director extends rehearsal scenes and uses conventional methods of staging the play as disciplinary tools against her partner.

A CLASSICAL APPROACH

In the new frame, characters are forced to interact with the text and the history of staging *Shrew*, and at times it appears that Shakespeare's play is imposing itself upon theatrical personnel rather than the other way around. To be clear, it is not Shakespeare's text itself that causes so much conflict but how it is staged. In two separate parts of the first half of the production, the Director emphasizes that her *Shrew* is taking a "classical approach," which she also defends as a strategy that is "unafraid to tackle the problems of a text that's outdated by looking them squarely in the eye."[17] This directorial category, at first, seems to refer to a period costume drama that lacks any overt signal to feminist or other contemporary paradigms. The Director's *Shrew* is played in Renaissance costume on an Italianate set of a piazza in front of the facade of Baptista's house with a balcony above Palladian arches. One reviewer noted that "the core *Taming of the Shrew* was an almost entirely conventional production in an Elizabethan setting."[18] The "conventional" part of the Director's "classical approach" not only refers to a style of set and costume design but extends to conventions of theatrical practice. The classical set design facilitated what might be called conventional or traditional blocking. For example, in act 1 of *Shrew*, Baptista stands in the piazza in front of his house and tells Bianca's suitors, Lucentio and Tranio, "I firmly am resolved you know: / That is, not to bestow my younger daughter / Before I have a husband for the elder" (1.1.48–50). When Baptista names his "younger" and "elder" daughters, Bianca (Katherine Cunningham) and Katherina appear in succession, at opposite doors in the balcony above the piazza. Audiences are familiar with the sort of conventional blocking that introduces the first appearance of characters as they are named. This example is a minor part of what the Director's classical approach entails, however, with the major part of it deriving from an iconic *repertoire* of staging *Shrew*.

The classical approach, while a construct of the fictional Director, intersects with a certain repertoire of staging Shakespeare and includes particular theatrical strategies associated with *Shrew*s of the past. *Repertoire*, according to Tracy C. Davis describes "an historical audience's competence to interpret performance" and "involves processes of reiteration, revision, citation, and incorporation."[19] In other words, repertoire explains the conventionality of the Director's Baptista introducing Bianca and Katherina as they open and step through separate French doors one after the other. The repertoire of the play-within-the-frame is not only about Renaissance iconography but is also and especially about "the recycling of material to encourage particular structures of reception" in audiences.[20] The CST *Shrew*, in fact, begins with an iteration of iconic theatricality that proves to be the method through which the Director humiliates her partner. The production opens to the cast and crew rehearsing the end of Katherina and Petruchio's (Ian Bedford) wedding reception in act 3. Katherina has entreated her new husband to remain and refused to set off with him to his home in Verona. But Petruchio ultimately wins this battle by challenging all listeners with laws of patriarchal property:

> I will be master of what is mine own.
> She is my goods, my chattels; she is my house,
> My household-stuff, my field, my barn,
> My horse, my ox, my ass, my anything,
> And here she stands. Touch her whoever dare,
> I'll bring my action on the proudest he
> That stops my way in Padua. (3.2.230–36)

At this point LaBute's Petruchio "manhandles Kate in a variety of ways, ending up with her over his shoulder and with his hand on her . . . ass," a bit of stage business that regularly shows up in productions of *Shrew*.[21]

At first glance, the image of Katherina slung over Petruchio's shoulder and being carted off to her new home at the end of their wedding scene is an innocuous one inasmuch as it is typical of conventionally staged *Shrew*s, such as this one. But the Director seizes upon Kate's vulnerability in this iconic position under the guise of her professional duties. She stops Kate and the actor playing Petruchio to work out a technical issue. As Kate remains over her fellow actor's shoulder, the Director walks toward them, looks up at the lighting booth, and asks, "Can I get more light on here," and uses her hands to frame Kate's clothed posterior. There is a blackout and then the stage is lit only by a few spotlights that noisily narrow their focus to accomplish the task requested by the Director, who responds, "Oh yes. . . . that's good."[22] This bit of rehearsal ends only when Kate asks, "Are we done here?"[23]

At this point audiences are unaware that Kate and the Director have a relationship beyond their theatrical one, but Kate takes personal offense to her partner's staging of the end of Katherina and Petruchio's wedding. Minutes later, during a break, Kate attempts to seduce Bianca (Katherine Cunningham) under the pretense of rehearsing a scene, the Director walks back on the stage in time to figure out what has occurred, and they have their first fight of the show. The Director lists her grievances with Kate's behavior, both past and present:

> You chase every girl I've ever cast . . . no matter what show we do, what lead part I give you, you just keep on—my Ismene, my Sonya, my, my . . . What's the other girl's name in *Midsummer*?
> **Kate:** I dunno . . . Titania . . . or Hermia?
> **Director:** My Titania! You're . . . wait a second, you didn't go after both, did you? DID YOU?! Hermia was *seventeen*! (NO RESPONSE) You are relentless. . . .[24]

This catalog of Kate's infidelity not only reveals to audiences her pattern of behavior but also reveals their shared professional repertory. The Director casts her partner in the leading roles of classical theater: Sophocles, Chekhov, and Shakespeare. This is a small detail but an important one for a frame story that examines the exploitation of a "classical approach" to Shakespearean comedy. Like *Shrew*, these other plays feature young women who resist their conscribed social roles in ancient Thebes, pre-Revolutionary-country-house Russia, and the Elizabethan vision of an Athenian forest. Although the frame offers no indication of the Director's previous approaches, it is possible that the Director has used the theater against her partner in the past. Moreover, the Director insists on calling her actors by the roles they play, rather than their given names, as part of the rehearsal process. For this reason, the Director refers to her partner only as "Kate" even during their intimate fights, as she has, presumably, in the past called her Antigone, Elena, and Helena, each time claiming her anew as *her* character in *her* show. The Director eventually identifies why her partner acts this way, and the reason is that it is actually a *re*action to her own directorial choices.

> You don't agree with my blocking and so you . . . do this?
> **Kate:** Maybe (BEAT) I mean, you just leave me hanging in mid-air while you played with lights on my *ass*, so . . .

The Director's accusation and Kate's affirmative response force us to revise our perceptions of the opening scene of the play. We thought we were watching a company make adjustments with lighting to play up the comedy of a scene staged in countless other *Shrews*, with Katherina slung over Petruchio's shoulder, but from the point of view of Kate, she was being disciplined by her partner. The Director, however, is able to ignore Kate's anger, because she holds the Shakespearean trump card: "I thought a classical approach to this play made a lot of sense."[25] In other words, the Director bears no responsibility for actions that humiliate her partner, because she can defer to a history of staging Shakespeare.

A fairly straightforward playing of acts 1 through 3 follows this replacement Induction, although there are metatheatrical moments that give the impression of the final dress rehearsal. For example, half of the main door to Baptista's house is missing, so that actors are forced to pantomime the business of opening and closing it. At the end of act 3, and amid much laughter, we return to the scene that began the performance. Up until this point, the only exaggeration in *Shrew* has been "velvet-covered, gold-trimmed" phallic codpieces, which provided a source of the bawdy and physical comedy of the production that critics unanimously praised.[26] The major surprise of the play-within-the-frame and the major exception to the Director's "classical approach" occurs when Petruchio arrives for his wedding in Padua. Usually, Petruchio arrives in Padua dressed in feathers, a jester's outfit, or resembling a vagabond beggar, but in this version he enters the stage wearing a sixteenth-century woman's cream-colored corseted shift, with the skirt tucked into a pair of brown leather ass-less chaps. He pairs this wedding dress with his sword, boots, belt, chest hair, beard, and a Venetian lace veil. Bedford's Petruchio is an imposing figure whose 6'4" 260-pound frame turns this costuming into an ugly drag show, but one that is not lacking in comedy.[27] Grumio, Petruchio's servant, wears a woman's gown and skips along as if he were his master's bridesmaid. When he refuses to change his clothing for the wedding, Petruchio, according to the text, tells his father-in-law, "To me she's married, not unto my clothes. / Could I repair what she will wear in me," but CST audiences heard a minor adjustment of this line (*Shrew*, 3.2.116–17). To better exploit Petruchio's lack of proper pants for full effect, he said, "To me she's married, not unto my clothes," and then turned with his back to the audience and spoke directly to Baptista, "But I will *bear* what she will wear in me," as he scratched his bare behind.[28]

This production has two Kates (a Katherina and the fictional actress playing her, both of whom are played by Amato), two Petruchios (Shakespeare's tamer played by Bedford and the Director played by Fisher), and now there are two brides in which the incongruent power between Katherina and Petruchio and Kate and her partner becomes obvious. Petruchio's demented bridal show contrasts with Katherina's own wedding dress and veil in a ploy for power. His feminine veil and undergarment combined with his bare-assed masculine riding gear mock his bride who has been forced to marry him. Petruchio, with his position, has the ability to put on and take off the accoutrements of femininity and masculinity to humiliate his wife as he rules her, but *she* is stuck, remaining in her role as his bride and in her bridal dress, which can be stripped off of her on his whim. Furthermore, the fictional Petruchio saunters on stage with an exposed ass to ridicule the wedding party, and the actor playing Petruchio does so with intentional agency for maximum comedic effect. Moments later we see his bride's ass exposed without her consent and for the purpose of ridiculing the actress who plays her.

Petruchio claims Katherina as his goods, chattel, house, and household stuff, flings her over his shoulder, threatens any member of her family or city who would defend her against his haste ("Fear not, sweet wench, they shall not touch thee, Kate; / I'll buckler thee against a million"), and is ready to exit the stage with his new bride, but the Director walks toward Katherina and Petruchio to arrange them (3.2.139–40). This time there is no call for a spotlight on Kate's rear. Instead, the Director pulls up her skirts, revealing powder blue underwear, and takes her surrogate's left hand and moves it toward his right shoulder so that it claps down on Kate's exposed blue bottom. Kate squirms down from Petruchio with a "Jesus!"[29] This scene occurs twice during the dress rehearsal, and both times the Director uses it as an opportunity to use theatricality against her partner and to force Petruchio to stand in as her proxy. The Director's "classical approach" is a means through which she can claim her partner, sling her over her shoulder, and humiliate her by publicly exposing her and grabbing her ass.

As expected, Kate and the Director fight, again. This time Kate expresses her distaste for "this role . . . even after all the times I've said I hated the whole . . . you know . . . theme of, of . . ." She fails to define the theme of *Shrew*, but she is able to name why her partner cast her as Katherina and lifted up her skirts: "You're using this show, a role like this one to control me. To put me in my place." The Director initially attempts to deny it but fails to do so when she vents her frustration with Kate, saying, "I want *you*. Maybe kids. I want stability and a woman I can trust." This exasperates Kate.

> Why? Why do you want the same junk that your mother had? Look at her— she's so unhappy! So was mine before she died—died without ever doing *one* thing she wanted to for herself. . . . Look at this goddamn play, we're doing—the way that women are treated. Right? And now just look how far we've come . . . people always bitch about it not being far enough and maybe

that's so, but I'll take it. . . . I want you too but not like some wife. I don't need to be in a *marriage*.[30]

Although Kate cannot identify the major theme of *Shrew* that offends her and makes her despise playing Katherina, she uses Shakespeare's play about a sixteenth-century Paduan woman's forced marriage as an instrument to measure women's cultural emancipation. Kate marks progress from and draws parallels between women's lives in *Shrew* and their mothers'. Her rejection of marriage, or a similar arrangement, rejects being controlled as a "wife," by "a lord, or king or governor . . . a husband."[31] This sort of comparison might come across as the banal observation that relationships, even or especially queer ones, that take on a marital arrangement risk dividing spouses into heterosexist husband and wife roles in which the former controls the latter, rather than maintaining equilibrium between partners. But more important, Kate's parallels situate the play in the present, which counters the Director's attempt to place the *Shrew*'s humiliating theatricality beyond the reach of her partner's present critique. The theme Kate does not name is the thing that makes the play a bummer for those of us who enjoy the sort of show within the fictional frame: a physical and farcical comedy of wooing, wedding, and taming in which Katherina's subjugation is a main point of the comedy, and the happy ending is attained because she submits to it. Although it is debatable whether her final submission is actual or ironic, the means through which Petruchio tames remain the same.

Kate and the Director leave rehearsal unresolved in their relationship, and the first half of the show ends. After intermission, the fictional cast of *Shrew* is no longer working through rehearsal. Time has progressed to the first preview performance with an invited audience, and the Director emerges from backstage to stall between the third and fourth acts. She directly addresses the audience to explain the delay but immediately devolves into a confessional monologue: "Obviously I'm out here covering for us as we had one more glitch during the break. . . . Our Bianca got a bit of a bump during act 1 and we're quickly getting her all—and my relationship is over . . . by the way."[32] The speech is long and rambling, switching from topic to topic, but it hints at a final reconciliation between the Director and Kate in its metatheatricality. The Director complains about her partner and her lack of fidelity, but she also adds, "God, I would run to her, crawl across broken glass to put my hands beneath her shoes—that's from the play. But she can't. No, it all has to be on her terms . . ."[33] Although the Director indicates that she would perform public acts of submission to repair her relationship with a woman who consistently rejects fidelity and commitment, she lacks any admission of remorse over her constant humiliation of her partner. What is absolutely absent from this confession is moral responsibility for abusing the power of her professional role to punish her personal partner. If Kate were to return to her partner without an apology for her manipulation, then that might be understood to be as masochistic as Katherina performing a straightforward public submission for the sake of the man who just subjected her to an abusive honeymoon. LaBute's original ending had an alternative *Kiss Me Kate* ending.

In Cole Porter's 1948 metatheatrical musical, an ex-husband-and-wife team is cast in a musical version of *Shrew*. They fight both on- and off-stage, but they reconcile within the play during the final scene. After *Kiss Me Kate*'s Lilli kneels and places her hand on the ground, she looks up at her ex-husband and mouths, "Fred," and he responds with "Lilli!" and then they finish the play as Katherina and Petruchio, performing a happy ending both within and outside of the play-within-a-play. In LaBute's original ending Katherina delivers her final monologue as the Director stands "at the back of the auditorium, taking in the speech. Kate is aware of her presence." She continues the monologue, but as the "Director starts to walk off—Kate went after her as she calls out" and directs the rest of her speech toward her partner while still trying to finish the scene traditionally. Petruchio speaks, "Why, there's a wench! Come on and kiss me, Kate," and then they begin to kiss. However, Petruchio aborts the scene. He stops kissing Kate, "looks around at everybody else and throws his arms up in the air" and tells his onstage partner, "Oh, go ahead and kiss her, for God's sake!" The Director and Kate walk toward each other and reconcile with a kiss as the cast ad-libs rhyming couplets and exits the stage, leaving the two women alone. They apologize to each other, and the Director tells her partner, "I'm a pain in the ass, so are you . . . but you're *my* pain in the ass! I don't want another ass. A new ass. A *different* ass. (BEAT) I want *you*." Then, instead of utilizing Petruchio's "Kiss me, Kate," she directs her partner, "Angela. (BEAT) *Kiss* me." In finally calling her partner by her real name and refusing to pattern her speech after Shakespeare's Petruchio, the Director seems to set aside her theatrical and personal control over her partner. The play ends with an ironic take on the moment in *Shrew* that caused so much conflict:

> The two women smile at each other. They draw close. And then closer. And then they kiss. Long and hard. Kate is up and into the Director's arms—Director holds Kate up with her hands on her ass. Two spots focus in on this timeless image. The lights begin to flicker and search for them. Music up. They are held in one light for a moment—like when Petruchio and Kate were

frozen at the beginning of the play—and then they are gone. Swallowed up by the dark.[34]

In LaBute's first version, which never played at Chicago Shakespeare Theater, the personal and theatrical conflict is set aside for the sake of romantic reconciliation. The ending does not revise Shakespeare so much as it revises *Kiss Me Kate*. In the Cole Porter musical, the reconciliation occurs between Katherina and Petruchio and the actors playing those roles simultaneously because the romance in both is heterosexual. It is impossible that Kate can simultaneously reconcile with her out-of-the-play romantic interest and play a Katherina that reconciles with Petruchio, because her world does not mirror the heterosexual romance of the play. Ultimately, this first frame for *Shrew* counters and revises contemporary assumptions about romantic possibilities in the world outside of the play, but it abandoned its initial interrogation of Shakespeare's text and a repertoire of staging in order to end as a comedy.

LaBute's revised version completely changed the trajectory of the narrative and resisted the romantic resolution of the *Kiss Me Kate* ending. In a further layer of metatheatricality, the two lead actresses, Amato and Fisher, and the production's actual director, Rourke, approached LaBute about revising the script because, through the rehearsal process, they felt that "the kind of happy submission ending . . . didn't feel credible," especially "at the height of a play in which the Director has emphasized and unromanticized the breaking of Kate's will."[35] Furthermore, these women felt that "the conflict at the core of the frame needed to be about the artistic interpretation of Shakespeare's play."[36] The original script was pared down, the Director's dominance emphasized, and what has been understood as a typical LaButian ending was actually born out of rehearsal and improvisation.

In the revised ending Katherina delivers the entirety of the famous speech that has left audiences and readers baffled—how could such a formerly spirited woman perform her own defeat? Unlike the first version, the Director begins the scene offstage and out of sight, and Shakespeare's characters exist only within the world of the play. At the end of the speech, the revised Katherina says, "My hand is ready, may it do him ease," and then kneels down to offer her open palm on a raised platform in the middle of the stage. Petruchio responds as expected, a little shocked, but delighted: "Why, there's a wench. Come on, and kiss me, Kate." But Katherina remains nearly prostrate, her head bowed into her arm. The actor playing Petruchio, thinking that Kate did not hear her cue properly, steps back and repeats himself, "Why, there's a wench. Come on—." Kate then cuts him off as she abruptly stands up and half speaks and half sings to herself, "No, no, no, no, no, no," unties her Elizabethan skirt, pulls it down, looks directly at the audience and exclaims, "Fuck this!" She steps out of the skirt and throws it at the Director, who has stepped onto the stage. She tells her, "*You* kiss him," and begins to exit the stage. The Director yells at her, "Kate, there's an audience!" but Kate continues her exit. In a last attempt to save the show, or, more likely, her relationship, the Director calls out, "ANGELA!" Only as Katherina/Kate quits the play and the manipulative relationship that uses the *Shrew*'s conventional staging as sexual manipulation does the actress receive her name back.

"I DON'T KNOW WHAT THAT MEANS IN THIS CONTEXT"

According to critics, the juxtaposition between the frame and the classical *Shrew* proved an uneven and confusing piece of theater. The *Chicago Tribune*'s Chris Jones wrote, "It all feels too much like one half of the show is apologizing for the other."[37] Terry Teachout echoed Jones's sentiment in the *Wall Street Journal*. Although he praised LaBute's "'Kiss Me, Kate'–like concept" for its "unexpected comic deftness" and Rourke's "well-cast mounting of the play proper . . . bold, bawdy and bluntly funny," Teachout ultimately decided that the "two halves of the show don't need one another."[38] M. G. Aune later documented the piece for the *Shakespeare Newsletter*, and her confusion over how the two parts of the show fit together is apparent from her review. She wrote that Kate's abortive act in the final scene made "sense to a modern audience" but is "unavailable to Katherina, who must always follow the text written for her in a time with a much more limited sense of female autonomy," although the "frame's interruption of the *Shrew*" also "reminded the audience that Shakespeare's characters are not real and that Katherina was not really being abused."[39] Andrea Stevens argued, in *Shakespeare Bulletin*, that "the contemporary frame created more problems than it solved (and I don't mean productive or theatrically productive problems)" and ended her own piece by quoting Caitlin Montayne Parrish's review from *Time Out Chicago*.[40] Parrish criticized LaBute's entire body of work as much as she rejected the specific frame—"[w]hat begins affectionately enough, a la *Noises Off* meta-theater dips into LaBute's predictable bile"—and she then told readers not to "look for meaning in the contemporary scaffolding. 'Fuck this!' is neither a thesis nor a revelation."[41] The jarring juxtaposition between LaBute's new Induction and a classical version of Shakespeare's play proved confusing because the poetics that audiences bring to LaBute's and Shakespeare's work, respectively, differ so greatly that they cannot even be said to be oppositional. Despite the frame's focus on the relationship between two women, the other framework for *Shrew*'s difficult sexual politics is the lack of relationship between two men: William Shakespeare and Neil LaBute.

The difficulty of interpreting the LaBute-framed *Shrew* begins with the playwright himself—not Shakespeare, but the other guy. Before audiences even set foot into CST's Courtyard Theater in April and May of 2010, many of them were expecting some interesting, and perhaps inflammatory, sexual politics. The CST advertised *Shrew* "with a new Induction by Neil LaBute" on promotional materials, including mailings and public transit posters. LaBute's reputation as a "politically incendiary"[42] playwright, screenwriter, and filmmaker already framed his new frame for *Shrew* and affected how audiences would later interpret the frame, the actual play, and the relationship between the two, as exemplified by Parrish's *Time Out Chicago* review in which she dismisses LaBute's work as "bile."

LaBute's plays and films regularly depict fraught relationships between men and women. Most of these harsh stories of power, sex, and manipulation offer glimpses into networks of friendships, neighborhoods, and office spaces in which gendered hierarchies of power and attractiveness give license to social criminals. In LaBute's first film, *In the Company of Men* (1997), an adaptation of his play of the same name, two men make a pact to avenge their gender by courting, duping, and rejecting a deaf woman who works as a secretary in their company. In *Your Friends and Neighbors* (1998), the masculine sociopathic cruelty is ratcheted up a notch by the creation of the character Cary (Jason Patric), a medical doctor who wears Notre Dame sweatshirts and has perfected terrorizing silent victims. In a steam room scene, after a group of friends has finished working out at the gym, Cary proudly narrates to the others how he raped a classmate in the locker room in high school without remorse. The same character later screams at his date through the bathroom door as he violently pounds on it, because she accidentally menstruated in his new sheets. Although masculine cruelty is a major theme of LaBute's work, women are also able to wield power over those who hold less sexual or social capital. In *The Shape of Things* (2001, play; 2003, film), a flaky MFA candidate manipulates the man who believes he is her boyfriend into making a series of temporary and permanent bodily changes and later exploits him as her "*human* sculpture."[43] And in the recent play *Fat Pig*, one of the main bullies is a woman threatened by the fact that her sometime lover could fall for a plus-sized woman. LaBute's Iagos are beautiful women and brutal men who have specific traits and attributes, but they are broadly drawn characters that are most specific and realistic in the peculiarity and particularity of their cruelties and transgressions. Unlike Shakespeare's *Othello*, however, LaBute's world lacks justice. Instead, these sociopaths graduate, receive promotions, and return home to their beautiful wives and girlfriends without a trace of their crimes following or haunting them.

LaBute's theatrical and cinematic imagination, alone, proves difficult for critics and audiences who question where the man exists in his work. Because his work contains misanthropic, misogynistic, and power-hungry characters, does this mean that his plays should be characterized similarly? If the plays are those things, then is LaBute as well, and if the playwright imposes such "bile" on the world, then shouldn't we reject his plays? These questions are rarely posed about Shakespeare, who, as Gary Taylor has argued, is treated as a singular unique genius.[44] Our interpretive strategies for Shakespeare are, obviously, far different than how we interpret LaBute, but attention to these differences helps to clarify some of the critical difficulty with this *Shrew*. Shakespeare is understood to be the creator of Petruchio, among other characters, and the certainty of his fixed genius keeps us from accusing him of *being* a Petruchio, whereas LaBute's ongoing career and current set of works leaves him open to misogynist and misanthropic speculation. Parrish's review reveals something even more important for performance criticism, however, and this is the assumption that theatrical performances are primarily the result of the mind of a singular playwright rather than an ongoing collaborative process between actors, designers, writers, directors, and producers. Through her assignation of blame to the male playwright for the LaBute-Rourke production's lack of thesis, Parrish was then able to dismiss and condemn the frame. It is ironic that LaBute is blamed as the sole author of the "Fuck this!" finale when it occurred in a piece of theater that showed that the "classical approach" *Shrew* was actually embedded with a repertoire of humiliation. The frame might be confusing, but the one thing it definitively demonstrates is that the process, and the problems, of theatrical meaning-making is a burden that belongs to a cast and crew.

The LaBute-Rourke *Shrew* specifically plays with the problem of interpretation. Although it might be assumed that the great moment of Bardicide occurs when Kate yells, "Fuck this!" and exits the stage, the only true instance comes early in the play, when the Director addresses her cast. If *Bardolatry*, a term coined by Shaw, is the worship of the mythic institution of Shakespeare, one that allows and encourages a poetics of absolute greatness and applicability, then *Bardicide* is a mechanism that counteracts it.[45] Near the end of scene 1, the Director attempts to clarify the goals of the dress rehearsal but gets derailed when she herself attempts to privilege Shakespearean inclusion over present meaning:

Director: Before we go, are there any questions?

Hortensio: Is this a "stop and start"? I mean, if we need to?

Director: Ummm, I think we got everything worked out in the morning session but I'm sure we'll need to tweak a few . . . you know . . . (Grins) We want it to be great. Right.

Hortensio: "He who runs fastest gets the ring."

Director: Exactly! (BEAT) I mean . . . no. I don't know what that means in this context. So . . .

Hortensio: Just running my lines . . .

Director: Oh.[46]

Hortensio's quoted line occurs during the opening scene of *Shrew*, in which he first competes with Bianca's other suitor. After the two men realize that neither of them can successfully court Bianca until Katherina is married, they make a pact to find a suitable match for her:

> **Hortensio:** . . . since this bar in law makes us friends, it shall be so far forth friendly maintained till by helping Baptista's eldest daughter to a husband we set his youngest free for a husband—and then have to't afresh. Sweet Bianca! Happy man be his dole. *He that runs fastest gets the ring.* How say you, Signor Gremio? (1.1.134–40 [emphasis mine])

Hortensio's phrase is not confined to the context of Hortensio and Gremio's rivalry and can even be used outside of Shakespeare's play, but it is not immediately applicable to the Director's clarification to her actors of the goals of the afternoon rehearsal. However, instead of assessing its applicability, she first accepts it as a meaningful gloss on her present speech before questioning *how* Hortensio's quoted line elucidates her direction to her actors. When she says, "I don't know what that means in this context," it is because she still assumes that a line of Shakespeare ex nihilo contains the stuff of meaning itself instead of assuming that one of her actors is running his lines—at rehearsal.

The LaBute-Rourke frame shows that a "classical approach" to *Shrew* requires some sort of lens for interpretation or an obvious indication that our discomfort with a straight version is warranted. The Director's claims about her fictional method might seem to trust *Shrew*'s audiences to enjoy the adept and precise artistry of a skilled cast performing Shakespeare while at the same time rejecting the play's embedded misogynistic abuse, but how is an audience supposed to recognize that the production is "attacking" and "tackling" the misogyny and abuse of the text from watching a classical approach alone? The collision between the two worlds of the 2010 *Shrew* at CST—the theatrical vision of sixteenth-century Padua and the twenty-first-century backstage drama—in fact emerges not only out of Kate's condemnation of the Director's staging but also through nonverbal signals that, at first, appear as necessary parts of theatrical rehearsal, in general, and rehearsal for the *Shrew*, in particular. Kate's contemporary undergarments counter the world of the play in three important parts. During the opening rehearsal scene, in which Kate is being hoisted over Petruchio's shoulder, she wears the voluminous burgundy and black Florentine printed skirt of her period gown with a black athletic racer-back tank top. At the play's abortive finale, Kate removes her skirt, throws it at her former romantic and professional partner, and steps away from both, wearing only her Elizabethan top and a modern pair of black leggings. In between the beginning with the black tank top and the end with the black leggings, in the middle of the *Shrew*, Katherina is wooed, wedded, and silenced in full costume. In act 3, after the spirited Katherina has sparred both verbally and physically with Petruchio, she shuts up as soon as the wedding date is set, and her formerly maidenly banter is replaced by her bridal pronouncement that "a woman may be made a fool / If she had not a spirit to resist" (3.2.221–22). But Katherina's spirit to resist is futile, because she has been sold off and become Petruchio's property, and not one citizen of Padua will support her "spirit to resist." During the end of 3.2, Bedford's Petruchio bellows threateningly as he delivers his "my goods, my chattels" speech in marked contrast to the more lighthearted faux-epic recitation from the opening rehearsal scene. Katherina is then slung over Petruchio's shoulder, and her partner lifts her skirts to reveal her twenty-first-century underwear beneath the yards of a beautifully constructed period gown fit for Katherina Minola or any of Shakespeare's women. And then Petruchio's hand is clapped over her ass. We laugh, but Kate, who is not Kate, does not. Beneath all of that Shakespeare is a woman who is suffering under the humiliation of four hundred years of making light of her forced marriage and subjugation. Feminist *Shrew*s of the past aimed to use moments like this to draw a parallel between a classical Katherina and contemporary women, but this one focuses the humiliation on a single, particular woman. The burden of representing Katherina affects the actress charged with assuming that role as the sexual manipulation of the fictional text is played out in reality against her.[47]

The end of the LaBute-Rourke *Shrew* might seem like Marowitz's act of feminist Bardicide, but it neither condemned Shakespeare nor made Katherina and Petruchio mirrors for contemporary relationships. Marowitz aimed to slaughter Shakespeare and indict ongoing misogyny in society simultaneously by juxtaposing a graphically violent version of the play with contemporary scenes of an abusive heterosexual relationship that, nonetheless, ends in marriage. In Marowitz's interpretation, the play is a disgusting account of the eternal return of sexual subjugation and manipulation. The abuse of power is still present in the queer relationship, but the major difference between past metatheatrical *Shrews* and the LaBute-Rourke production is that Katherina's parallel *leaves* as a by-product of experiencing her humiliating taming rather than mirroring a romantic reconciliation. "Fuck this!" is not a thesis, but in explaining Kate's f-word exit I will arrive at the crux of mine.

Kate quits the reconciliatory end of *Taming of the Shrew* and its *Kiss Me Kate* metatheatrical by-product because Rourke, Amato, and Fisher found it incredible that Kate would reconcile with a woman who had used classical theater as a disciplinary weapon against her and, in doing so, had sexually humiliated her. The Director's rambling contemporary and colloquial soliloquy at the beginning of the second half of the play expressed a willingness to reconcile, but the more the women discussed the frame's trajectory for Kate, the more they found it incredible that she would reconcile with a partner who "emphasized and unromanticized the breaking of Kate's will."[48] The actual women charged with playing the Director and Kate required a revision. They improvised and arrived at the ending that appears in LaBute's revised script and is explained in the stage directions: "We set out to move Kate as far away from her origins as possible—when we began that was to put her in a lesbian relationship but by the end of rehearsal we found that it was even better to let her stand up as her own woman, not to be undone by any other man or woman."[49] How strange is it that these women could not accept that Kate would use Katherina's lines to metatheatrically reconcile with her longtime romantic partner, but the rest of us would accept over and over again that a formerly spirited and resistant woman, who may prefer to remain eternally unmarried and unbedded—to use a Shakespearean phrase in context—*by a man*, at least, performs a humiliating monologue after a humiliating taming and a humiliating forced marriage? Are we really to believe that Petruchio is just "as peremptory as she proud-minded, / And where two raging fires meet together / They do consume the thing that feeds their fury" (2.1.130–32)?

Contrasting throughout the play with the comedic banter of parity—that Katherina "being mad herself, she's madly mated" and "Petruchio is Kated"— is the incongruence of power between Petruchio and his new wife (3.2.245–46). The parallel incongruence and imbalance of power between the two women, which seems relatively minor when placed to scale next to the sixteenth-century rights of a husband, caused Amato and Fisher to abort the metatheatrical romantic reconciliation scene. In refusing to perform Katherina's scripted compliance, Kate leaves her abusive relationship, but in her stripping off the heavy gown that made her Katherina and kept her in the play, the "Fuck this!" simultaneously addressed the text and her partner and rejected both a theatrical and an actual romantic reconciliation. Through her experience of embodying Katherina in *The Taming of the Shrew*, a comedy about the subjugation of a resistant woman, the actress playing her *refused* to mirror her character's taming. Out of all of Shakespeare's plays, this specific one made it impossible for Kate to ignore the manipulation or humiliation she had suffered, and when she encountered the full force of it in an artistic representation of it in a 400-year-old monologue. In revising a new piece by a contemporary playwright that some critics and audiences hold in contempt, the women of the Rourke-LaBute *Shrew* proved that Shakespeare, too, could be revised.

NOTES

1. George Bernard Shaw, *Shaw on Shakespeare: An Anthology of Bernard Shaw's Writings on the Plays and Production of Shakespeare*, ed. Edwin Wilson (New York: E. P. Dutton, 1961), 180; Michael Billington, "A Spluttering Firework," *Guardian*, May 5, 1978, 10.

2. Chris Jones, Review of *The Taming of the Shrew*, *Chicago Tribune*, April 16, 2010, 8.

3. All citations of the text, unless otherwise noted, are from William Shakespeare, *The Taming of the Shrew*, third series (Arden), ed. Barbara Hodgdon (London: Methuen, 2010), Induction.2.136.

4. *A pleasant conceited historie, called The taming of a shrew As it was sundry times acted by the Right honorable the Earle of Pembrook his seruants* (London: By Peter Short and are to be sold by Cutbert Burbie, at his shop at the Royall Exchange, 1594), G2^v.

5. Hodgdon, "Introduction," *Taming of the Shrew*, 105–18.

6. See also Paul Yachnin's article "'To Kill a King': The Modern Politics of Bardicide," in *Shakespeare and Modern Theater: The Performance of Modernity*, ed. Michael Bristol et al. (London and New York: Routledge, 2001), 36–54. In this essay, Yachnin examines the revisionist work of Charles Marowitz and Jane Smiley, among others.

7. Irving Wardle, "The Taming of Shakespeare," *Times* [UK], December 24, 1975.

8. Charles Marowitz, *The Shrew* (London: Calder and Boyars, 1975), 76.

9. Marowitz, "Shakespeare Recycled," *Shakespeare Quarterly* 38.4 (1987): 471.

10. Ibid., 473.

11. Michael D. Friedman, "'I'm not a feminist director but . . .': Recent Productions of *The Taming of the Shrew*," in *Acts of Criticism: Performance Matters in Shakespeare and His Contemporaries*, ed. Paul Nelsen and June Schlueter (Madison, NJ: Fairleigh Dickinson UP, 2006), 162.

12. Ibid., 163.

13. Ibid., 168.

14. Nicholas de Jongh, Review of *The Taming of the Shrew*, *Evening Standard* [London], April 24, 1995, 7.

15. See Sarah Werner, "*The Taming of the Shrew*: A Case Study in Performance Criticism," *Shakespeare and Feminist Performance: Ideology on Stage* (London: Routledge, 2001), 69–95.

16. Ian Bedford, interview with the author, August 21, 2011.

17. Neil LaBute, *Shrew Scene(s)*, scene 1 and scene 2. I am grateful to Mr. LaBute for sending me his unpublished manuscript of the frame and granting me permission to quote from it. The manuscript he sent me, titled *Shrew Scene(s)*, is divided into four scenes; therefore, I cite by scene rather than page or line number. I have silently amended most of LaBute's stage directions, which appear in all capital letters in his manuscript. I have retained the case for directions that appear within parentheses in parts of dialogue, such as "(BEAT)," but I have altered it when quoting more extensive directions, such as "MANHANDLES KATE IN A VARIETY OF WAYS."

18. M. G. Aune, "*The Taming of the Shrew* at Chicago Shakespeare Theater," *Shakespeare Newsletter* 60.1 (2010): 2.

19. Tracy C. Davis, "Nineteenth-Century Repertoire," *Nineteenth Century Theater and Film* 36.2 (2009): 6, 8.

20. Marvin Carlson, *The Haunted Stage: The Theater as Memory Machine* (Ann Arbor: U of Michigan P, 2001), 16.

21. LaBute, *Shrew Scene(s)*, scene 1.

22. Ibid.

23. *The Taming of the Shrew*, directed by Josie Rourke, archival recording, Chicago Shakespeare Theater.

24. LaBute, *Shrew Scene(s)*, scene 1.

25. Ibid.

26. Aune, "*Taming of the Shrew* at Chicago Shakespeare Theater."

27. Ian Bedford, interview.

28. *Shrew*, archival recording, CST.

29. LaBute, *Shrew Scene(s)*, scene 2.

30. Ibid.

31. Ibid.

32. Ibid., scene 3.

33. Ibid.

34. Ibid., scene 4, First Version.

35. Mary Beth Fisher, interview with the author, August 21, 2011.

36. Ibid.

37. Jones, Review, 8.

38. Terry Teachout, "Better than Broadway," *Wall Street Journal Online*, May 28, 2010, accessed September 1, 2011.

39. Aune, *Taming of the Shrew* at Chicago Shakespeare Theater, 22.

40. Andrea Stevens, Review of *The Taming of the Shrew*, *Shakespeare Bulletin* 28.4 (2010): 495.

41. Caitlin Montayne Parrish, Review of *The Taming of the Shrew*, *Time Out Chicago*, April 22–28, 2010.

42. Jones, Review, 8.

43. Neil LaBute, *The Shape of Things* (London: Faber, 2001), 119.

44. Gary Taylor, "Singularity," in *Reinventing Shakespeare: A Cultural History from the Restoration to the Present* (New York: Weidenfeld & Nicolson, 1989), 373–411.

45. The term "Bardicide" first appeared in Richard Levin's article "The Poetics and Politics of Bardicide," *PMLA* 105 (1990): 491–504. In this article, Levin argued against new critical interventions of the time, such as New Historicist and feminist projects.

46. LaBute, *Shrew Scene(s)*, scene 1.

47. In using the phrase "the burden of representing her," I take up David Wiles's argument that "[e]very actor brings personal and cultural issues into performance. So does every audience." See "The Burdens of Representation," in *Method Acting Reconsidered: Theory, Practice, Future*, ed. David Krasner (New York: St. Martin's Press, 2000), 169–78.

48. Fisher, interview.

49. Ibid.

BIBLIOGRAPHY

Anonymous. *A pleasant conceited historie, called The taming of a shrew As it was sundry times acted by the Right honorable the Earle of Pembrook his seruants*. London: By Peter Short and are to be sold by Cutbert Burbie, at his shop at the Royall Exchange, 1594.

Aune, M. G. "*The Taming of the Shrew* at Chicago Shakespeare Theater." *Shakespeare Newsletter* 60.1 (2010): 2, 15–16, 22.

Billington, Michael. "A Spluttering Firework." *Guardian*, May 5, 1978.

De Jongh, Nicholas. Review of *The Taming of the Shrew*. *Evening Standard* [London], April 24, 1995.

Friedman, Michael D. "'I'm not a feminist director but . . .': Recent Productions of *The Taming of the Shrew*." In *Acts of Criticism: Performance Matters in Shakespeare and His Contemporaries*. Ed. Paul Nelsen and June Schlueter. Madison, NJ: Fairleigh Dickinson UP, 2006.

Jones, Chris. Review of *The Taming of the Shrew*, directed by Josie Rourke. *Chicago Tribune*, April 16, 2010.

LaBute, Neil. *The Shape of Things*. London: Faber, 2001.

———. *Shrew Scene(s)*. Unpublished script.

Levin, Richard. "The Poetics and Politics of Bardicide." *PMLA* 105.3 (1990): 491–504.

Marowitz, Charles. "Shakespeare Recycled." *Shakespeare Quarterly* 38.4 (1987): 467–78.

———. *The Shrew*. London: Calder and Boyars, 1975.

Parrish, Caitlin Montayne. Review of *The Taming of the Shrew*. *Time Out Chicago*, April 22–28, 2010.

Shakespeare, William. *The Taming of the Shrew*. Third Series (Arden). Ed. Barbara Hodgdon. London: Methuen, 2010.

Shaw, George Bernard. *Shaw on Shakespeare: An Anthology of Bernard Shaw's Writings on the Plays and Production of Shakespeare*. Ed. Edwin Wilson. New York: E. P. Dutton, 1961.

Stevens, Andrea. Review of *The Taming of the Shrew*. *Shakespeare Bulletin* 28.4 (2010): 401–95.

Taylor, Gary. "Singularity." *Reinventing Shakespeare: A Cultural History from the Restoration to the Present*. New York: Weidenfeld & Nicolson, 1989. 373–445.

Teachout, Terry. "Better than Broadway." *Wall Street Journal*. May 28, 2010.

Wardle, Irving. "The Taming of Shakespeare." *Times* [UK]. December 24, 1975.

Werner, Sarah. "*The Taming of the Shrew*: A Case Study in Performance Criticism." *Shake-

speare and Feminist Performance: Ideology on Stage. London: Routledge, 2001. 69–95.

Wiles, David. "The Burdens of Representation." *Method Acting Reconsidered: Theory, Practice, Future.* Ed. David Krasner. New York: St. Martin's Press, 2000. 169–78.

Yachnin, Paul. "'To Kill a King': The Modern Politics of Bardicide." *Shakespeare and Modern Theater: The Performance of Modernity.* Ed. Michael Bristol et al. London: Routledge, 2001. 36–54.

Michael Bogdanov
An International Director's The Winter's Tale *at Chicago Shakespeare Theater*

BRADLEY GREENBURG

One of the most important aspects of Chicago Shakespeare Theater in its history as a preeminent site of Shakespeare's drama in the United States is its ability to lure directors from all over the world. The theater has been especially keen to offer productions helmed by top British directors, including Peter Brook, Peter Hall, Mark Rylance, Josie Rourke, and Michael Pennington (just to mention those discussed in this volume). This consistent feature of the theater demonstrates the lengths to which CST goes to produce ever-changing, ever-evolving stage productions of the Shakespearean canon. One example of this is the production of *The Winter's Tale* by acclaimed Welsh director Michael Bogdanov in the spring of 2003.

THE PRODUCTION

In a recent *New Yorker* review of a Central Park performance of *The Winter's Tale*, theater critic Hilton Als wrote:

> I have a grudge against Shakespeare's late romance "The Winter's Tale," whose burden of whimsy exhausts me about halfway in. I find it to be a dishon-

est play—dishonest in its forced imaginativeness and in its depictions of its young lovers, Florizel and Perdita, who spend much of their time in blissful ignorance in an unreal Bohemia and then suddenly start speaking as if they knew something about life and grief. The second half of the play is basically "Godspell," without the songs or Jesus.[1]

As funny and clever as this is, and however accurately it captures the particular production Als saw, it fails to grapple with what is admittedly a challenge in understanding the play. *The Winter's Tale* presents us with a paradox: in the midst of great contentment and celebration (boyhood friends Leontes, king of Sicilia, and Polixenes, king of Bohemia, reunited for a lengthy visit at Leontes' court), Leontes' jealousy causes him to attempt the murder of Polixenes; to berate, threaten, and imprison his wife, Hermione; and to cause the death of his young son, Mamillius. Out of the raw materials of comedy emerge the makings of a tragedy. But not quite. The critical invention of "romance" as a subgenre emerging from comedy identifies redemption and renewal among its key tenets. And though Mamillius dies and Perdita is cast out of Sicilia, there is indeed a path of change that differentiates such a play from a tragedy. What Als identifies here as "whimsy" and "forced imaginativeness" is the paradox the play presents to its viewers as it brings late comedy into a structural relation with tragedy.

When I read Als's review I was reminded of Bogdanov's production. Not because it suffered from being a song-less play without a groovy Jesus but because it took the difficult paradox inherent in this strongest of the romances and made it accessible and believable. I was also reminded of a remark by the psychoanalyst D. W. Winnicott: "Paradoxes are not meant to be resolved; they are meant to be observed."[2] For those accustomed to realism, which would not have included theatergoers in Shakespeare's lifetime, the clashes, reversals, and even contradictions of *The Winter's Tale* can be jarring. The salutary approach Bogdanov takes in his production is to observe the paradoxical nature of the play instead of attempting to resolve it.

The production opened with the entire cast assembling onstage, spread out in no apparent order, to sing an a cappella version of Christina Rossetti's Christmas carol "In the Bleak Midwinter." If this opening song's lyrics created a somber tone, it was lightened when we recognized that the community of the play was caroling the audience. The stage was bare, apart from a tall hearth rising behind the actors, which, added to the caroling, offered an oasis of comfort and domesticity to what might otherwise be a forbidding season. The lights dimmed as the cast moved to a choral position behind and to stage left. The lights came up as Hermione, who did not appear at all pregnant, was seated and as the chorus continued quietly to sing the song. Behind her chair stood her husband and a few men and women of the court. The scene and costumes suggested a comfortable Victorian or Edwardian drawing room. She asked Mamillius to tell her a tale. He responded that he'd tell it to her in her ear. She leaned forward, and he began to tell the tale as the scene froze and the lights dimmed, leaving us with this tale-telling tableau. Here is the text as it appears in 2.1, where Bogdanov has taken it to form this opening scene:

> **HERMIONE:** Come sir, now
> I am for you again. Pray you sit by us,
> And tell's a tale.
> **MAMILLIUS:** Merry or sad shall it be?
> **HERMIONE:** As merry as you will.
> **MAMILLIUS:** A sad tale's best for winter. I have one
> Of sprites and goblins.
> **HERMIONE:** Let's have that, good sir.
> Come on, sit down, come on, and do your best
> To fright me with your sprites. You're powerful at it.
> **MAMILLIUS:** There was a man—
> **HERMIONE:** Nay, come sit down, then on.
> **MAMILLIUS:** Dwelt by a churchyard. —I will tell it softly,
> Yon crickets shall not hear it.[3]

Bogdanov made cuts and rearrangements so that this moved more quickly and was focused on the happy playfulness between mother and son. This served to frame the ensuing action with the possibility that it was all just a winter's tale, and a frightening one. Perhaps this, suggested Bogdanov, was the kind of story a precocious young boy might tell his mother, where he dies and there is tragedy but all comes right in the end. The scene faded to black. Music continued to be sung.

When the lights came up, the stage was backlit by a white background fronted by a geometric pattern of rectangles that lent a modern, art deco look to an otherwise spare setting. A large crystal sculpture sat conspicuously at the rear of the stage on a stand. It was nonfigurative and composed of intersecting planes of clear glass that formed a kind of bent or distorted star. The two chairs and settee that constituted the only properties onstage were not modern, returning to the Victorian/Edwardian look of the framing scene. The sculpture was flanked by two white-coated waiters.

The play now opened as it does in the text, with Camillo (of Sicilia) and

Archidamus (of Bohemia) in dialogue about their respective kings and countries. They both wore formal evening attire, Camillo in a white tuxedo and Archidamus in black. They were followed onto the stage by the Sicilian court, and we saw that there was a large cocktail party taking place in which everyone was in formal evening dress. There were no shades of gray or other colors: the only colors were white and black.

Once the principal characters were present, the scene's action developed into a leave taking. But rather than offering a valediction, Hermione urged her husband's best friend to stay longer. From this initial genial atmosphere we were suddenly confronted with Leontes' mounting discomfort as he observed his wife and best friend in intimate, flirtatious conversation. He began to simmer visibly, the lights dimmed (except for a spotlight on Leontes and Polixenes/Hermione on the settee), and the action onstage froze, except for Leontes, who raged about his jealous suspicions to a single discordant tone (from offstage). Leontes was in black, while Polixenes and Hermione were in white, as though a better-matched pair. The light picked them out as the subject of his jealousy and rage. This brought into clear focus the extent to which Leontes had lost his rational mind, though without providing a reason. The audience had little evidence for believing Hermione to be anything but sincere in her desire to convince Polixenes to stay on her husband's behalf. Leontes' excessive emotional outburst and subsequent ruthless actions were hard to fathom, because they seemed an asymmetric response to an understandable kindness. Bogdanov's production did not try to mitigate this. Instead, Leontes' disproportionate anger was affixed to his inability to relate to anyone else in the scene; his isolation was a visual and verbal cue that what jealousy of this variety causes is a break in community and friendship as well as social relations. This is the paradox *The Winter's Tale* explores and which proves a challenge for readers and performers of the play: how such an abrupt and severe reversal can occur and cast the play from its apparent path. The breakdown in the world of Sicilia that follows can't be readily resolved. What Bogdanov's production did, with skillful patience, was to allow us to observe the consequences of such extreme, contradictory behavior.

In an article on the production, the critic Michael Phillips writes that "the 'romance' tag, Bogdanov says, is 'absolutely, fundamentally misleading.' The power of these late Shakespeare adventures, he says, lies in 'treating the fantastic as a matter of fact.'"[4] *The Winter's Tale*'s structure splits the world the play presents into two spaces and times. It does this by setting up the plot in Sicilia, then jumping forward in time sixteen years, after which the action moves to Bohemia. In Sicilia we encounter extreme jealousy, a murder plot, the incarceration of a faithful, pregnant wife, the death of a son and birth of a daughter, the attempted murder of that daughter, her rescue and adoption. None of these elements are conventional comedy fare. There are no young people blocked from love or marriage, no clowns, no mistaken identities, no disguise. As my list of plot turns demonstrates, *The Winter's Tale*'s initial time in Sicilia is bleak, as though it were the desperate heart of winter.

After a passage of sixteen years the play opens in Bohemia, and we find conventions of comedy in ready supply: it's a festive season (sheep-shearing time), the desire of young lovers drives the plot, a father disguises himself to check the relationship of his son with a girl of whom he does not approve, there is a trickster clown, no deaths or life-threatening situations mar the plot. As the comedy gains complexity, conflict causes the young couple to flee Bohemia for Sicilia, led by the old councilor (Camillo) who left with Polixenes in the first part of the play. Camillo arranges for the couple's acceptance at the Sicilian court, which opens the final part of the play as a reconciliation between all the remaining characters. Even Leontes, the character who propelled the drama furthest toward tragedy, finds redemption as his wife and daughter are returned to him.

Bogdanov's approach to the play is to contrast the two sites and times of the drama as dual genre-specific spaces: Sicilia and tragedy, Bohemia and comedy. If he rejects the "romance" label, he does so by attending to the play's paradox as a productive source for what is a realistic set of conflicts. In refusing to succumb to presenting *The Winter's Tale* as mere "whimsy," he offers instead a serious meditation on the protean nature of masculine authority. His male protagonists disrupt amity with jealousy, cause death through willfulness, interfere in courtship, and disown sons out of a lack of control and propriety. This is a failure of fatherhood. It is consistent across both halves of the play and brought to a resolution—at least at the level of the social fabric, if not for the men themselves—only with a revelatory ending in which Hermione comes to life, Perdita is revealed to be the lost princess, and Leontes is returned humbly to his family. For Bogdanov, this means juxtaposing a place of stark court manners, where there is no culture beyond political and sexual intrigue, with a pastoral place of craft and sociability, where nature and human beings are in a relationship of reflection and responsible stewardship.

This difference between failed husband and accomplished husbandry strikes us the moment the lights go up on Bohemia. Bogdanov's scene opened with young women hanging laundry on clotheslines, laughing and carousing, until a bicycle-riding Autolycus chased them playfully and stole a few pieces of clothing. Their playfulness and sexuality already exceeded the sum total of such liveliness in the first part of the play. This continued with Florizel's courtship of Perdita, which followed a timeworn comic path. The tone and energy of the play's Bohemia was driven by festivity and communal labor. The sheep shearing and the celebration that followed, even when invaded by a thief (Autolycus), provided a sharp contrast with Sicilia, both visually and thematically.[5] The only threats to this pastoral scene were the court figures (Polixenes and Camillo) posing as rustics so that they may spy on Florizel. While this is a standard element of plotted comedy (though typically in Shakespeare with the father attempting to control his *daughter*), its threat in this play was not quite parental. It was instead the court with its attendant judgments and demands, its culture, disrupting the country. In the world *The Winter's Tale* offers, and that Bogdanov's production emphasizes, there can be no liveliness, no peace, no spirit of communal trust and collaboration where court culture reigns.

What happened, then, when we returned to Sicilia in the final act? All of the main characters had gotten themselves there—Perdita and Florizel, in search of a safe place away from Polixenes; Camillo, to see his homeland again; and even the shepherd and his son, supposed father and brother of Perdita. Paulina had kept Hermione hidden for all these years while Leontes, like a penitent monk, sought forgiveness and apparently found it at least in part in religion. Bogdanov set up a giant cross at the back of the stage to emphasize this and to project the idea of redemption and sacrifice over the closing of the play. That this was heavy-handed is intentional, for the swift and easy redemption the play offers both fathers was treated with a dose of skepticism. Bogdanov does not understand the play to have a simple, happy ending. He does not find a neat resolution to the serious set of events that lead to it.

> Fed in secret, exercising in secret, waiting for the moment when Perdita would return. There is to be no miraculous resurrection; the statue trick is a cold, careful, calculated plan. Deception as an art form. A huge con trick posing as a miracle . . . .
>
> Paulina knows that the time is fast approaching when the game will be up. She will not be able to hold off the heir-seeking court jackals much longer. After the revelations of Perdita's identity comes the news of the statue carved in Hermione's likeness. Of course no one is allowed to touch it. The "statue" comes alive. Shock, horror, not a dry eye in the house. The penny drops:

LEONTES: . . . for I saw her,
As I thought, dead; and have in vain
Said many a prayer upon her grave. (act 5, scene 3)

Do you mean I have been on my knees for sixteen years for nothing? The deception boomerangs back.

What lessons have been learned? Polixenes has been let off the hook; he doesn't have to make a choice. Leontes is miffed that no one told him about Hermione and is throwing his weight around again. Hermione says not a word to Leontes in the last scene, preoccupied as she is with Perdita. But that silence is eloquent. Is she going to forgive Leontes for causing her to be incarcerated for sixteen years, for leaving her baby in the wilds (what a bit of luck it was found, eh?), for bringing about the death of her son? Is the winter over for the man who dwelt by a churchyard? Questions.[6]

In his Chicago production, Bogdanov staged this final scene as a return, visually, to the play's opening. The costuming was once again formal court attire, the set was spare and modern. Gone were any indications of pastoral Bohemian culture; even the shepherd and his clownish son were dressed to the nines. If we expected the ending to provide a change to this Sicilia, an infusion of life to the grim, cold court space, it was not in evidence. Even when the statue was revealed, that symbol of renewal that activates the "romance" structure of the play as one of redemption, a distancing took place. As Bogdanov has already indicated, Hermione attended only to her daughter. She did not speak to and was not touched by her husband. Leontes regained a wife and a daughter, but there was no evidence of the rapprochement we would expect. Polixenes had learned his new daughter-in-law was a princess, though this did not resolve the fact that his son had not gotten his permission for his choice of a wife. At the play's close, after revelations and reunions led unhappy actions to a happy ending, Bogdanov left Leontes on stage, alone, to circle the now-empty pedestal that had held his now-animate wife. As the music of "The Bleak Midwinter" played offstage, he was lost in thought and did not seem at all joyful as he left the stage. We were provoked to wonder what he was thinking about here where the comedy is meant to keep us from contemplation. After all, the ideological force of the comedic ending is typically one of consensus, of social convention affirmed. Why would this production possibly leave us with an unsettled version of the "reformed" king? Had he "awakened his faith"? Or was it wavering or growing weary here as he went offstage and we faded to black? Was he thinking about what he'd done or what he would do? Were his thoughts on his dead son, on time lost, or perhaps on how he would keep his wife in line? After all, Polixenes was back, and we were, though minus Mamillius, right where we started.

If there are unresolved tensions as *The Winter's Tale* nears its close, we should not be surprised. Every comedy including and after *Measure for*

21. Cast of *The Winter's Tale* (2003), directed by Michael Bogdanov. Photo by Liz Lauren

Measure ends thus to a greater or lesser extent. Regardless of how miraculous the resolution, or how many people get married or reenter the world of the living, something goes unresolved. The store of anger, resentment, bad faith, or even ill will has not been entirely depleted. Order is temporary, knit together insecurely, and likely to be unraveled in due time. At the end of Bogdanov's *The Winter's Tale*, hope lay not with the older characters, who seemed unwilling or unable to shed their skins and change their behavior. It was instead with the young couple. And not because they were a young couple who happened to be royalty, heirs to two thrones. This can be no guarantee of good behavior. In the Shakespearean universe it is most likely a warrant for its opposite. For Bogdanov, what makes Perdita a redemptive figure is her upbringing in a Bohemia that values something missing in Sicilia: "A sense of value, of place, of community. Perdita would have helped in the house, around the farm; would know all about animals, the seasons, the countryside, wild flowers. . . . These values are those of an unpretentious rural community at one with itself. She will carry them with her to the Sicilian court, along with her accent. It is these values that Florizel falls in love with.["][7] Earlier in the production we saw Florizel participating in the sheep shearing. He was there getting his hands dirty, a part of the action while his father spied on him, disapproving of his choice of woman and of lifestyle. And now at production's end, our prince and princess, she with her rural accent and he with his broadminded choice of partner and wider experience than his father, offers a different kind of future. The marriage of Sicilia and Bohemia.

MICHAEL BOGDANOV, LIFE AND WORK

Michael Bogdanov is known as a versatile director of stage productions across a range of genres and styles. He is also an experienced, award-winning film, television, and radio director and producer.[8] What sets him apart as a director of Shakespeare is his avowedly political approach to staging the plays. This is not, as Bogdanov makes clear in his writing and through the evidence of his productions, a cheap attempt to politicize the plays by using them as an instrument to take up contemporary issues. Seeing just one of his productions might give such an impression, but this would ignore the larger body of work and its evolution. As Bogdanov tells it, he learned first what it meant to modernize Shakespeare—to make him, in Jan Kott's words, "our contemporary." From there it was a question of how this contemporaneous dramatic energy could afford to ignore the forces animating the context out of which such a production was conceived and played. No audience, no

22. Cast of *The Winter's Tale* (2003), directed by Michael Bogdanov. Photo by Liz Lauren

theater company, no staged production exists in a vacuum. On modernizing Shakespeare, here is Bogdanov on his first breakthrough production, of *Romeo and Juliet* in Leicester in 1974:

> In rehearsal the story had been coming over hard, clear and very exciting.
> . . . When the production moved from the rehearsal room and arrived on
> to the stage, somehow the clarity and the hardness, the linear quality of the
> story, had gone. What was more, audiences weren't responding either to the
> production or the play. At the last moment, after the very final preview, I cut
> the whole of the end scene, where the Friar recaps the story for the benefit of
> Escalus and, after the death of Juliet, I switched to a press conference around
> the unveiling of the two gold statues that Capulet and Montague erect to the
> memory of each other's child.
>   Rock music built to a crescendo during a blackout and, when the lights

came up, the entire company was assembled in modern dress in front of Romeo and Juliet, now dressed in gold cloaks and masks standing on the erstwhile tomb. Muzak played "Fly Me to the Moon." . . . Escalus, the Duke, read the prologue as an epilogue from a cue card, as if inaugurating an unveiling ceremony. "I hereby name this ship." . . . The main protagonists were photographed in front of the statues, shaking hands, the Nurse holding up a rope ladder, Escalus attempting to bring about the familial reconciliation with a three-way hand clasp. Jimmy Carter's smile of the time as he handed over the presidency to Reagan.

The transformation had an extraordinary effect. People in the audience shouted, people walked out, people cheered, people bravoed, people booed, and I thought, "For three hours they have been bored out of their minds and suddenly something has challenged them. A moment of real theatre." It was an anarchic stroke and it turned the whole evening around in a most remarkable way. More importantly, it served to emphasize that I was going up the wrong path in attempting to ape what I thought was a traditional way of performing Shakespeare. There are many directors in many parts of the globe who are able to tell a Shakespeare story with tremendous power and clarity without having to go to the lengths that I have described, but that is how I discovered a way to tell the stories. By removing the barriers that exist between the language and the audience, by allowing them to identify with the characters clearly, by associating the events with contemporary politics, I allowed the plays to breathe.[9]

It is clear from this anecdote that Bogdanov's Brechtian approach to the plays is not didactic but dialectical: arguments and propositions in constant motion that need not be resolved into moral certainty or even narrative certainty.

In the mid-1980s, Bogdanov founded the English Shakespeare Company with Michael Pennington. Their goal was to form a touring company outside the auspices of the larger Royal Shakespeare Company and to have free rein in doing Shakespeare's history plays.[10] The story of this collaboration, told in meticulous detail (and registering genuine astonishment that they ever pulled it off), in which Bogdanov and Pennington produced their "Wars of the Roses," is told in their book *The English Shakespeare Company: The Story of the "Wars of the Roses," 1986–1989*.[11] A blurb from Mel Gussow of the *New York Times* at the beginning of the book sums it all up: "In a marathon lasting more than 23 hours, seven interrelated plays were performed: *Richard II*, followed by *Henry IV Parts 1 and 2*, *Henry V* and the three *Henry VI* plays distilled to two, followed by *Richard III*. It was, in all senses, a prodigious undertaking, most of all for those theater-goers who experienced the complete and indispensable Shakespearian event."[12] Over a four-year period, "The Wars of the Roses" toured England, Canada, the United States, Japan, Germany, Australia, Holland, and finally Wales (to be filmed for television).

From the beginning, this ambitious, massive production was meant to be political. Here is Bogdanov describing his state of mind in 1986 when they were figuring out what sort of tone they wanted to set in the production:

> I was burning with anger at the iniquity of the British electoral system. Eleven million people had voted for Thatcher, fourteen million against. Scotland, Wales and the North were almost totally Labour and only in the fat, green, get-rich-quick Yuppie haven of the South did the Conservative Party hold sway. Moreover, Boadicea had rallied her troops around her with a senseless war of expediency, sailing heroically (in some people's eyes) twelve thousand miles to the Falklands to do battle for "a little patch of ground that hath in it no profit but the name / To pay five ducats, five, I would not farm it." The parallels were plain. *The Henrys* were plays for today, the lessons of history unlearnt. The Grand Mechanism of the Polish critic, Jan Kott, in full sway, the escalator shuttling mice and men up to the top, where the golden crock of Imperialism shone brightly, waiting for the next attempt to snatch it from its podium.[13]

Clearly this was not a production that unselfconsciously presented English history as triumphant or as a means to rally a nation as Olivier had done during WWII.

Bogdanov's sensitivity to politics and historical context stems from his view that Shakespeare wrote and played at a time of rich multiculturalism and political upheaval:

> How do we deal with the plays in the twenty-first century in an increasingly multicultural society? And anyway, has there ever been a time when these islands were not multicultural? I suspect that the courtyards of Elizabethan England teemed with "masterless men," the tongues of a hundred regions grappling with the sound of a language comprised of the scraps and leftovers of a dozen other languages. Hard enough today for some people to distinguish Cork from Glasgow, Liverpool from Birmingham, Newcastle from Cardiff, Belfast from Bethnal. London then was the polyglottal stopover for regional runaways, a bubbling linguistic British brew, the pot full of the still succulent sounds of French, Latin, Goedelic, Brythonic, Norwegian, Saxon, Platt-Deutsch, Hoch-Deutsch, Middle-High Deutsch, fresh

words entering the language (in a variety of spellings: Mr. Shakesshaft, Shagsboar, Shakespear with or without an "e") at a faster rate possibly than at any other time.[14]

His sensitivity to this is no doubt heightened by his Welshness. Included as part of a United Kingdom, colonized Wales is very self-conscious not only of its own culture and language but of its long, complex, and often repressed history with England. While Wales and Welshness in Shakespeare's plays have garnered increasing scholarly attention in recent years, Bogdanov has been a fierce advocate of this on the stage, as well as for Welsh theater more generally.[15] In 1996, he made a BBC drama documentary film based on *The Tempest*, shot in the working-class Tiger Bay section of Cardiff, called *The Tempest in Butetown*.[16] The film restages the play as intensely political and reflecting the immediacy of the political conflict that was at the time ripping through that part of the city. The local people were set upon by outside forces that sought to alter their world for the purpose of "development" without their consent. Bogdanov used this tempest in Butetown to frame the political urgency latent in Shakespeare's play by using locals involved in the controversy as actors.

Bogdanov has been a keen observer of the subject of Wales and the Welsh in the Henriad. On his work with the history plays, he notes, "I was very interested when we were doing 'The Wars of the Roses' with the English Shakespeare Company how much Welshness there is in the plays."[17] His lecture "The Welsh in Shakespeare" presents a convincing argument about the positive representation of Welsh culture in Shakespeare's work. This extends to the comedies as well. On *Cymbeline*: "When I looked at *Cymbeline*, suddenly Wales became the civilizing force of nature away from the autocratic fascism of the English court—let's call it Westminster—and its stifling autocratic ethos."[18]

CONCLUSION

It is no coincidence that *Cymbeline* and *The Winter's Tale* sit side by side in the group of late plays that have come to be known as "romances," marked by a volatile fusion of the comic and tragic sensibilities. Like Bogdanov's view of *Cymbeline*, in which Wales civilizes while England corrupts, his *Winter's Tale* for Chicago Shakespeare Theater depicted Sicilia as the bleak wintery world of tragedy, Bohemia as the springtime world of comedy. Making no attempt to suggest that these two worlds could be effectively fused in a comic resolution tacked on to a vexed plot, Bogdanov succeeded in letting the play's paradoxical nature govern his production. In so doing, he achieved, as he had with his *Romeo and Juliet* in 1974, a moment of "real theater."

NOTES

1. Hilton Als, "Shakespeare on Park," August 15 & 22, 2011, 86.

2. From the chapter "Children Learning," in W. D. Winnicott, *Home Is Where We Start From: Essays by a Psychoanalyst* (New York: Norton, 1990), 148.

3. *The Winter's Tale*, 2.1.22–33. All citations from the play taken from *The Norton Shakespeare*, ed. Stephen Greenblatt et al., 2nd ed. (New York: Norton, 2008).

4. Michael Phillips, "Bogdanov Returns for Thrilling 'Tale,'" *Chicago Tribune*, March 30, 2003.

5. "We go from the austerity and sterility of the Sicilian court to the celebration at the end of shearing time in Bohemia. Shearing is hard. I know. I've done it. Two or three hundred times a day (not me, I hasten to add) wrestling with a hundredweight of sheep and wool, turning, twisting, shearing. It's communal and traditional." Michael Bogdanov, *Shakespeare: The Director's Cut*, vol. 1 (Edinburgh, UK: Capercaillie Books, 2003), 96.

6. Ibid., 100–102.

7. Ibid., 98–99.

8. Bogdanov was born in Neath, Wales (near Swansea), and lives in Cardiff. He is a founding member (with Michael Pennington) of the English Shakespeare Company (1986) and of the Wales Theatre Company (2003), has directed eight productions for the Royal Shakespeare Company, was associate director of the Royal Shakespeare Company (1980–1988), and has directed major productions in Ireland, Germany, Italy, Canada, Japan, and the United States. As joint Artistic Director of the English Shakespeare Company, he directed the company's inaugural productions of "The Henrys" and, in 1987, the seven-play history cycle of "The Wars of the Roses," which toured worldwide. For this ambitious program he earned the 1990 Laurence Olivier Award for Best Director. He is a former Intendant of The Deutsches Schauspielhaus, Germany's largest National Theatre, where he is remembered for his many successes, among them *Hamlet*, *Reineke Fuchs*, *Julius Caesar*, *The Ginger Man*, *Under Milk Wood*, and *The Tempest*. In addition to directing musicals, opera, and innovative productions of *Beowulf* and *Sir Gawain and the Green Knight*, he has been nominated for a BAFTA for *Shakespeare on the Estate*. Most recently he has been associated with the Hamburger Kammerspiele, where he has twice won the Ralph Mares Preis for Best Director.

9. Bogdanov, *Shakespeare: The Director's Cut*, vol. 1, 3–4. See also his further, more detailed comments on this production in his interview with John Drakakis, in "Theatres for Shakespeare," *Shakespeare Survey* 60 (Cambridge: Cambridge UP,), 196–213, at 202.

10. In Bogdanov, *Shakespeare: The Director's Cut*, vol. 2 (Edinburgh, UK: Capercaillie Books, 2005), Bogdanov explains: "In spring 1986, Michael Pennington and I sat in a coffee bar around the corner from the Arts Council of Great Britain in Piccadilly and plotted the downfall of the acceptable face of British theatre. Our plan was to launch a radical alternative to the Royal Shakespeare Company by producing highly politicised versions of *Henry IV, Parts 1 and 2*, and *Henry V* with a company of 25 actors, and tour them all around Britain" (10).

11. Michael Bogdanov and Michael Pennington, *The English Shakespeare Company:*

The Story of the "Wars of the Roses," 1986–1989 (London: Nick Hern Books, 1990).

12. Ibid., i.

13. Ibid., 23.

14. Bogdanov, *Shakespeare: The Director's Cut*, vol. 1, 5–6.

15. On Wales and/in Shakespeare, see Willy Maley and Brian Schwyzer, eds. *Shakespeare and Wales: From the Marches to the Assembly* (London: Ashgate Press, 2010); Garrett A. Sullivan, Jr., *The Drama of Landscape: Land, Property, and Social Relations on the Early Modern Stage* (Stanford: Stanford UP, 1998), 127–58; Patricia Parker, "Uncertain Unions: Welsh Leeks in *Henry V*," in *British Identities and English Renaissance Literature*, ed. David J. Baker and Willy Maley (Cambridge: Cambridge UP, 2002), 81–100; Brian Schwyzer, *Literature, Nationalism, and Memory in Early Modern England and Wales* (Cambridge: Cambridge UP, 2004); Bradley Greenburg, "Romancing the Chronicles: *1 Henry IV* and the Rewriting of Medieval History," *Quidditas* 27 (2006): 34–50.

16. For details on the production and Bogdanov's reasons for making it, see Drakakis interview, "Theatres for Shakespeare," 196–99. See also Bogdanov's chapter on *The Tempest* in *Shakespeare: The Director's Cut*, vol. 1, 49–70.

17. Drakakis interview, "Theatres for Shakespeare," 200.

18. Ibid.

BIBLIOGRAPHY

Als, Hilton. "Shakespeare on Park." *New Yorker*, August 15 & 22, 2011.

Bogdanov, Michael. *Shakespeare: The Director's Cut*. Vol. 1. Edinburgh, UK: Capercaillie Books, 2003.

———. *Shakespeare: The Director's Cut*. Vol. 2. Edinburgh, UK: Capercaillie Books, 2005.

Bogdanov, Michael, and Michael Pennington. *The English Shakespeare Company: The Story of the "Wars of the Roses," 1986–1989*. London: Nick Hern Books, 1990.

Drakakis, John. "Theatres for Shakespeare." *Shakespeare Survey* 60. Cambridge: Cambridge UP. 196–213.

Greenburg, Bradley. "Romancing the Chronicles: *1 Henry IV* and the Rewriting of Medieval History." *Quidditas* 27 (2006): 34–50.

Maley, Willy, and Brian Schwyzer, eds. *Shakespeare and Wales: From the Marches to the Assembly*. London: Ashgate Press, 2010.

Parker, Patricia. "Uncertain Unions: Welsh Leeks in *Henry V*." In *British Identities and English Renaissance Literature*. Ed. David J. Baker and Willy Maley. Cambridge: Cambridge UP, 2002.

Phillips, Michael. "Bogdanov Returns for Thrilling 'Tale.'" *Chicago Tribune*, March 30, 2003.

Schwyzer, Brian. *Literature, Nationalism, and Memory in Early Modern England and Wales*. Cambridge: Cambridge UP, 2004.

Shakespeare, William. *The Norton Shakespeare*. 2nd ed. Ed. Stephen Greenblatt et al. New York: Norton, 2008.

Sullivan, Garrett A. *The Drama of Landscape: Land, Property, and Social Relations on the Early Modern Stage*. Stanford: Stanford UP 1998.

Winnicott, D. W. *Home Is Where We Start From: Essays by a Psychoanalyst*. New York: Norton, 1990.

Risky Business

Rose Rage *at Chicago Shakespeare Theater*

CLARK HULSE

For Ivan

Chicago Shakespeare Theater took extravagant artistic risks when it staged *Rose Rage* in 2003. Imagine launching a six-month run, with a four-and-a-half-hour-long running time—plus intermissions and dinner break—for Shakespeare's least-popular history plays, about a famously and fatally weak protagonist, set in a slaughterhouse, with an all-male, twelve-actor cast playing thirty-three speaking characters plus messenger, rebels, and soldiers, all led by a director in his American debut.

But then, the *Henry VI* plays, which are restaged in *Rose Rage*, presented similar risks when Philip Henslowe opened them at the Rose Theater in 1591–1592. He challenged the ascendancy of Christopher Marlowe's moral-revenge tragedies, with politically risky material, unstable acting companies, and an untried, undereducated actor-turned-playwright with the bawdy name of Will Shake-speare.

The CST–Edward Hall production of *Rose Rage* in Chicago and New York in 2003–2004 was a high point on the long arc of theatrical innovation and risk taking that makes up the history of the *Henry VI* plays. It is a 412-year-long story of innovation, running from the inception of the plays as individual works to their knitting together as a trilogy in the First Folio, to the epic productions of the mid-twentieth century, to the triumph of the CST-Hall production.

Risk takes many forms in the theater. There is straightforward business risk, there is theatrical risk, and there is artistic risk. Of course, the historically available risks of 2003 were different from those of around 1592, and the specific risks facing Ed Hall and CST were different from those facing Shakespeare, Henslowe, and the companies of Lord Strange's Men or the Earl of Pembroke's Men. But shared among them is the catalyzing effect that risk brings to the theater.

Take the business risk of a theatrical production. The space is blocked out on the calendar or rented; artistic property licensed; director and designer hired; actors contracted; production crew at work on sets; advertising, marketing, and fund-raising in gear—all burning money long before the first patron walks through the door. A few fortunate theaters can be assured of advance ticket sales or subscriptions. Most have little idea until the reviews come out whether the thing will pay off or ruin its producers.

Business risk and reward are to some extent quantifiable: the play pays its costs, and then some, or it does not. The profit provides a market-competitive return on investment, or it does not. But in longer-term ways, business risk and reward are more qualitative: the profits are turned into insightful investments in the next season—or plowed into over-reaching blunders. The success or failure of the play may attract new scripts to be acted and may hold or draw the best actors and directors. At this point, business risk begins to shade into theatrical risk.

Theatrical risk is first of all physical. Actors and directors must challenge themselves, to the extent of their abilities, and challenge each other—what athletes call "leaving it on the playing field." This may include vocal challenges and challenges to physical endurance. In epic plays about violent episodes of history, it may mean unexpected risks to life and limb. And the acting space itself dares the company with its capabilities and its limitations. Shakespeare compares the stage to a cockpit, and the phrase is nearly literal: a tiny, confined area of physical contact, with animal spirits aroused and the possibility, even likelihood, of blood.

Hardest to define is artistic risk. The phrase conjures images of the solitary writer, inventing new forms of expression that may or may not be understood in his or her lifetime. Emily Dickinson risked using too few words. Shakespeare—in Ben Jonson's famous critiques—risked using too many, in forms that were too tortuous and yet insufficiently steeped in Latin and Greek.[1]

But we also know reflexively that the solitary writer offers us too narrow a model for the artistic work of theater. Henslowe's payments to writers and the intricate text of *The Play of Sir Thomas More* remind us that writing often demanded multiple hands cobbling together disparate scenes. The intrusion into *Macbeth* of a song known to be written by John Fletcher reminds us that scripts were reworked as they were remounted, and the recorded or extant early versions of *King Lear* and *Hamlet* remind us that Shakespeare himself was the master reworker.

Collaboration was also between actors and writers. Marlowe's great tragedies and what is now *Henry VI Part 1* seem to have been written expressly for the great Edward Alleyn in the lead role. From 1594 on, with the establishment of the Lord Chamberlain's Men, Shakespeare was able to write with the assumption that Richard Burbage would be available for the lead, and a stable group of actors (Heminges, Condell, Kemp, Cowley, Shakespeare himself) would be available for the other parts. Hence, theatrical artistry itself must have been highly collaborative, with the production evolving rapidly through rehearsal and performance. This leaves us with a maddening lack of key evidence about the artistic risks of sixteenth-century productions but a wealth of record and report about modern productions.

As separate as business, theatrical, and artistic risk may be in theory, they are all creative, and in the heat of action they run together. In *English Shakespeares*, Peter Holland identified some of the mundane practical decisions made about English productions of the 1990s that had profound effects on acting, audience reaction, and box office. How long is the production? (A running time that goes beyond eleven o'clock makes it hard to catch the last train to the suburbs.) How long is it from curtain to the interval? (That is, how long will the audience have to wait to urinate?) How will the length of the interval affect the bar sales? And incidentally, do you time the interval in *King Lear* for before or after the blinding of Gloucester?[2]

The CST *Rose Rage* production faced these issues at an unprecedented level. Would audiences be willing to commit six hours to the production, plus travel time to and from the theater? Would anybody want to sit down to a meal in the midst of the butchery and mayhem? Could the actors maintain the stamina and focus required to put the show on four times a week? Could the set withstand a constant pounding with knives and staves, and would the stage floor—slippery with blood and offal—cause some horrible accident? And above all, would purists and innovators alike recognize and respond to a distinctive style that was a combustive mix of Shakespeare and Chicago?

The roots of these challenges to *Rose Rage* ran deep into the play text, and deep into its early Shakespearean staging as three distinct plays about the long and troublesome reign of King Henry VI.

By any measure, the 1591–1592 theater "season" in London was one of ferment. "Season" is a bit of a misnomer since it implies a set schedule with set venues and companies, and none of those things were yet fully in place. In the summer, when plague stalked the narrow places of London, the acting companies generally went away to play in the provinces. They returned in the late fall, and the best were then invited to the court to perform during the December–January holidays. And as occasion bid, they might play at this or that castle, manor, or townhouse for their own lord, or some other.

Likewise the places of playing were still in flux. At the city inns used for playing—the Red Lion, the Bull, the Bell, the Bel Savage, the Cross Keys—the actors had to compete with other forms of leisure as well as contend with the regulations of the city fathers. Outside the city to the north, Burbage's Theatre was the scene of regular shouting matches and brawls over the gate receipts.[3] Its chief rival, Henslowe's Rose, was limited in audience and production capacity. Companies seem to have moved from playhouse to playhouse, depending on the shifting dynamics of audiences and impresarios.

Not least, the companies themselves were in flux. The Queen's Men and the Admiral's Men seem to have collapsed around 1588 to 1590, and their members joined and split in various combinations as Sussex's, Strange's, and Pembroke's Men in their search for steady work. This is one of the most murky and vexing periods for theater historians. During these two years and the subsequent period of June 1592 to December 1593, when the theaters were closed for the plague, all but one of the major companies underwent radical reorganization or change of status. Only with the reopening in 1594 did the Admiral's Men and Lord Chamberlain's Men establish themselves as the dominant groups for the next decade.

Here's what we do know.

In 1591, Edward Alleyn of the Lord Admiral's Men had joined with Lord Strange's Men and was playing at James Burbage's Theater when he had a falling out over receipts.[4] Alleyn and Strange's Men bolted across town to the rival Rose Theater, taking their playbooks with them, which included Christopher Marlowe's *Tamburlaine* and *The Jew of Malta*, as well as Thomas Kyd's *Spanish Tragedy*.

In the first months of 1592, Philip Henslowe rebuilt the Rose in Southwark at considerable cost, expanding the audience capacity from around 2,000 to about 2,400, but still short of the capacity of the Theater, which stood at over 3,000. More important, he deepened its shallow stage and added an upper structure that could accommodate both machinery and playing areas.[5] The effect was to make it a better home for the large-scale spectacles that Marlowe had introduced to London audiences. Henslowe laid out an average of six shillings a week to "Master Tilney's Man," that is, to the agent of Edmund Tilney, who licensed plays on behalf of the Lord Chamberlain.[6] Then, in mid-February 1592, he launched his season, featuring the amalgamated Admiral's/Strange's Men in plays by Robert Greene, Thomas Kyd, and Christopher Marlowe. It was, in a very real sense, the turning point in the history of English theater.

But something was missing. To be exact, Marlowe was missing. He had a habit of disappearing, and it is difficult to know how much his companions in the theater could guess about his espionage activities, though they certainly knew about his dangerous opinions and violent temper.[7] But as Henslowe opened the remodeled Rose, his most popular plays in hand were two or three years old, and their hold on the audience could not last forever. With Marlowe gone, it must have been clear that there would be no immediate additions to match *Tamburlaine* or *The Jew of Malta*. Henslowe, Alleyn, and Strange's Men needed an infusion of new material.

By March 3, 1592, Marlowe was back in London, but under guard, arrested for counterfeiting in the Netherlands, and facing execution. On that exact day, Henslowe recorded in his account book the opening of *Harry the VI*, with receipts of 76 shillings, the biggest single day's gross of the season. He records fourteen more performances of the play by June 22, more than any other play, including *The Spanish Tragedy*, *The Jew of Malta*, or *Mullah Mulluca*.[8] By August, Thomas Nashe had come out in print with lavish praise, and by September the dying and jealous Robert Greene—whose *Friar Bacon* was eclipsed—had lashed out at its author, as an "upstart Crow, beautified with our feathers, that with his *Tygers hart wrapt in a Players hyde,* supposes he is as well able to bombast out a blanke verse as the best of you: and being an absolute *Johannes fac totum,* is in his owne conceit the only Shake-scene in a country."[9] Shakespeare the actor-turned-playwright had arrived.

Nashe's late-summer praise is for the staging of the death of Talbot in what we now know as *Henry VI Part 1*, while Greene's attack mimics lines from what we now know as *Henry VI Part 3*. Most theater historians agree that Henslowe's play at the Rose is Part 1, with Edward Alleyn as Talbot. Versions of Parts 2 and 3 were printed in 1594 with the titles *The First part of the Contention betwixt the two famous Houses of Yorke and Lancaster . . .*, and *The true Tragedie of Richard Duke of Yorke, and the death of good king Henrie the Sixt, with the whole contention betweene the two Houses Lancaster and Yorke.* The title page of Part 3 adds that it had been "sundrie times acted by the Right Honorable the Earle of Pembrooke his servants."

There are two reasonable theories to explain all this. The most commonly accepted one is that all three parts of *Henry VI* were played by Strange's Men, and when the theaters were closed in July 1592, the company broke into two major parts and went to tour the provinces, dividing their play scripts between them.[10] This would explain how Pembroke's Men suddenly turn up as a top company in possession of *Henry VI Parts 2* and *3* and Marlowe's *Edward II*. It requires, however, that the pragmatic and thorough Philip Henslowe simply forgot to note or mention that he had all three blockbusters on his boards. And it fails to explain why internal linkages between Parts 1 and 2 are absent, while they are strong between Parts 2 and 3.

Just as likely is that all three parts of *Henry VI* were being played by 1592, at different theaters by different companies, and were most likely not conceived of as a single three-part set. Indeed, two-part plays like *1 & 2 Tamburlaine* or the two parts of *The Spanish Tragedy* were doing very well in the theater around 1589–1592, so it is perfectly reasonable that what is now *Henry VI 2* and *3* were playing on one side of town with a start-up company of Pembroke's Men as the first and second parts of *The Contention betwixt the Two Famous Houses,* while the prequel *Harry the VI* was running at the Rose with Strange's Men. It was common for the theaters to run contending plays on similar subjects: *Friar Bacon* ran against *Faustus* as plays on the occult; Greene's *Battle of Alcazar* ran against *Mullah Muhamed* (author unknown). And Marlowe—mysteriously out of jail by early May—quickly wrote *Edward II* for Pembroke's Men, competing with Shakespeare's *Harry the VI* with Strange's Men. Clearly, the playwrights—none were sharers in the companies as Shakespeare would later be with the Lord Chamberlain's Men—were happy to write for either side or both.

From this blurry, bubbling morass of actors, audiences, playwrights, and playhouses emerged some clear results. In *1* and *2 Henry VI*, Shakespeare and his actors matched Marlowe's Tamburlaine, Barabas, and Faustus with bold Talbot and the vaunting Suffolk and York, bombasting in blank verse. And they took Marlovian spectacle and added a new level of physical theater in the form of continuous combat.

In *3 Henry VI*, Shakespeare and some talented boy actor created an entirely new kind of character, one that Marlowe had not yet been able to imagine—Queen Margaret, with a "tiger's heart wrapped in a woman's hide." This violent, resolute woman taking bold action in the world of men was the creation that brought Greene's envious attack and became Shakespeare's signature. He repeats and develops the Margaret figure with Tamora, Queen of the Goths in *Titus Andronicus*, with Regan in *King Lear*, and above all with Lady Macbeth.

Again with Margaret, Shakespeare gave his audience the first glimpse of a new dramatic language that breaks out of the bonds of blank verse:

> Where are your mess of sons to back you now?
> The wanton Edward and the lusty George?
> And where's that valiant crookback prodigy,
> Dickie, your boy, that with his grumbling voice
> Was wont to cheer his dad in mutinies?[11]

Or later:

> . . . Thou shouldst be mad;
> And I to make thee mad do mock thee thus.
> Stamp, rave and fret, that I may sing and dance. (1.4.89–91)

The lines scan iambic. But the monosyllables, underlain with syncopated rhythms and mixed with the colloquial diction of "Dickie, your boy" and "dad," foretell a poetry of the human voice that will refashion English drama in short time.

Finally, *Henry VI* in 1592 marks the creation of a new genre: the English history play. The three *Henry VI* plays are not yet at this point knit together into the trilogy presented by the First Folio, much less into the double tetralogy that modern producers and directors sometimes imagine. But the history play itself is established—and ratified by imitation in Marlowe's *Edward II*. And the core of the cycle structure is there in the internal linkage between Parts 2 and 3.

This last creation is the most collaborative of all, the joint work of Shakespeare, the actors, the two companies, the impresarios, and the audiences by their pennies and applause. It was a creation that would have long endurance, but above all it was born of the moment and reverberated within the moment. *Tamburlaine* and *The Jew of Malta* had resonated with the events, disturbances, and fears of recent history, but the *Henry VI* plays brought those resonances onto English soil.

The plays are not directly topical in the way that plays like *The Isle of Dogs* must have been to bring direct suppression, or that *Richard II* was, when revived on the eve of the Essex rebellion. But the mood in England in 1591–1592 was ripe for the Henry material. It was a time of not quite peace and not quite war. The crisis of the Spanish Armada was three years in the past but a low-grade conflict with Spain remained. Drake, Frobisher, and Hawkins were pirating and privateering, and Grenville had died at the hands of the enemy, his ship the *Revenge* gone to the bottom. Spain fought in France to bar Henry IV from the throne, and England fought as Henry's reluctant but necessary ally against Spain, his enemy. English forces landed on French soil but were decimated by disease and want of supply. The old court rivals Leicester and Hatton and Walsingham and Burghley were dead or declined, but the new rivals Cecil and Essex were put on the Council. The threat of Mary Queen of Scots had been shortened by a head, but there were rumors of new plots to assassinate Elizabeth. Perhaps Marlowe was among the plotters. Perhaps the goal was to place on the throne none other than Lord Strange, the patron of the players.

And there were ominous signs. For the second year in a row, 1592 brought severe drought, and there was a miraculous ebbing of the River Thames. In London, a man named Hacket proclaimed that he was Jesus Christ returned in judgment for a sinful world. He was arrested, hanged, cut down, and drawn and quartered. But who was he really?[12]

The *Henry VI* plays, like Shakespeare's later history plays, refer directly to none of this. Instead they take connective bits and pieces—futile wars in France, bickering factions at court, miseries in the land, and people who hear voices—and swirl them around in suggestive juxtapositions. The history plays are never quite topical, and never without relevance. They take the mood of anxiety and dread, the fear of being consumed in violence, and work it through and through.

On June 12, 1592, the Lord Mayor, fearing riots, petitioned the Council to close the theaters, so as to prevent "great multitudes of people assembled together."[13] His wish was granted on June 23. The magical season was over. The actors broke into small groups, went into the country, and did not return until December of 1593. By then, Greene was dead of debauchery. Marlowe was murdered—most likely assassinated by the government. Kyd, arrested and tortured, was "utterly undone" and likewise died. Shakespeare alone grew and prospered.

If *The Contention betwixt the Two Famous Houses* with Pembroke's Men and *Harry the VI* with Strange's Men constituted a two-part play and a competing prequel, their transformation into a three-part epic was rapid. Shakespeare himself must have rewritten them at least once, as the Lord Chamberlain's Men played them repeatedly. By the time of the publication of the First Folio in 1623, they had been improved, lengthened, and knitted together to make the *Henry VI 1–2–3* that we now know.

They had also become period pieces. Their lofty, bombastic style was undercut by the new dramatic language that Shakespeare had molded with Margaret's sneer at "dad" and "Dickie, your boy." In the *Henry IV* plays and again in the Player's speech in *Hamlet*, a confident Shakespeare could mock the earlier style that he had made famous along with Kyd and Marlowe. That said, the plays seem to have held the stage throughout Shakespeare's career. In them, Shakespeare had first developed the core of his style, wedding literary language with theatrical physicality.

The Restoration and eighteenth-century production history of the *Henry VI* plays is a story of readaptation, with pieces of the plays woven into other material to create topical political commentary. In the nineteenth century and into the twentieth, it is more a story of building monuments to English history. The plays are firmly treated as a sequence, in deference to the First Folio, and presented in their entirety or as self-conscious fragments. By the end of World War II, the "first tetralogy" had acquired a curiously positive arc, as if a century of mayhem were leading British audiences to see past the feuding of Yorkists and Lancastrians to a redemptive ascendant of the Tudor dynasty—and to see in the plays the origins of their own antifascist and still imperial present.

Two productions in the second half of the twentieth century stand out as marking a dark turn for the Henry VI material, creating the immediate reference points for *Rose Rage*. Peter Hall's "Brechtian"[14] *Wars of the Roses* with the Royal Shakespeare Company in 1963–1964 was a three-part play formed out of the three *Henry VI* plays plus *Richard III*. The Michael Bogdanov–Michael Pennington "post-Falklands-War"[15] *Wars of the Roses* with the English Shakespeare Company in 1989 took on both the first and second tetralogies (*Richard II, 1–2 Henry IV, Henry V, 1–2–3 Henry VI, Richard III*) in a twenty-three-hour mammoth production. While both maintained period costuming, the positive gloss and glorious memory of war were now gone.

Compared to these productions, Edward Hall's conception for *Rose Rage* is not so massive after all. It is actually a theatrical *compression* of material that had expanded to gargantuan proportions. The nucleus of *Henry VI* material has a two-part structure in both the Peter Hall and Bogdanov *Wars*, with Parts 1 and 2 joined together and Part 3 standing on its own. Ed Hall follows a version of that structure, but instead of Renaissance costumes, multiple sets, and epic gestures, he compresses the action into a flexible space with minimum furniture, set below the audience, which peers into the abattoir. Instead of pitched battles, butchers in white aprons smash apart entrails and cabbage heads with ax handles, cleavers, and knives. The sound alone sticks in the heads of audience members a decade later. Reviewers persistently called the production "bloody," though there was only a small quantity of real blood. Instead, extremes of physical action were arrested just short of physical contact and displaced onto symbolic violence. In Hall's hands, the play became an anatomy of the human capacity for spiraling hatred and deliberate viciousness.

Ed Hall was in his early thirties when he launched the *Rose Rage* project. As a young director, Hall risked being defined through his relationship to his famous father, Sir Peter Hall. On the surface, doing a Henry VI cycle looked like the awakening of a competition with the elder Hall's renowned *Wars of the Roses* at Stratford. Furthermore, *Wars* held an iconic position in the narrative of Peter Hall's life. In his memoirs from his time as director of the National Theater opening the new South Bank complex, Peter Hall constantly invokes *Wars of the Roses* as the play that pushed him into a spiral of overwork and collapse four years before the birth of his son Edward. Not just a "breakthrough" production, it was his "breakdown" play, leading to the breakup of his first marriage.[16]

There is little trace of a psychological signature, however, in *Rose Rage*. By age nine, Ed Hall had witnessed forms of spectacle ranging from *Planet of the Apes* and *Jack and the Beanstalk* to Arsenal football matches, had been babysat by Harold Pinter, and could tell the difference between a very good *Hamlet* and an ordinary one.[17] The *Wars* of Peter Hall and Bogdanov–Pennington had simply gone as big as you could go with the material. *Rose Rage* was a radically different play in a different style in response to different times.

To begin with, although the text of *Rose Rage* (developed by Hall with the scholar Roger Warren) is based on the First Folio, in many ways it harks back to the *True Contention* of Pembroke's Men.[18] The Joan of Arc sections that make up so much of *Henry VI Part 1* are eliminated, and the focus of what remains—essentially shorter versions of Parts 2 and 3—are tightly focused around the two warring houses. The text of *Rage* comprises twenty-five scenes, divided into two parts, each with an interval. The first five-and-a-fraction scenes derive from *1 Henry VI*. The remainder of *Rose Rage* Part 1 (slightly less than eight scenes) derives from *2 Henry VI*. The whole of *Rose Rage* Part 2—comprising twelve scenes—hails from *3 Henry VI*. This recasting of three parts into two parts, with two halves each, allows a restructuring of an amorphous historical action into digestible segments. It is roughly depicted in Table 12.1.

TABLE 12.1

Part 1.1	Scenes 1–7	*Regency of Duke Humphrey:* Death of Henry V and accession of Henry VI; plucking of red and white roses; death of Talbot; wooing of Margaret by Sussex; marriage of Margaret to King Henry; impeachment of Duke Humphrey.
INTERVAL		
Part 1.2	Scenes 8–13	*Things Fall Apart:* Murder of Duke Humphrey; exile and murder of Sussex; death of Cardinal Beaufort; Jack Cade's rebellion; rise of York and victory at St. Albans.
INTERMISSION		
Part 2.1	Scenes 14–19	*Revenge & Counter-Revenge:* Henry accepts York as successor; Margaret defeats York at Wakefield, tortures and kills him; York's sons are victorious at Towton, torture and kill Clifford, and capture King Henry; Edward IV is crowned king and woos Lady Grey; Richard vows to kill everybody.
INTERVAL		
Part 2.2	Scenes 20–25	*The Fall of Lancaster:* Margaret wins support from France; Warwick switches sides and is killed; Edward IV defeats Margaret's army in Battle of Tewkesbury, and Edward of Lancaster is killed; Richard murders King Henry; Edward IV celebrates as Richard plots to take the throne.

By this re-sectioning of the play, Hall and Warren reduced over a hundred parts to thirty-three, which, with careful doubling, could be covered by just twelve actors. By contrast, *Henry VI Part 2* by itself requires a company of twenty-six actors, and *Henry VI Part 3* requires twenty-five, according to the doubling charts developed by the Arden editors.[19] Hall and Warren have, in effect, re-created a play that could be mounted by an Elizabethan company reduced from full strength to the size of a touring company.

Rose Rage was developed for performance by the Propeller Company, with Ed Hall directing, at the Watermill Theater, Newbury, and then on tour. Barbara Gaines and Criss Henderson with Ed Hall made the three-and-a-half-hour trip to Huddersfield in a driving rain to see it and then drove back to London again. "It was the longest day in my life," recalls Gaines.[20] But Gaines and Henderson agree that there was never a question they would invite Hall to Chicago to mount it with Chicago actors. It felt to them like a Chicago play.

This was a critical moment at CST. The company had opened the new theater on Navy Pier in 1999. In its first three seasons on the Pier, it had explored and mastered the possibilities of its main stage and had successfully begun importing touring productions from France, Great Britain, and the Stratford Festival of Canada. But as Henderson and Gaines planned their fifth season in the new house, the Thoma Theater—CST's upstairs black box theater—remained a bit of a puzzle. Gary Griffin had scored successes with an imaginative production of Sondheim's *Pacific Overtures* and would do so again the following season with *Sunday in the Park with George*. But the Thoma had been built to house innovative projects of all kinds. Its full dramatic potential was still not known, and it had not yet acquired a distinctive, cutting-edge style of its own. Furthermore, CST's subscriber audience had mostly not yet ventured from the comfort of the downstairs main stage to the smaller upper reaches.

At first blush, booking a twelve-actor, six-hour performance for six months into a venue with about 175 seats looks like a recipe for financial disaster. However, it was also a heady time for sponsorship of theater in Chicago. Boeing, new to the city, was eager to underwrite innovative work, and so *Rose Rage* got a head start with an unusually large proportion of its budget underwritten, and hence a smaller-than-usual dependence on box office sales. With the Boeing sponsorship in hand, CST could shift its focus from financial to creative risk taking. Analogies between the conditions of patronage in 1592 and 2003 must not be pressed too far, but in each case the willingness of patrons to provide the spaces and materials for creative risk was essential to what happened.

Casting for *Rose Rage* began in early April 2003. One hundred and fifty actors read at the initial call; a week later, twenty-four were called back to audition when Hall visited Chicago. The part of Henry VI himself proved the most difficult to cast and was completed via a visit by Hall to New York for final readings.

The audition readings ran the gamut of vocal styles needed for the production, from the rapid-fire exchanges of single lines in scenes of confrontation to the long, soaring speeches—especially by Talbot, York, and Margaret—that marked symphonic high points of the drama. Hall had worked out the doubling plan very tightly, so the grouping of characters that a single actor would play determined the physical type and style of each. Plus, there were musical requirements—some had to carry the lyrics that punctuated the scenes of violence, while everyone had to be able at least to carry a tune. Hence, the actor playing Margaret of Anjou and Vernon should "use slight French accent, a good singer (tenor), not a drag act." In contrast, the actor handling both the Earl of Warwick and Jack Cade needed to be a "thunderously powerful noble, a lot of military muscle" and then switch to "anarchistic rebel, larger than life, anarchic street-wild man—Jack Cade rap."

Meanwhile, in London, Hall was preparing to direct Kenneth Branagh in David Mamet's *Edmond* in the Olivier Theater at the National. *Edmond* opened on July 17, 2003, and closed on October 4. It was in many ways the exact opposite of *Rose Rage*: a modern play with twenty actors to play twenty characters, overshadowed by a dominant leading man, with a 112-minute running time in a 1,150-seat theater. But *Edmond*—even though it is set in New York City—is a quintessential Mamet and Chicago play, with rapid dialogue, mounting to angry confrontation and an outburst of violence. In some ways the production was almost like a long scene from *Henry VI* in modern dress. And by an uncanny coincidence, CST's *Pacific Overtures* was running at the same moment across the Thames at the Donmar Warehouse in Covent Garden.

CST and Chicago therefore offered a clear set of advantages for *Rose Rage*, advantages that Hall understood well. First and foremost was Chicago's recent tradition, coming out of its legendary storefronts, of all-out, "balls to the wall" acting (to quote one CST member). If companies like Steppenwolf had become famous for contemporary "dysfunctional family theater," then a historical extended family of Plantagenets and their kin carried no surprises. Chicago had a surplus of actors who, with the right direction, would be willing to do anything.

Furthermore, a lot of those actors were young males who could bring a very physical style to the stage. There was some serendipity, since the "leading male" types are readily skimmed off by touring companies and often are in short supply. But the moment was right for a cast that would require a dozen male actors with skill and experience with Shakespeare and the stamina to handle multiple roles, intense action, and long performances. The majority of the actors came out of CST's own established pool, so in a direct sense its years on the small stage of the Ruth Page Theater and its five years at Navy Pier paid off in development of that reservoir. The shared memory among CST personnel about the acting company can be summarized as "there was a lot of testosterone on that stage."

In the auditions, the actors were warned that the play would be visceral and extremely physical, though the violence itself would be symbolic. Though half of them could aspire to be leading men, it was an ensemble production, and they would need to be team players. And it would be exhausting. The unusual nature of the play required additions to the usual Equity contracts. The length and extreme physicality of the play necessitated the addition of a "marathon" side-letter in which the actors agreed to the extended lengths of rehearsals and performances that would be required. A rider specified that "the Actor understands that properties in *Rose Rage* include raw meat, animal by-products and cutlery. Actor agrees to handle these props." And further, "The Actor understands that *Rose Rage* is an Ensemble-based production and each actor will execute staging including movement of scenery and properties; the sweeping of the stage following the battle scenes and the set up of raw meat and butcher equipment." The play was, in effect, visceral about viscera, and the actors' willingness to deal with offal became a factor in the casting process. Vegetarianism was fully accepted—indeed, the play may have won some converts—but squeamishness was not.

The text as performed by CST was 95 percent identical to the text published in 2001. It used the rigorous doubling scheme developed by Hall and Warren, again with twelve actors. Eleven of the twelve went on tour to NYC, with the one actor who dropped out being replaced by an actor who had done the play in the UK with Propeller. By multiple accounts, the actors were exhilarated at the prospect of doing the play and grasped that as actors they would be challenged to do things they might not have another chance to do in front of an audience.

The set for *Rose Rage* presented its own set of challenges. The small stage, measuring about forty feet wide by twenty-four feet deep, was surrounded on three sides by lockers (minus their backs) with steel-mesh fronts, shrinking the main playing area to just thirty-five feet by nineteen feet. Above the lockers was a catwalk, also around three sides. The catwalks extended beyond the stage along the sides of the seat risers, so that they combined with the passageway behind the top row of seats to create a 360-degree upper playing area. Ladders on each side of the set, plus the center aisle through the audience, gave the players ready access between upper and main play spaces. Stage furniture was limited to two oblong boxes—roughly coffin-sized—whose tops served primarily as chopping blocks but, alternatively, as hills, thrones, and beds. In its main characteristics, the CST *Rose Rage* playing space, with its small size, upper playing areas, and minimal furniture, was roughly similar to the remodeled Rose Theater of 1592.

The set was acoustic as well as spatial in design. The soundscape of the play was intensely percussive, calling on the actors to create distinctive and recurring noises by scraping knives across the wire-mesh locker fronts and banging on the blocks, lockers, and corner supports with knives and ax handles. The set took such a pounding it had to be extensively rebuilt by the end of rehearsals—and rebuilt again before the show went to New York. Ultimately the actors were told they didn't have to hit things quite so hard.

The soundscape included not just the metallic cutting instruments but also songs. The lyrics were interwoven with the action in often ironic ways. Each half of *Rose Rage* began with Blake's poem "And did those feet in ancient time" in a lilting tune:

> And did those feet in ancient time
> Walk upon England's mountains green:
> And was the holy Lamb of God,
> On England's pleasant pastures seen?
> And did the Countenance Divine,
> Shine forth upon our clouded hills?
> And was Jerusalem builded here,
> Among these dark Satanic mills?[21]

During the murder of young Rutland, Young Clifford and the butcher chorus sing "Lullaby, lullaby, lulla-lulla-lullaby." Other deaths are accompanied by snippets of the Requiem Mass: "sanctus . . . kyrie eleison . . . " The songs were performed in a choral style that hovered between Anglican hymn and English music hall, but there was nothing religious about them. Quite the opposite—they both emphasized a human degeneration in which all that is good becomes evil and underscored the sheer lack of conscience or remorse among the perpetrators. While the texture of the play is severely secular, the juxtaposition of song and action gave the violence an apocalyptic quality, and its perpetrators became what Blake himself described in the lines prefacing his poem as "a Class of Men whose whole delight is in Destroying."[22]

Even as the songs injected a diabolic tinge, they heightened the symbolic distancing of the violence from its physical enactment. For the audience, the songs frequently aroused astonishment and laughter that relieved the tension and horror of witnessing murder. They provided a modern way of capturing a key, mysterious element of early Shakespeare, from the *Henry VI* plays to *Titus Andronicus*: human suffering made into cruel humor.

Counterpointing the Blakean song was the cacophony of Jack Cade. He appeared suddenly as a British street hip-hopper, storming the stage, racing up the center aisle, chanting,

> Down with the gentry
> Down with the gov'mint
> No Taxation!
> Reformation!
> Long live—
> Jack Cade![23]

Cade is less rational than the aristocrats but just as casually cruel and destructive. His shift in cadence and injection of pure disorder widens the frame of reference around the aristocrats and throws in relief their irresponsibility for letting order and legitimacy disintegrate from within the regime. But the self-obsession of Cade's lyric equally affirms that there is no redemption available from outside either.

Costuming was neither modern nor Shakespearean. It was based on photographs of Victorian dress, especially for the nobles. The main perpetrators of violence were particularly distinctive: Warwick in a long brown leather military coat; Young Clifford in red riding coat with white riding pants; the three older sons of York in city dress, with George especially elegant, leaning on a cane that sheathed his sword. Cut and color helped the audience to keep the characters straight, while the contrast between upper-class dress and brutal actions underscored the casual sadism of the action. All of the actors put on and took off butcher's smocks throughout, as they moved between character and ensemble, emphasizing the shared investment in violence, across class lines and historical epochs. When all are dressed in white, and stained with blood, there are no good guys and bad guys.

Props presented perhaps the greatest challenge of all. If wear-and-tear on the set was extensive, even greater was the damage to the knives that did the wearing and tearing. The knives were not only hitting lockers, blocks, and steel supports. They were also constantly grinding against one another to create distinctive, rhythmic, clinking and scraping sounds. This created two problems. First, the knives were continually chipped, making them both dangerous in themselves and liable to break and fly apart. Second, and unexpectedly, the scraping was sharpening the knives beyond what was tolerable on stage. Daily knife checks, with sharp edges being ground down to dullness, became routine, until the knives were ground to almost nothing and had to be replaced. All told, CST spent nearly $2,000 on fine cutlery, blowing the line item in the budget, and no doubt missing an opportunity for an in-kind sponsorship.

But the greatest challenge came not from the knives. It came from the meats and vegetables used as the objects of symbolic violence. The severing of heads was represented by smashing red cabbages. In a few instances, the cabbages were sliced with the ever-sharp knives, but most often—and especially in Part 1—they were placed on the chopping blocks and smashed with ax handles. As the hickory handle hit them, the cabbages would make a wondrous squishy sound and explode, spraying purple-red cabbage shards across the stage.

The meats garnered even more attention than the vegetables. Hall specified pig meat and offal—kidneys, livers, and intestines. The meat was not readily available in the weekly quantities required for the production, and there were health regulations involved in its use. The meat had to be picked up from a slaughterhouse, brought to the theater, and cleaned. This was done at first in a catering kitchen near the black-box stage. During rehearsal, the smell of it got into the HVAC system and permeated the theater building. So the meat preparation site was moved to the trap area under the main stage, where the props manager worked in a small black space with a steel table for cleaning and cutting and a steel refrigerator for storage. The stage had to be disinfected and cleaned with bleach after each rehearsal and performance, on a rigorous schedule so that the odors would dissipate before the next performance.

The meat had an electrifying effect on the audience, often setting them tittering nervously, exactly as the violence mounted. Bagged, the meat could be hung up to represent a severed head. When the bag was split, the meat would spill out into a bucket with a distinct "plop." Sight, sound, and idea merged into a sensation of ludicrous horror. For those in the first or second row, the smell was part of the experience.

The stage became slippery with ooze and blood as each performance wore on. In one of the final segments, depicting the Battle of Towton, Yorkists and Lancastrians line up and run at each other screaming and brandishing their

23. Cast of *Rose Rage: Henry VI Parts 1, 2 and 3* (2003), directed by Edward Hall, adapted by Edward Hall and Roger Warren. Photo by Michael Brosilow

knives. At one point in rehearsal, it simply became too much. Whether the actors became afraid for their own safety or simply wanted management to recognize what they were doing, there was a rebellion of sorts. The Equity steward was called in, discussions were held, changes were offered—with the result that the house lights were turned up so that the actors could see their way through a remarkable piece of precisely choreographed stage fighting—with real meat.

The mini-rebellion sits differently in different memories within the CST company—what it was about, how serious it was. Otherwise, the recollections of rehearsals all converge. They were intense. Hall provided a tight structure with the doubling scheme, the soundscape, and the overall conception. He demanded ensemble acting but let each actor take his characters where the instincts and characteristics of that actor would take them. The group became tight-knit, even a bit cut off from what was happening on other floors of the theater. "They would do anything for Ed," "they would do whatever he asked them" are typical recollections. It traveled the narrow edge, becoming "Ed's play" and a thoroughly Chicago and CST play at the same time.

The distinctive experience of *Rose Rage* in performance came through the assembly of all of these elements—varied play-spaces, strong actors, bombastic language, muscular action, percussive sound, raw meat—not so much woven together as heaped upon one another. The easiest way to convey the experience is through a single, climactic passage: the death of the Duke of York in which all elements are interwoven, with action carefully driven by cues within the text. (Long speeches are shortened in this excerpt; material within square brackets is my description of stage action):

MARGARET: Yield to our mercy, proud Plantagenet.
CLIFFORD: Ay, to such mercy as he showed my father. . . .
   [Clifford swings butt of knife; butcher strikes chopping block with double cleavers]
EXETER: What would your grace have done unto him now?
MARGARET: Come, make him stand upon this molehill here,
That wrought at mountains with outstretched arms. . . .
   [Cleavers strike block twice: whack—whack as Clifford and Essex strike York]
   [They stand York on box downstage right; he grabs iron rings with both hands]
What, was it you that would be England's king?
Was't you that reveled in our Parliament,
And made a preachment of your high descent?
Where are your mess of sons to back you now,
The wanton Edward and the lusty George?
And where's that valiant crookback prodigy,
Dickie your boy . . . [audience titters at "Dickie"]
Or with the rest, where is your darling Rutland?
   [Margaret downstage right turns toward audience, sticks out tongue gleefully, then speaks very slowly; holding napkin aloft and waving it]
Look, York, I stained this napkin with the blood . . .
And if thine eyes can water for his death,
I give thee this to dry thy cheeks withal. . . .
   [M. crosses and waves napkin in York's face; he grimaces and averts face; she stuffs it in the top of his shirt; he begins to weep]
I prithee grieve, to make me merry, York.
What, hath thy fiery heart so parched thine entrails
That not a tear can fall for Rutland's death?

[York's stoic silence grows louder and louder]
Why art thou patient, man? Thou shouldst be mad,
And I, to make thee mad, do mock thee thus.
Stamp, [She smacks upstage right block with whip handle]
rave, and fret, that I may sing and dance. . . .
York cannot speak unless he wear a crown.
    [M. picks up paper crown]
A crown for York, and lords, bow low to him.
[M. tries to place crown; Y. pushes her away; Clifford intercedes with knife
drawn; Essex smacks him; cleavers whack block; Y. writhes in pain; C. and E.
bind his arms; M. places crown as Y. groans]
Hold you his hands whilst I do set it on.
Ay marry, sirs, now looks he like a king. . . .
    [Louder: as command]
Off with the crown, and with the crown his head,
And whilst we breathe, take time to do him dead.
    [M. turns and walks downstage right]
CLIFFORD: That is my office for my father's sake.
    [Goes to strike; Y stretches out arms to receive the blow]
MARGARET: Nay, stay—[M. turns; Clifford halts] let's hear the orisons he
makes.
YORK: She-wolf of France, but worse than wolves of France, . . .
O tiger's heart wrapped in a woman's hide!
How couldst thou drain the life-blood of the child
To bid the father wipe his eyes withal,
And yet be seen to bear a woman's face? . . .
This cloth thou dipped'st in blood of my sweet boy,
And I with tears do wash the blood away.
Keep thou the napkin and go boast of this.
There, take the crown, and with the crown, my curse . . .
    [Y. falls forward, legs up on block, arms outstretched]
    [M. gestures to Clifford to continue]
CLIFFORD: Here's for my oath,
    [C. mounts block, strikes from above and behind; cleavers whack other block]
    here's for my father's death.
MARGARET: And here's to right our gentle-hearted King.
    [M. walks from downstage right and kicks upward into Y.'s face; cleavers
    whack; Y. falls backward; M. returns downstage right; hums tuning note to
    Chorus; "Never . . . One-Two-Three-Four . . ."]
ALL: Never weather-beaten sail [Thomas Campion hymn]

More willing bent to shore
[M. picks up knife, holds toward Y's head with knees bent, stabs; cleavers whack]
Never tired pilgrim's limbs
Affected slumber more
[Clifford, in front of Y., knife in right hand; reaches down and mimes grasping Y's genitals in left hand; turns gleefully toward audience; chops with knife; cleavers whack; slight gasp from audience]
Than my wearied sprite now longs to
Fly out of my troubled breast
[M., C., and Prince Edward now dance around York singing; C. hands knife to Prince Edward; his mother Margaret guides his hand for downward thrust into Y's back. Cleavers whack. PE now fully initiated, holds knife down, pinning Y on it, who cries out]
O come quickly
O come quickly
O come quickly
Sweetest Lord
[into York's face] and take my soul to rest.
[PE pulls knife out; cleavers whack; Y. pitches forward.]
YORK: Open thy gate of mercy, gracious God:
My soul flies through these wounds to seek out thee.
[He dies]
MARGARET: Off with his head and set it on York gates,
So York may overlook the town of York.
[C. takes knife from Edward; delivers beheading stroke; butcher tosses him plastic bag filled with offal; C. hangs it on hook stage left; Exeunt omnes.]

The effect of the scene depends on the tight choreography of movement and dance; on the intricate soundscape of percussive cleavers, dramatic voices, and song; on the precise correlation of stabbing motions and cleaver whacks; and on the intermixing of extreme pathos and macabre humor.

The reviews were instant raves, though the most important review complained about ticket prices at $70. Audiences did not seem to feel that was unreasonable for a six-hour theater experience and accepted the concept of a play that would make them uncomfortable, a play in which, as Artistic Director Barbara Gaines put it, "there was nothing enlightened. No hearts are mended."[24] The house quickly filled up and stayed full for most of the run.

The play topped the list for Joseph Jefferson Awards for the year, including Best Production, Best Direction, Best Ensemble, and Best Supporting Actor (Scott Parkinson for Margaret).

Coincidentally, while *Rose Rage* was playing upstairs, CST hosted a run of *Twelfth Night* by the Shakespeare's Globe Theater Company on its main stage, with Mark Rylance as Olivia. Both were all-male companies; there the resemblance ended. *Twelfth Night* emphasized "original" production techniques; *Rose Rage* was thoroughly contemporary. *TN* had a London cast; *RR* a Chicago cast; *TN* was suave and elegant; *RR* was brutal and elegant. *TN* was a novelty. *RR* sticks in the memory.

Rose Rage closed in Chicago in January 2004 and became the first CST production to travel to New York. It was, relatively speaking, a simple show to move. The set (once it had been rebuilt again) fit onto a single truck. The cast (once a key actor had been replaced) moved intact. All fit nicely into the Duke Theater on 42nd Street, with a stage similar to the one in Chicago. Opening on September 17, 2004, and running for a month, it had little competition early in the New York season, drew the theater crowd, and got superb notices. The play fundamentally altered New York attitudes toward Chicago and CST and contributed directly to CST's Regional Tony Award of 2008.

The manifold risks of *Rose Rage* produced palpable outcomes: the company realized the potential of the Thoma Theater for innovative drama; drew a distinct audience, about half from subscriber core, half new; tested their limits with Chicago-style physical theater; tested themselves against international performance standards; and succeeded in New York.

Rose Rage was, in Criss Henderson's summation, "a capacity-building production,"[25] expanding audience, but above all, expanding the theater's sense of its own capabilities. It was an artistic, theatrical, and commercial speculation that is nonetheless firmly within Shakespeare's own practice of undertaking risky business and making good on it.

Fast Forward: in 2012, Chicago Shakespeare Theater will be the only US theater company participating in the London Cultural Olympics, performing a hip-hop version of *Othello*. It is, arguably, the latest legacy of *Rose Rage*.

> Down with the gentry
> Down with the gov'mint
> No Taxation!
> Reformation!
> Long live—
> Jack Cade!

NOTES

Dedication: This essay was conceived and written during a transitional period punctuated by intense conversations about how to think and write, especially about the performance of culture, with Ivan Karp, NEH Professor of Humanities and Director of the Center for the Study of Public Scholarship at Emory University. Sadly, just as I began writing, Ivan was hit by an onslaught of illness and died. A brilliant social anthropologist, he revolutionized our understanding of how third world cultures are "staged" in modern museums. There is much we can learn from his work about how premodern Western culture is staged through our productions of Shakespeare.

Acknowledgments: I am grateful to the members of Chicago Shakespeare Theater who generously shared their time and insights during interviews for this essay, especially Barbara Gaines, Criss Henderson, Marilyn Halperin, Bob Mason, and Chris Plevin.

1. Ben Jonson, "Timber, or, Discoveries," in Ian Donaldson, ed., *Ben Jonson* (Oxford: Oxford UP, 1985), 539–40; "To the Memory of My Beloved, The Author, Mr William Shakespeare, And What He Hath Left Us," in ibid., 453–54.

2. Peter Holland, *English Shakespeares: Shakespeare on the English Stage in the 1990s* (Cambridge: Cambridge UP, 1997), 1–20.

3. E. K. Chambers, *The Elizabethan Stage*, vol. 2 (Oxford: Clarendon Press, 1923), 388–93.

4. Andrew Gurr, *The Shakespearean Stage, 1574–1642*, 3rd ed. (Cambridge: Cambridge UP, 1992), 36–38.

5. Julian Bowsher, *The Rose Theatre: An Archaeological Discovery* (London: Museum of London, 1988), 43–51.

6. R. A. Foakes, ed., *Henslowe's Diary*, 2nd ed. (Cambridge: Cambridge UP, 2001), 15.

7. For a probing and detailed analysis of Marlowe's opinions and behavior, and the seditious milieu of the early 1590s, see David Riggs, *The World of Christopher Marlowe* (New York: Holt, 2004).

8. Foakes, ed., *Henslowe's Diary*, 16–19.

9. William Shakespeare, *King Henry VI Part 3*, ed. John D. Cox and Eric Rasmussen (London: Thomson Learning, 2001), 6.

10. This theory has its origins in Chambers's *Elizabethan Stage*, 129–31, and is endorsed and refined by Gurr, *Shakespearean Stage*, 38–39.

11. Shakespeare, *Henry VI Part 3*, 1.4.73–77. Citations of Shakespeare's plays throughout are to the Arden editions and are referred to parenthetically after the first citation.

12. William Camden, *The History of . . . Elizabeth*, 4th ed. (London, 1688), 444–55.

13. Riggs, *World of Christopher Marlowe*, 293.

14. Inga-Stina Ewbank, "European Cross-Currents: Ibsen and Brecht," in *The Oxford Illustrated History of Shakespeare on Stage*, ed. Jonathan Bate and Russell Jackson (Oxford: Oxford UP, 2001), 128–29.

15. Michael Dobson and Stanley Wells, eds., *The Oxford Companion to Shakespeare*, (Oxford: Oxford UP, 2001), 202.

16. Peter Hall, *Peter Hall's Diaries: The Story of a Dramatic Battle*, ed. John Goodwin (New York: Harper & Row, 1984), 51, 316.

17. Ibid., passim.

18. Edward Hall and Roger Warren, *Rose Rage* (London: Oberon Books, 2001). Subsequent citations of the text of *Rose Rage* are to this edition, with the exception of the

songs, which are omitted from the printed text. All statements about the songs and stage directions are based on CST video and annotated scripts.

19. *King Henry VI Part 2*, ed. Ronald Knowles (London: Thomson Learning, 1999), 434–36; William Shakespeare, *King Henry VI Part 3*, 413–20.

20. Conversation with Barbara Gaines, July 11, 2011.

21. William Blake, introductory poem to *Milton*, in *The Complete Poems*, ed. W. H. Stevenson and David V. Erdman (London: Longman, 1971), 488–89. The text of the song does not appear in the printed version of *Rose Rage* (see note 18) or in the call script in CST archives.

22. Blake, *Complete Poems*, 288.

23. Consistent with its form, Jack Cade's rap admitted variation and improvisation in performance. The version excerpted here is as recorded in performance by CST. The call script preserves another version. The rap is omitted from the published text.

24. Conversation with Barbara Gaines, July 11, 2011.

25. Interview with Criss Henderson, August 12, 2011.

BIBLIOGRAPHY

Blake, William. *The Complete Poems*. Ed. W. H. Stevenson and David V. Erdman. London: Longman, 1971.

Bowsher, Julian. *The Rose Theatre: An Archaeological Discovery*. London: Museum of London, 1988.

Camden, William. *The History of . . . Elizabeth*. 4th ed. London, 1688.

Chambers, E. K. *The Elizabethan Stage*. Vol. 2. Oxford: Clarendon Press, 1923.

Dobson, Michael, and Stanley Wells, eds. *The Oxford Companion to Shakespeare*. Oxford: Oxford UP, 2001.

Donaldson, Ian, ed. *Ben Jonson*. Oxford: Oxford UP, 1985.

Ewbank, Inga-Stina. "European Cross-Currents: Ibsen and Brecht." *The Oxford Illustrated History of Shakespeare on Stage*. Ed. Jonathan Bate and Russell Jackson. Oxford: Oxford UP, 2001.

Foakes, R. A., ed. *Henslowe's Diary*. 2nd ed. Cambridge: Cambridge UP, 2001.

Gurr, Andrew. *The Shakespearean Stage, 1574–1642*. 3rd ed. Cambridge: Cambridge UP, 1992.

Hall, Edward, and Roger Warren. *Rose Rage*. London: Oberon Books, 2001.

Hall, Peter. *Peter Hall's Diaries: The Story of a Dramatic Battle*. Ed. John Goodwin. New York: Harper & Row, 1984.

Holland, Peter. *English Shakespeares: Shakespeare on the English Stage in the 1990s*. Cambridge: Cambridge UP, 1997.

Riggs, David. *The World of Christopher Marlowe*. New York: Holt, 2004.

Shakespeare, William. *King Henry VI Part 2*. Ed. Ronald Knowles. Arden. London: Thomson Learning, 1999.

———. *King Henry VI Part 3*. Ed. John D. Cox and Eric Rasmussen. Arden. London: Thomson Learning, 2001.

PART IV

13

In Defense of Ruffled Feathers

MICHAEL BILLINGTON

I paid my one and only visit to Chicago Shakespeare Theater in the summer of 2004, and it was memorable for many reasons. The jazzy excitement of Navy Pier. The volatile enthusiasm of Barbara Gaines. And then there was the strange sensation of entering the 500-seat theater and feeling immediately at home: I felt I could be back in the Swan at Stratford-upon-Avon. But what hit me most was the play itself: *King John* directed by Gaines with political urgency, so that when Greg Vinkler's king wrapped himself in the flag to justify his military chauvinism, one was reminded less of a medieval English monarch than of George W. Bush. I couldn't quite believe that I was seeing one of Shakespeare's least-loved plays speaking so directly, in the course of a sold-out ten-week run, to an audience that seemed like a cross-section of Chicago in its mix of middle-class Shakespeare buffs, blue-collar workers, and students.

I've often thought about that experience because it told me something important: that the common assumption that certain Shakespeare plays are automatic box-office poison is outdated, conservative, and naive. In Britain I've noticed that in recent years we have started to divide Shakespeare's plays, like football teams, into three separate leagues. First, there are the plays that are always popular and capable of endless revival: *Hamlet, King Lear, Macbeth, Othello, Twelfth Night, A Midsummer Night's Dream, As You Like It, Much Ado About Nothing, Julius Caesar, Antony and Cleopatra,*

Richard III. There is then a whole group of plays that are revived either because a director has a strong conceptual vision or because they attract star performers: a category that includes the bulk of the history cycle, *The Comedy of Errors*, *The Merry Wives of Windsor*, *Coriolanus*, *All's Well That Ends Well*, and a late masterpiece, *The Winter's Tale*. Finally come the unloved brethren that are rarely revived, and then more often out of a sense of duty than from any overwhelming conviction: *Titus Andronicus*, *Timon of Athens*, *Pericles*, *Cymbeline*, *Two Gentlemen of Verona*, *Henry VIII*, and, very much bringing up the rear, *King John* itself. Individual plays are capable of promotion and relegation: a work like *Measure for Measure*, partly because of its portrait of the hidden face of political corruption, chimes with the times and has lately been elevated to the major league. But you can go years without seeing *Timon of Athens*, while *A Midsummer Night's Dream* is never off the public stages.

Inspired by my visit to Chicago, I would like to plead for a restoration of the entire Shakespeare canon so that we can see the man's work in its entirety. I would also argue that the plays that, not least in America, ruffle modern sensibilities should be regularly revived. And we all know what they are: *The Merchant of Venice* and *The Taming of the Shrew*. In my experience the problems the plays present have a way of disappearing in intelligent productions. Rupert Goold's 2011 Royal Shakespeare Company revival of *The Merchant*, for instance, brilliantly relocates the play to Las Vegas and reminds us that the play is much more about money than race: Patrick Stewart's Shylock is an assimilated casino owner, and Susannah Fielding's Portia a ritzy game-show hostess in a society predicated on gambling. The gender issues that plague *The Shrew* were also resolved some years ago in a Gregory Doran production at Stratford. Jasper Britton's Petruchio was a drunken wreck, still mourning the death of his father, who was taken in hand by Alexandra Gilbreath's sparky Katharina so that her seeming submission became an act of redemptive therapy. In the case of both productions, the problems of political correctness simply didn't arise.

But my larger point is that we should look to the neglected plays in the canon and bring them back into the fold. And, since I saw it work so vibrantly in Chicago, where better to start than with *King John*? In the late eighteenth century it was popular, largely because it allowed a great actress, Sarah Siddons, to display her "eagle-like power" as the grieving mother, Constance. And in the late nineteenth century it was staged as a lavish historical pageant: Beerbohm Tree even interpolated a scene showing the signing of the Magna Carta, which Shakespeare had somehow forgotten to write. But lately the play has fallen out of fashion since it seems messily chaotic in its account of the political machinations between England and France. Yet look more closely and *King John* seems strikingly modern in its reflection of the cynicism, opportunism, and as Barbara Gaines realized, the bogus appeals to patriotism that accompany societies at war. It is all beautifully summed up in a speech by the Bastard after the English and French have patched up their quarrels with a hastily arranged diplomatic marriage. According to the Bastard, this displays the ultimate triumph of "that smooth-faced gentleman, tickling commodity": in other words, "expedient self-interest." And, having railed against it, the Bastard admits that he too is susceptible to its power. "Since kings," he concludes, "break faith upon commodity, Gain be my lord, for I will worship thee."[1] You could hardly have a clearer account of the way the individual is corrupted by the values of the society; which is one of the many reasons that *King John* still speaks to us today.

I would also argue that it is high time we integrated *Timon of Athens* back into the Shakespeare family or at least gave it more than the occasional random revival. It is admittedly problematic in its portrait of a reckless plutocrat who, on losing his wealth, turns into a friendless misanthrope and crazed hermit: until, that is, he comes on another stash of gold. The text is also thought, in Dr. Johnson's words, to be "perplexed, obscure and possibly corrupt." But, on the rare occasions I see the play, I am always struck by its moral force, the opportunities it provides for a star actor, and also its sheer poetic power. You see this clearly in the scene where the isolated Timon, digging in the ground for roots, turns up gold, which he variously addresses as a "yellow slave," a "sweet king-killer," a "bright defiler of Hymen's purest bed," and a "visible god / That sold'rest close impossibilities / And mak'st them kiss."[2] It was this speech that Karl Marx avidly seized on, claiming that it showed how money acts as "the universal whore" and results in "the alienation of human capacity" in early capitalist societies.[3] But, while it would be specious to argue that Shakespeare was writing a proto-Marxist tract, *Timon* is eminently worth reviving in an age like ours, when capitalism is in crisis, when the gulf between rich and poor is cavernous, and when economic depression can produce individual suffering.

Another play that remains, unfairly, on the margins is *Titus Andronicus*. I suppose I am deeply attached to it partly because I was present, as a fifteen-year-old Warwickshire schoolboy, on a historic occasion when Peter Brook directed its first-ever Stratford production: one that starred Laurence Olivier and Vivien Leigh and that turned what many thought to be a piece of Marlovian barbarism into an event of stylized beauty. I have seen a handful of revivals since. One, staged in Bristol by Adrian Noble with Simon Callow as Titus, treated the play as a bloodbath at which even Sam Peckinpah might

183

24. John Douglas Thompson in *Henry IV, Parts 1 and 2* (2006), directed by Barbara Gaines. Photo by Stewart Hemley

have winced. Deborah Warner also directed a memorable revival with Brian Cox, which reminded us that it is not so much a play about violence as about stoical suffering in response to extreme provocation. There was also wit and humor in Warner's production, with Cox whistling a tune from Disney's *Snow White* as he set about preparing a cannibalistic banquet. But what startles me is the modern theater's squeamish nervousness about a play that is often seen as a catalogue of horrors: when you consider the graphic violence of today's cinema, TV, and comic books and the ability of modern audiences to accept plays like Edward Bond's *Saved* and Sarah Kane's *Blasted*, it seems strange that we should still regard *Titus Andronicus* as almost beyond the pale.

Of course, we occasionally see a *Titus*, a *Timon*, and a *King John* as well as the other marginalized Shakespeare plays. But I still believe it is impossible to understand Shakespeare without a total immersion in the canon: even a play like *Two Gentlemen of Verona*, which is undoubtedly an immature early work, is full of fascination for its intimations of the later comedies and for its obsession with the overarching Shakespeare theme of the falsity of appearances. What I am arguing is that we are in danger of losing sight of the kaleidoscopic richness of Shakespeare and restricting our appreciation to a dozen surefire box-office hits, which also crop up, time and again, on examination syllabi. Which brings me back, strangely enough, to *King John*. I studied it for what were then called A-Level school exams when I was seventeen, though I gather now it would never be a prescribed text. I also saw it seven times in a single summer at Stratford-upon-Avon. And when I saw it memorably revived at Chicago Shakespeare Theater, I fell on it once more with delight. But what was moving was to see it with an audience that palpably shared my pleasure in the play. And, for me, this was living proof that the growing tendency to diminish the Shakespearean repertory to a dozen or so golden oldies is arbitrary and nonsensical. The rest of the world could learn a lot from Chicago.

NOTES

1. William Shakespeare, *King John*, ed. John Jowett, in *The Oxford Shakespeare: The Complete Works*, 2nd ed., ed. Stanley Wells and Gary Taylor (Oxford: Oxford UP, 2005), 2.1.574 and 598–99.

2. William Shakespeare, *Timon of Athens*, ed. John Jowett, in *The Oxford Shakespeare: The Complete Works*, 2nd ed., ed. Stanley Wells and Gary Taylor (Oxford: Oxford UP, 2005), 4.3.384–91.

3. Karl Marx, "Economic and Philosophic Manuscripts of 1844: The Power of Money," Marx/Engels Internet Archive, accessed December 25, 2011.

"Never did young man fancy"
Troilus and Cressida *and Chicago Shakespeare Theater*

PETER KANELOS

It was autumn 1987. The El rumbled down the tracks, shuddering to a stop at stations along our route—Bryn Mawr, Wilson, Fullerton, Belmont—as passengers, bundled against the Chicago cold, entered and exited. My new overcoat barely kept out the chill; having grown up in a warmer climate, I had not yet mastered the art of layering. I wasn't even sure how to tie a scarf properly.

Two friends, Sharon and Kate, shared the row of molded plastic seats with me. It had been Sharon's idea, I believe, that we head into the city to see a play. We were all freshmen at Northwestern, living in the same hall. The three of us had frequently taken the train to explore an urban landscape that was thrilling in its complexity and unpredictability. On an earlier trip, we had met a group of gypsy musicians on the Howard platform and followed them to a gig at a back-alley club. College, I learned quickly, offered much more than textbooks and lectures; it provided a kind of liberty that I had never quite imagined—an open space that I was responsible for filling myself. I embraced this charge enthusiastically.

Shakespeare was, for me, as exotic as a band of traveling gypsies. I had never seen a production of a Shakespearean play. In fact, I had never heard of the play that we had tickets to see, *Troilus and Cressida*. Not that I let my companions know this. I was embarrassed that I was as green as could be when it came to "culture," and I colored over this as best I could—luckily, I was a fast talker and quick to adapt to new situations. I faked it, I think, quite well.

The El had descended underground by the time we exited at Division Street. As we climbed the stairs to street level, a chilly gust caught us and my scarf unwound, flapping about in the wind. Kate took a moment to teach me how to wrap it securely around my neck, and the three of us headed down Dearborn Street.

I don't remember entering the Ruth Page Theater (aka the Ruth Page Dance Studio). Nor do I remember all the small things that happened prior to the curtain. What I do remember quite vividly was my first sight of the stage. I had never seen a thrust stage. My idea of a theater (and it was an *idea*, since I had never, truth be told, been to a proper theater of any sort) included a proscenium arch, a curtained stage, and a long, sloping auditorium.

When the Prologue emerged to introduce the play's action, I was immediately taken with the play. Something was happening in front of me, literally in front of me by a few feet. The drama penetrated the way films never had. This was a singular event, a happening in the here and now. There was something so utterly human, both vulnerable and powerful, that the machine-driven cinema could never replicate. And I was experiencing something quite transformative—not that I knew it then, nor have ever really considered it until quite recently.

When I took on the task of coediting a volume of essays on the twenty-five-year history of Chicago Shakespeare Theater, I originally planned that my own contribution would address the question of whether there was a distinctive "Chicago style" in the performing of Shakespeare in the city. I had written a rather nice abstract, I thought, and had plans to interview Chicago actors who had worked with the theater extensively. I was looking forward to the project. But in the back of my mind, there was a niggling *something*.

Then I found the program from 1987. I had forgotten that it was at the earlier incarnation of Chicago Shakespeare Theater that I had seen my very first Shakespeare, a quarter of a century ago. I realized now how remarkable this coincidence was. In fact, I had seen all three of the CST productions of *Troilus and Cressida* over the intervening years. In the meantime, I had gone from green university student to university professor, specializing in Shakespeare. Looking retrospectively at the history of Chicago Shakespeare Theater, I was also looking at my own history.

Looking over that original program, I now realize that the company, then called Shakespeare Repertory, was nearly as green as I was. The program, really just a section of a *Stagebill* from 1987, provides a brief introduction by Barbara Gaines:

> The Chicago Shakespeare Repertory began four years ago as a workshop of 30 professional actors dedicated to celebrating the human spirit through performing the works of William Shakespeare.
>
> With each performance, our enthusiasm and acclaim grew, particularly after our production of *Henry V* at the Red Lion Pub in August 1986.
>
> And so we began to dream of becoming more—a complete Shakespeare Repertory Theater, the only company of its kind in Chicago.[1]

There was certainly something proleptic about this pronouncement, a sort of "if you build it they will come" confidence. And it was confidence that was clearly not misplaced, as is evident to anyone today who visits the Tony Award–winning Chicago Shakespeare Theater in its impressive Navy Pier digs. Chicago Shakespeare Theater has become an institution, one that has very much taken its place in the city's landscape of cultural institutions.

Back in 1987, however, this was a company just getting off the ground. *Troilus* was its first production in what would become its longtime home, the Ruth Page Dance Studio. Of course, I had no idea then that there was anything fringe about Shakespeare Rep. This *was* Shakespeare, as far as I knew. And what had I found Shakespeare to be? To my great surprise, I found something exciting, engaging—enthralling, even.

Memory is a tricky thing, of course. Hamlet is right to remind us that it holds its seat in our "distracted globe." What I remember of my original encounter with *Troilus and Cressida*, with Shakespeare Rep, with "Shakespeare," is filtered through the kaleidoscope of what I have experienced since. There is no recording of the 1987 production for me to check my memories against. It is not just our minds, our own "globes," that are frustratingly mercurial; the stage itself, the other Globe, presents spectacles that fade as quickly as they materialize. Ben Jonson's sense of loss for his own masque, *Hymenai*—"that it lasted not still, or, now it is past, cannot by imagination, much less description, be recovered to a part of that spirit it had in the gliding by"[2]—captures the beguiling elusiveness of the theatrical experience as well as one might ever hope.

But I knew nothing about Ben Jonson then—not that he was a contemporary and rival of Shakespeare, that he would chide Shakespeare for his "small Latine, and lesse Greeke," even as he recognized the "genius" of the "Sweet

25. Barbara Gaines directs Bruce A. Young, Jeannette Schwaba, Timothy Gregory, and Kevin Gudahl in *Troilus and Cressida* (1987). Photo by Bill Hogan

Swan of Avon" in the memorial poem he penned for the posthumous collection of Shakespeare's works, the First Folio. The only thing I knew in that moment was that there was a spectacle unfolding right in front of me that demanded my full attention.

What do I remember? Swords. Swords so close (I was seated in the first row, off the right side of the stage) that I recoiled as they flashed in front of me. I remember more flesh than I expected to find in something as highbrow as a Shakespearean play—not only enough skin from Cressida and Helen that I was a bit embarrassed to be in the company of two female friends, but the broad, hairy back of Ajax and the trim, toned form of Achilles. I remember hearing the reference to Helen and a "thousand ships" and thinking, "Ah! This is where that came from" (not knowing, of course, that Shakespeare was riffing off of Marlowe).

What I remember most of all, however, was that the language, shockingly, made sense. There was clarity. The story of the equivocating Cressida, her oily uncle, Pandarus, her wet-noodle of a boyfriend, Troilus, seemed

189

very much alive. And that it was wrapped within the events of the Trojan War! I had no idea that Shakespeare had written about the Trojan War. Yet here were Ulysses, Agamemnon, Ajax, Hector, Achilles—an Achilles, by the way, who was scandalously treacherous. This was not the *Iliad* that I, having grown up in a rather insular Greek community, knew and loved. This was a provocative, iconoclastic retelling of the tale. Shakespeare, apparently, who I had always assumed to be the bedrock of everything canonical and conservative, was much more complex than I had imagined.

After it had glided by, I wanted more. While many of the details of the production will forever elude me, what I know beyond a doubt is that my encounter with this play at this time in this setting by this company propelled me into a relationship with Shakespeare that has lasted for twenty-five years and counting.

The only review of the production that I have been able to find is a particularly unkind one, by the former theater critic of the *Reader* Tom Boeker. He found the play highly problematic and the production uneven.

> As is, it's a long haul through one of the great master's unfinished works. I wouldn't recommend this show to a friend, but then none of my friends are Shakespeare fanatics. Those of you who are will see many of the things you're used to seeing (gray plastic armor and unconvincingly choreographed fight scenes) and hear the things you're used to hearing (recorded trumpet flourishes and resonant diphthongs). You'll even enjoy a relatively skilled caliber of acting, that is, relative to other American productions of Shakespeare. And— far more uncommon—although this production fails to cull and nourish it, you'll see Shakespeare, one of the most buoyant and hardy souls in English literature, gag a little on his own ideals. And if you see that, you can see the Jacobeans following the Elizabethans, as the night follows the day.[3]

It should be noted that Boeker described himself as one of Chicago's most "reviled" critics. He was a crank. He was jaded. I am sure, however, that he was not entirely wrong. If we were to stack that performance up against one from CST today, we might be inclined to agree on certain points. Perhaps the armor was plastic, the fights less than convincing, and the trumpets canned.

But I'm glad that I saw what I saw. I am sure that it was the rawness that held me to a certain extent, that made it accessible in a way that I needed Shakespeare to be accessible at that point in my life. Had my first exposure to Shakespeare been at an established, refined theater—at Stratford, Ontario, or Stratford-upon-Avon, or even at the present Chicago Shakespeare

Theater—would I have responded differently? It is difficult to say. Whatever Shakespeare Rep lacked in resources and polish, it clearly made up for in commitment and enthusiasm. And it is these qualities that are integral to theatrical success, as the subsequent history of the company has made profusely evident.

By 1995, I had become inured to winter. I was living in Boston but returning to Chicago often to nurture a long-distance relationship. I was then in graduate school, in an interdisciplinary program at Boston University, working on my MA thesis. Shakespeare Rep was putting on *Troilus and Cressida* during the holiday break and I was eager to see the production: I had by now developed the habit of seeing Shakespeare at every given chance and, more important, had not seen *Troilus* since my initial experience and was eager for a reprise. Once again I was bundled and making my way down Dearborn Street.

Of course, as Heraclitus notes, "No man ever steps in the same river twice, for it is not the same river, and he is not the same man." (To which an astute student once appended, "But you can't step in the same river *once*.") I was a different person than I had been when a freshman in college—or if not a different person, at least one who had traveled down a series of branching paths over the intervening eight years (I had been at the fall of the Berlin Wall, had seen my first poem published in *Poetry*, had taught the children of migrant farmworkers in the Rio Grande Valley). My experience of the play this time around would be seen through the prism of who I had become and who I was becoming.

Similarly, Shakespeare Rep had evolved. The 1995 program sums up that moment in time in its development:

> Approximately 70,000 people will attend the company's 1994–95 season, including 20,000 secondary and middle school students. . . . Each year Shakespeare Repertory receives widespread critical acclaim for artistic excellence and its accessible, creative approach to Shakespeare—the hallmarks of this company's work. The coveted Joseph Jefferson Awards have honored Shakespeare Repertory's artists with 12 awards, including the two highest honors awarded in Chicago theater: Best Production and Best Director for Barbara Gaines' productions of *King Lear* (1993) and *The Tale of Cymbeline* (1989).
>
> Guided by the vision of Artistic Director Barbara Gaines, Shakespeare Repertory is creating a national center for the performance and appreciation of Shakespeare in Chicago—a significant and singular landmark upon this city's uniquely rich cultural landscape.[4]

Shakespeare Rep was well on its way to becoming exactly what it had set out to become. I was on my way to becoming something beyond what I had ever conceived at that moment in my life. What I was most immediately setting out to do, however, was to finish the MA thesis on Thomas Hobbes that I was writing, and which would, surprisingly, color my experience of *Troilus and Cressida* that evening.

While still an undergraduate at Northwestern, I had taken a class on seventeenth-century literature with Wendy Wall. One of our texts was *Leviathan*, and in the way that some works impress themselves on the impressionable, I'd had a running argument with Hobbes (at least on my side) ever since my first encounter with the man from Malmesbury. Hobbes famously characterized the life of man in the state of nature as "solitary, poor, nasty, brutish and short." Driven by passions—most powerfully by the passionate fear of a violent death—man, who would otherwise prefer to live at liberty, can be corralled into ceding his rights to a higher, necessarily absolute, authority—the Leviathan. The passion of men, Hobbes argued, can be managed by the right operation of reason.

Hobbes's totalitarian vision and mechanistic view of human beings were troubling. But it is often those things that trouble us most that push us in profitable directions. When it came time for me to settle on a topic for my thesis, I had circled back to *Leviathan*, inspired by further reading in a seminar at Boston University with Geoffrey Hill, the eminent British poet. Hill, who gives a jeweler's attention to each facet of language, pressed me to consider the entirety of Hobbes's text before making any conclusions about his work. And what I discovered in the process was something quite unanticipated.

Hobbes seems to most to be a calculating rationalist—and with good reason, given the systematic approach in his political writings. But at the front of his most famous work, *Leviathan*, is an epistle dedicating the work to his friend Sidney Godolphin. Godolphin had perished in the civil conflict then raging in England; Hobbes held him up as a paragon of humanity: "For there is not any vertue that disposeth a man, either to the service of God, or to the service of his Country, to Civill Society, or private Friendship, that did not manifestly appear in his conversation, not as acquired by necessity, or affected upon occasion, but inhærent, and shining in a generous constitution of his nature."[5] But Hobbes's world, at war with itself, was too dangerous a place for one with such a gentle nature, which Hobbes lamented greatly. When viewed through this lens, through this tender evocation of friendship, the *Leviathan* appears to be more than a super-rational tract, suborning humanity to the power of a political juggernaut: rather it was Hobbes's very human answer to a very human problem. The purpose of the state is not to suppress the liberty of its citizens but to provide the preconditions by which the fullest of human relationships might thrive. And the greatest impediments to these relationships are chaos and its attendant violence.

This was what was swirling in my head at the moment I saw the 1995 *Troilus and Cressida*. The play, as I had not really noticed the first time around, is very much about the brutality of war and the fragility of human relationships. But there is not—except in the last few scenes, and in spite of my memories of swordplay from the 1987 production—really much fighting in the play. War hovers on the edges of the action, just out of sight. Yet the pervasive threat of violence, which sets quaking the foundations of normal human interaction by generating suspicion and distrust, is pernicious, forcing people to fall back upon the only thing they can count on, their own self-interest. This was pure Hobbes, the "war of all against all." Fear of betrayal trumps reason; passion undermines order.

As a sign of the company's growing repute, David Bevington, one of the world's premier Shakespeareans, contributed to the program of the Shakespeare Rep's 1995 production; his notes touched on this very sentiment: "Troilus, Cressida, and Pandarus are trapped in the events of a great war, the most famous of all antiquity. . . . Morale suffers on both sides. Leaders quarrel among themselves and jockey for position in dispiriting emulation; the lower ranks jeer at their leaders. . . . What can we hope for then in the love relationship of Troilus and Cressida?"[6] Given the voluminous rattling of spears and the titanic clashing of egos, what hope could there be for something as fragile as intimacy?

Of course the Trojan War itself was a conflict, ostensibly, initiated by a breach of intimacy. Gaines's production reminded us of this at its opening: the stage was covered with an immense, gauzy sheet; tittering and giggles emerged from a heap upstage; as the sheet was pulled back, Helen and Paris were revealed in a romantic embrace, blissfully uninterested in the rest of the world. They were exposed by Pandarus, who broke into the play's opening soliloquy as the lovers scampered away.

Here, in essence, was the problem. Paris and Helen had exempted themselves from the rules that governed their world. In the version of the story that Shakespeare was working from, that of Chaucer, Helen took very well to her abduction. She was relieved to leave her boorish husband, King Menelaus, and to find herself in the arms of the dashing Paris. Thus, we find these two forming a private alliance at odds with the public good. The rules of their society, designed to prevent conflict and disorder, demanded that men, particularly powerful men, were honored in accord with their position. Any deviation from the rules, any infraction of personal honor, triggered an overwhelming response. When the aggrieved parties were kings, war was at hand. There is invariably tension between what is private and what is public; in a society as close to the state of nature as was Homeric Greece, private desire must be subject to public will. Love is shielded only by the most delicate and diaphanous of coverings, which are stripped away at a moment's notice.

The most striking figure in my mind in this production of *Troilus and Cressida* was Ulysses, played by Greg Vinkler. With a salt-and-pepper beard and a stalking gait, this Ulysses seemed particularly wolfish. He understood well the demands of the pack. The war was being stalled, Greek victory delayed, because of another private concern: Achilles, the Greeks' greatest warrior, has sequestered himself with his boon companion, Patroclus. The two of them spend their time mocking the leaders of the Greek expedition. Ulysses gets to the heart of the matter:

> O, when degree is shaked,
> The enterprise is sick. How could communities,
> Degrees in schools and brotherhoods in cities,
> Peaceful commerce from dividable shore,
> The primogeneity and due of birth,
> Prerogative of age, crowns, scepters, laurels,
> But by degree stand in authentic place?
> Take but degree away, untune that string,
> And hark what discord follows.[7]

To steal a wife or fail to honor the greatest warrior according to his due is to dispel order and reduce relationships to an elemental level. Strength asserts itself through force. Those who can take will take. As Ulysses continues:

> Then everything includes itself in power,
> Power into will, will into appetite;
> And appetite, an universal wolf,
> So doubly seconded with will and power,
> Must make perforce an universal prey
> And last eat up himself. (1.3.119–24)

It takes a wolf to know a wolf. In response to Achilles' intransigence, Ulysses (of Trojan Horse fame) plots. He must persuade Achilles to rejoin the war effort, if the Greeks are going to have a chance at victory. To bring Achilles back into the fold, however, Ulysses contravenes the very hierarchy he attempts to reaffirm. He arranges to have Ajax, who, although an able warrior, is clearly inferior to the mighty Achilles, praised publicly as the most valiant of the Greeks. Ajax, it is announced, will venture forth against the great Trojan champion, Hector. Ulysses chooses policy over primogeneity, manipulation over machismo.

In Gaines's 1995 production, Ajax was a hirsute mountain of a man, as thick in the skull as he was in the midsection, played as a grotesque. Seeing this figure praised, Achilles' pride is pricked and he is nearly stirred to action; but at the last minute a letter comes from the Trojan queen, Hecuba, reminding him of his promise to her daughter, Polyxenes (whom Achilles loves), that he not fight. Achilles chooses to honor this private pledge over his public allegiance: "Fall, Greeks; fail, fame; honour, or go or stay; / My major vow lies here; this I'll obey" (5.1.42–43). His companion, Patroclus, however, disguises himself in Achilles' armor and ventures forth to face Hector.

Although Shakespeare and Hobbes were circling the same subjects, the fundamental difference between the two was stark; it was, in fact, the fundamental difference between poetry and philosophy. Shakespeare worked through the medium of character, Hobbes through the force of argument. While Shakespeare's characters used argument to achieve their objectives, Hobbes, by animating the figure of Sidney Godolphin, used a character to achieve his objective, which was persuasion.

It was this distinction that struck me more than anything in Shakespeare Rep's *Troilus and Cressida*. Rather than considering the great questions that underlie the human experience in some sort of abstract way, through the cold, geometrical prism of rationality, I was witnessing Achilles' hot anguish as he stalked the stage in seeking vengeance. Patroclus was Achilles' Sidney Godolphin, the great friend who could not pass unharmed through the Scylla and Charybdis of armed factions. But where philosophy brought the calculations of the mind to bear on the tragedy, drama brought the orchestrations of the heart. As Achilles, spurred by rage, set his Myrmidons quite ingloriously upon Hector, it seemed to me that Shakespeare was hitting upon the truth about humans in the state of nature in a way much more complex, and more compelling, than Hobbes could manage.

This was the substance of my conversation with Saul Bellow, the Nobel novelist, a few weeks later when I returned to Boston. Bellow had recently joined BU's University Professors Program, where I was studying, and we were seated next to each other at a student/faculty luncheon. I think Bellow was more amused than impressed by my thoughts on Shakespeare and Hobbes, but being a peddler of poetic truth himself, he was, he claimed, inclined to agree with me. More important, he asked me why I was not studying in the Committee on Social Thought at the University of Chicago. This was the program that Bellow had taught in for many years. It is famously interdisciplinary and, in some circles, notorious. I had heard of Social Thought but, frankly, did not think I could ever get into a graduate program at the University of Chicago.

I was never certain that Bellow wrote a letter on my behalf, but I do know that a former professor of mine from Northwestern, Joseph Epstein, did, and I was admitted into the Committee on Social Thought, largely on the recommendation of others. When I entered the University of Chicago in the fall, I did so with a twofold commitment: first, I wanted to be sure that I did not let down those who had helped place me there and, second, I wanted to write a dissertation on the plays of William Shakespeare.

Chicago Shakespeare Theater's 2007 *Troilus and Cressida* opened with a tableau that recalled the 1995 production: the stage was similarly covered from front to back in gossamer. I experienced, twelve years later, a jolt of déjà vu. But rather than philandering and Pandarus, the audience heard heavy, rhythmic breathing, then watched as ghostly half-naked figures attired in helmets from wars of many periods processed slowly beneath the diaphanous expanse. This was a production, the opening assured, that intended to foreground war, not love.

Now Chicago Shakespeare Theater, the company had taken up residence at Navy Pier in 1999, and *Troilus and Cressida* was selected, quite appropriately, to be included in its 2006–2007 twentieth-anniversary season. In the two decades since its first *Troilus*, the company had expanded, matured, moved, and garnered profuse accolades:

> Chicago Shakespeare Theater is one of the most vibrant producing and presenting theater institutions in America. CST currently produces a 50-week season encompassing 600 local performances, as well as regional, national and international tours. . . . During the most recently completed season, CST welcomed 225,000 patrons. . . . The visibility of CST on Navy Pier places a strong emphasis on our company's ability to make Shakespeare and his theater accessible to people of all walks of life. In accepting this mandate, Chicago Shakespeare Theater seeks to serve the citizens of Chicago and the broader community by creating a first-rate international center for the performance and appreciation of Shakespeare and the performing arts.[8]

The range of offerings at CST in the 2006–2007 season bordered on the epic.

26. Andrew Rothenberg and Chaon Cross (below) with Kevin O'Donnell (above) in *Troilus and Cressida* (2007), directed by Barbara Gaines. Photo by Michael Brosilow

The Subscription Series featured *Hamlet, The Two Noble Kinsmen, The Three Musketeers*, and *Troilus and Cressida*. The World's Stage Series brought to Chicago a *Twelfth Night* from Russia, *Amajuba: Like Doves We Rise* from South Africa, and from Italy, the *Marionette Macbeth*. Moreover, CST sent its own *Henry IV, Parts 1* and *2* to the Royal Shakespeare Company. The company also produced the CST Family Series, including *MacHomer; Seussical the Musical; Witches, Wizards, Spells and Elves: The Magic of Shakespeare; Short Shakespeare: The Taming of the Shrew*; and *How Can You Run with a Shell on Your Back?* This effusion of theater was remarkable, and it was supported by the corporate community, which had fully embraced CST: American Airlines, Citigroup Private Bank, ComEd, Hyatt, and Kraft Foods were all featured sponsors of the season.

In the twelve years since the last CST *Troilus and Cressida*, I had indeed written a dissertation on Shakespeare and earned my PhD from the Committee on Social Thought. After a stint at Stanford, I was now teaching at the University of San Diego. I had morphed into a professor of English, but my interest in the theater had also led to an appointment in the Old Globe MFA program, where, as the resident Shakespearean, I taught graduate courses in a classical actor-training program and served as dramaturg on productions at the Old Globe Theater. The bulk of my writing and research was centered on Shakespeare and performance. I had acquired, for better or worse, a professional interest in Shakespeare.

My return to CST to see the latest *Troilus* was more calculated this time around; I was working on the subject of Shakespeare and the Greeks and was trying to take in as many productions as possible of Shakespeare's "Greek" plays. It had struck me that whereas Shakespeare's "Roman" plays (*Titus Andronicus, Julius Caesar, Antony and Cleopatra*, and *Coriolanus*) were commonly grouped together by critics, scholars, and theater professionals, there was no parallel discussion of the plays that Shakespeare had set in Greece. In fact, I had made it a habit to bet my literary colleagues that they could not name all of Shakespeare's "Greek" plays—and more often than not they were forced to treat me to a cocktail. The difference between Shakespeare's Greece and Shakespeare's Rome is that the Roman plays are set in a rather homogeneous and familiar Roman world, while the Greek plays—*The Comedy of Errors, A Midsummer Night's Dream, Twelfth Night, The Winter's Tale, Timon of Athens, Pericles, Two Noble Kinsmen*, and *Troilus and Cressida*—are found across a scattered archipelago of locales, periods, and genres. Where the Roman plays are realistic, grounded in verisimilitude, the Greek plays are fanciful, taking great liberties with representation. This has led many scholars to complain that Shakespeare's portrayal of the Greeks is at best whimsical, at worst naive, disparaging, and slanderous.

CST's 2007 *Troilus and Cressida*, which I was catching during the summer break, had received near universal acclaim. Alan Bresloff wrote, "Chicago Shakespeare Theater, now in its 20th year, offers us Shakespeare's infrequently produced *Troilus and Cressida*, and it will knock your socks off."[9] In a similar vein, Tony Adler noted that the production "keeps things lively, sumptuous—even occasionally thought provoking—over approximately 175 minutes of running time."[10] In *New City*, Fabrizio O. Almeida was most taken with the image of phantom warriors that opened and closed the play:

> Memorable characterizations, strong performances and satisfying text work would have been more than enough for me, as well as justified the production's nearly three-hour length, but Gaines' pièce de résistance is an eerie and beautifully haunting processional of dead warriors that bookends the play, reminding you that although Shakespeare mercilessly satirized all of his characters with delicious aplomb, 'tis far better to be a foolish lover than a foolish warmonger.[11]

I make it a habit not to look at reviews of a play before going to see it, so as to be able to shape my own opinion as freely as possible, so I had no idea before the fact that this *Troilus* had been so well received. I had, however, stumbled across an interview with Barbara Gaines while the show was still in rehearsals and, injudiciously it seems, allowed myself to read it. The short piece, by Chris Jones, the theater critic for the *Chicago Tribune*, discussed Gaines's approach to the production:

> Talk to Barbara Gaines, the artistic director of Chicago Shakespeare Theater, about her upcoming "Troilus and Cressida" and you wonder what happened to the other Barbara Gaines—the one that, for years, has talked about her shows in romantic language, long sentences and measured tones.
>
> Apparently, she's been locked away somewhere.
>
> "We are angry as hell," Gaines said the other day, as I almost dropped the phone. "Every artist comes to the point where they have to draw a line in the sand and say, 'no more.'"
>
> The topic that has Gaines so upset is the ongoing war in Iraq, which she clearly and intently opposes.
>
> Her production of "Troilus and Cressida," she says, is designed to shed some more light on the folly of that endeavor.[12]

I generally take issue with productions of Shakespeare that attempt to establish a direct analogy between the events of the play and some contemporary situation we find ourselves in. I find such approaches to be reductive, the idea of a one-to-one correspondence between "Shakespearean topic X" and "twenty-first-century political issue Y" too narrow. Every time a director insists that *this* Renaissance play corresponds to *that* facet of contemporary life, I can't help but begin to think of all the ways it does not. So when Gaines claimed to be mounting a *Troilus and Cressida* that would comment explicitly on US involvement in the Middle East, my guard went up. I had just seen an absurd *Titus Andronicus* that attempted to cover the same ground, replete with Abu Ghraib imagery, camouflage, and antiwar ballads, doing no credit to Shakespeare's play or to those who wished to be critical of the war.

I do not mean to argue that Shakespeare, or any artist from a period not our own, could not have relevance for us today (although the pervasive *insistence* on "relevance" is, I believe, a symptom of our narcissism). But it seems to me that the work of Shakespeare best provides illumination by being placed in proximity to our own world, not by being laid on top of it. By chance, as I write this essay, I happen to be reading Olivia Manning's Balkan Trilogy, which follows a young British couple, Guy and Harriet Pringle, caught up in the tumult of World War II. In the first book, *The Great Fortune*, the Pringles are living in Bucharest where Guy, an English teacher, decides to mount a play to distract his students and the expatriate community from the incipient dangers of German aggression. His choice is Shakespeare's *Troilus and Cressida*. While neither the novel's narrator nor any of the novel's characters remark upon the correspondence between the Trojan War and the events at hand, when the novel closes with the news of the fall of Paris reaching the audience just after they've witnessed the performance of the fall of Troy, the reader is left gasping at the eternal recurrence of human vice and human folly.

So I entered the Courtyard Theater at CST braced for an argument. I was prepared, as I had been with the recent *Titus Andronicus*, to analyze away any pretensions the director might have toward making Shakespeare "relevant." From the start, it felt like a turkey shoot. The soldiers, while visually arresting, seemed heavy-handed. There was a tower stage right that loomed like a gigantic silo, practically shouting—"Look! Your high-school English teacher was right—there are phallic symbols *everywhere!*" For the first few scenes, everything seemed too calculated: the acting, the lights, the blocking. I felt the barometric pressure of a Message beginning to push down upon me.

But then something happened. I will admit that I have developed a problem when it comes to watching Shakespeare: spending so much time reading, teaching, writing about, and coaching the plays, it becomes very difficult to pull away from the text during a production. I imagine a concert violinist is subject to the same occupational hazard when attending a symphony. It is a challenge to dial down the critical voice in one's head and simply experience the performance at hand. Yet, in the same way that one begins to stop noticing subtitles in foreign films, I found, without quite being aware of it at the time, my critique of the directorial choices slipping away. I began to respond to the play—to the characters, the plot, the language—guided by the invisible hand of the theater artists who were responsible for the production. I was no longer watching Ross Lehman, a CST stalwart, but witnessing the habitually caustic Thersites tramp about. I was no longer wondering whether the costume designer, Nan Cibula-Jenkins, had picked up her hues from the 1981 BBC televised version of the play. I was no longer, that is, outside the theatrical experience but, rather, was inhaling the play, the way one inhales air, not quite cognizant of the process. And what I was taking in had nothing directly to do with Iraq, nothing to do with George W. Bush or WMDs. The play—about lovers whose love becomes collateral damage of war, a war initiated, ironically, on the premise of violated love—was asking us to query the world in which such things could happen. Or, rather, insisting that we do, the way theater does, by displacing our quotidian reality and presenting a spectacle so compelling we have no wish to turn away, even when it is harrowing. The program notes, tellingly, make no mention of Iraq; Stuart Sherman's short essay declares:

> The penalties of ambition and distraction are apparent everywhere in a world whose preoccupations center (as Thersites repeatedly insists) on "wars and lechery." But it is in the inspired intensity of its uglification and derision that the play sets itself apart from anything else in Shakespeare, perhaps anything in literature, compassing the realms of love and war in what one character describes as "monumental mockery."[13]

Gaines, as she confessed to Chris Jones, clearly had ideas, even convictions, that animated her production. But she trusted the core story, and the core company of artists she had worked with for so many years, to convey what it was that she felt so passionately about.

What was most remarkable to me was how similar the production felt to the earlier ones. Although the theater space was upgraded and the performances impeccably professional, the texture and tenor of this *Troilus and*

Cressida was very much like the two that had preceded it. There were no gimmicks, no assault rifles, no video screens blasting CNN reportage from the front lines. Other than the subtle nod at the opening and closing to the generations of warriors that have fallen, and will continue to fall, there was nothing explicitly linking the past to the present. Gaines trusted her audience, and because of that, I allowed myself to trust her.

Of course there were differences between this production and the other two I had seen, but these were variations of degree rather than kind. What emerged most vividly from the 2007 production was the pervasiveness of license, the slackening of morals, the lack of empathy that is so disquieting in Shakespeare's play. Gaines's 1995 *Troilus* had retained a strand of romance, albeit strained and ultimately snapped. Her 2007 production was sexualized so insistently that one could not help but agree with Thersites that "all the argument is a cuckold and a whore" (2.3.71–72).

Indicative of this shift, the second act of the CST production began with Patroclus and Achilles lolling around on a rug, passionately embracing. They did not attempt to hide their romantic relationship, kissing each other while Ulysses, shifting uncomfortably, waited for Achilles. In fact, they seemed to be provoking Ulysses, who had earlier been critical of their intimate connection. While the possibility that the rumors of Patroclus serving as—in Thersites' colorful elocution—"Achilles' male varlet," his "masculine whore" (5.1.14, 16), are often confirmed by directors, Gaines herself had resisted this reading in the 1995 production (frankly, I can't recall what happened in this regard in 1987). Her choice to eroticize their bond, while not radical, was an interesting one, given that underlying her vision for the production was a critique of war. It served as part of the general amping up of lust, the physicalizing of relationships that seemed to displace sexuality from the realm of romantic love to another field of contention.

The scene where Troilus and Cressida are separated from each other, as she prepares to embark for the Greek camp as part of a prisoner exchange, contains the play's last gasp of romance, with the lovers swearing loyalty to each other and exchanging tokens of their commitment even as they are ripped apart by circumstance. Again, Gaines chose to sexualize the moment: Troilus and Cressida were seen making love beneath sheets for a long while, until Pandarus broke in to announce that it was time for Cressida's departure. That this was staged as an aubade scene, the dawn after a lovers' night together, recalled quite explicitly the most famous of aubades: Troilus and Cressida's soon to be failed relationship is seen in contradistinction with that of Romeo and Juliet. Cressida would become the byword for faithlessness, Romeo and Juliet the gold standard for fidelity; yet as we are asked to consider the difference between the couples, we are faced with the rather dispiriting conclusion that the constancy of love is dependent upon the concatenations of circumstance.

It was with Cressida's entrance into the Greek camp that Gaines dissolved entirely the boundaries between sexuality and violence. As the scene reads in Shakespeare's play, Cressida is escorted in by Diomedes, then greeted with a series of kisses by the assembled Greek warriors. The moment devolves into a sort of kissing contest, with Menelaus, the cuckold, as the butt of the joke. Cressida banters wittily along with the men, holding her own, and leaving Ulysses, who refuses to kiss her, to conclude once she departs, "Fie, fie upon her! / There's language in her eye, her cheek, her lip, / Nay, her foot speaks; her wanton spirits look out / At every joint and motive of her body" (4.5.55–58). While there is jostling for power, Ulysses, whose opinion the audience is generally inclined to credit, sees the balance tipping toward Cressida.

There was no balance whatsoever in the 2007 production. The air was electric with menace, as Cressida was thrust among the Greeks by Diomedes. Agamemnon, who greets her in the text with the courtly line, "Most dearly welcome to the Greeks, sweet lady" (4.5.19), grabbed her breasts violently, then tossed her to the old man, Nestor. In 1995, Nestor pecked sheepishly at Cressida; in 2007, he groped at her and shoved his staff between her legs. The others handled her in turn, Patroclus licking Cressida salaciously. Cressida, propelled from one man to the next, pushed back in desperation. When mocked by her, Menelaus pulled out a knife with every intention of carving her up in place of his unfaithful wife. Over the course of the scene, Cressida, out of fraught necessity, began to experiment with her sexual power, by turning flirtatious. She was clearly walking a fine, dangerous line; but she was called out, seemingly unjustly, by Ulysses, who grabbed her by the throat, then threw her back to the camp, for claiming "the sluttish spoils of opportunity" (4.5.63).

What did all this have to do with Iraq? The war, as Gaines admitted to the *Tribune*, was the undergirding inspiration for this production. Yet I had been wrong to assume that this would lead to a warping of the play to make a political point. In fact, Gaines stayed absolutely faithful to *Troilus and Cressida*. Her work—the proper work of all theater artists, I would contend—was to elevate, accentuate, make explicit elements embedded in the play, so as to stimulate response and reflection. Iraq was inevitably in our thoughts in 2007. Rather than bring the particularity of that war to the play, Gaines made us consider the impulses that lead to war and the consequences of giving these impulses free rein. Any thinking person would naturally use those lenses to think through the war at hand.

An artist focuses our attention on certain objects—love, betrayal, lust, ambition—and presents, in the most compelling way possible, the complex relationship between the pied elements of the human condition. Artists of integrity induce the audience to grapple with the thorny things of life, without insisting on a particular conclusion. The audience should be responsible for working toward its own conclusions. To insist on a singular interpretation, to constrict narrowly, even oppressively, the interpretive range of one's audience is to produce propaganda. If there is any hope for humanity to avoid the dark and despair interwoven into *Troilus and Cressida*, it is not to be garnered by pressing out of the play a singular message but, rather, by producing an audience that is capable of reflection and empathy on its own cognizance. While I did take away from the CST's 2007 *Troilus and Cressida* ideas that would be useful for my scholarship, as I hoped, the most important thing the production made me reconsider was the relationship of the artist to his or her art. Since its first appearance, *Troilus and Cressida* has resisted categorization; it was, it seems, inserted at the last minute into the First Folio (the first collection of Shakespeare's body of work, published posthumously in 1623 by his most intimate colleagues), wedged in between the Comedies and Tragedies, as if it could lean either way or was an admixture of both. Seeing Gaines's production clarified something for me that I had been unable to sort out for myself up to that point. In art, complexity is infinitely preferable to simple categorization. Yet artists, who of necessity must make choices and must embrace their own particular visions, may produce work that is capacious, expanding rather than constricting our sense of the world.

CODA

As I write this essay, a circle is closed. Nearly a quarter of a century ago, I saw my first Shakespearean play at Shakespeare Rep; today, I am one of the editors of the volume honoring the first twenty-five years of Chicago Shakespeare Theater. Moreover, I have returned to teach in Chicago; I am in my third year in the Department of Fine and Performing Arts at Loyola University. Now that I am back in the city, I have had the opportunity to work rather extensively with CST: I lead workshops on Shakespeare for CST's Bardcore program and frequently deliver PreAmble lectures before performances. In fact, I have had a chance to write the very sort of program notes for a CST production that I have turned to throughout this essay as a record of scholarly perspective on the theater's work.

Throughout my career, my work has centered on Shakespeare. I have taught Shakespeare to thousands of university students, served as drama-

27. Cast of *Troilus and Cressida* (2007), directed by Barbara Gaines. Photo by Liz Lauren

turg on many productions of Shakespeare, directed Shakespearean plays, attended dozens of Shakespearean conferences across the globe, and spoken to thousands of theatergoers, both in the United States and abroad, about Shakespearean drama. I have held both National Endowment for the Humanities and National Center for the Humanities fellowships for research on Shakespeare. I have published many articles and several volumes on Shakespearean performance, and I've recently been named an editor of a new series of books entitled *Shakespeare and the Stage*. Reflecting back on this mass of lived experience, I realize how very different my course would have been had I not been convinced to take the El into the city on a cold autumn evening to see a play.

But the point of this essay has not been simply to show the originary point of a career dedicated to Shakespeare. Rather, my intention has been to illustrate how vibrant the relationship between a single theater, a single person, and a single play might be. The intersections have been rich and varied: I shared a conference panel with Wendy Wall, whose class was a shaping influence on my choice to become an English major, last summer in Prague, and afterward we discussed her contribution to this volume over a pint of Czech beer; David Bevington, who not only contributed the program notes to the 1995 production but edited the Arden edition of *Troilus and Cressida* that I use exclusively for reference in this essay, invited me to be his teaching assistant at the University of Chicago and has influenced me in innumerable ways ever since; Ross Lehman, whose 2007 Thersites was the best I have ever seen, collaborated with me on a project this past spring and will be doing so again in a few months. Most important, however, the work of Chicago Shakespeare Theater, as evident through the prism of these three productions of *Troilus and Cressida*, has over the years pushed me to work harder, challenged me to think more deeply, and pressed me to reconsider my assumptions about my own work and my own life.

NOTES

1. Chicago Shakespeare Repertory, *Stagebill*, Fall 1987, 18.
2. In *Ben Jonson: The Oxford Authors*, ed. Ian Donaldson (Oxford: Oxford UP, 1985), 229.
3. Tom Boeker, Review of *Troilus and Cressida*, *Chicago Reader*, October 22, 1987.
4. Chicago Shakespeare Repertory, *Stagebill*, Winter 1995, 10.
5. Thomas Hobbes, *Leviathan*, ed. C. B. Macpherson (London: Penguin, 1987), 75.
6. David Bevington, *Stagebill*, Winter 1995, 15.
7. *Troilus and Cressida*, Arden third series, ed. David Bevington (London: Methuen, 1998); 1.3.101–9. All quotes from the play are from the Arden edition and will be referred to parenthetically hereafter.
8. Chicago Shakespeare Theater, *Bill*, Spring 2007, 5.
9. Alan Bresloff, Review of *Troilus and Cressida*, directed by Barbara Gaines, *Epoch Times*, May 4, 2007.
10. Tony Adler, Review of *Troilus and Cressida*, directed by Barbara Gaines, *Chicago Reader*, May 3, 2007.
11. Fabrizio O. Almeida, Review of *Troilus and Cressida*, directed by Barbara Gaines, *New City*, May 3, 2007.
12. Chris Jones, interview with Barbara Gaines, *Chicago Tribune*, April 20, 2007.
13. Stuart Sherman, *Bill*, Spring 2007, 34.

BIBLIOGRAPHY

Adler, Tony. Review of *Troilus and Cressida*, directed by Barbara Gaines. *Chicago Reader*, May 3, 2007.
Almeida, Fabrizio O. Review of *Troilus and Cressida*, directed by Barbara Gaines. *New City*, May 3, 2007.
Boeker, Tom. Review of *Troilus and Cressida*. *Chicago Reader*, October 22, 1987.
Bresloff, Alan. Review of *Troilus and Cressida*, directed by Barbara Gaines. *Epoch Times*, May 4, 2007.
Chicago Shakespeare Repertory. *Stagebill*, Winter 1995.

Chicago Shakespeare Theater. *Bill*, Spring 2007.

———. *Stagebill*, Fall 1987.

Donaldson, Ian, ed. *Ben Jonson: The Oxford Authors*. Oxford: Oxford UP, 1985.

Hobbes, Thomas. *Leviathan*. Ed. C. B. Macpherson. London: Penguin, 1987.

Jones, Chris. Interview with Barbara Gaines. *Chicago Tribune*, April 20, 2007.

Shakespeare, William. *Troilus and Cressida*. Arden third series. Ed. David Bevington. London: Thomson, 1998.

15

At Home with Shakespeare
Merry Wives *on Stage*

WENDY WALL

As you entered Chicago Shakespeare Theater in April 2004, you were invited to fix your gaze onto an enormous stage set comprised of two interlocking and gabled houses. These imposing structures boasted an intricate set of working staircases, windows, and balconies. It almost seemed as if this structure were an architectural space in the process of being made: a man on a ladder sang as he painted the outer beams of one house, while others carried out various labors and chores to sustain the household. You quickly saw that these seventeenth-century houses were unusual, namely, because they lacked walls. People outside the home thus had full access to and view of all that went on within it and, indeed, could look straight through the houses to the autumn sky behind them. The line between private and public areas seemed almost nonexistent in this scenario. While it is common, of course, for rooms presented on a theater set to lack a fourth wall in order to permit audiences to peer into the interior action, the particular design of these houses allowed fictional characters onstage to see readily into their neighbor's domestic space. And yet the houses presented the skeletal outline of an imagined wall that *should* have obscured access; you might say that these houses *gestured toward* the idea of being closed and sealed off even as they offered the fiction of full transparency, both to the audience and to the

28. Don Forston (front) with the cast of *The Merry Wives of Windsor* (2004), directed by Barbara Gaines, set designed by James Noone. Photo by Dan Rest

characters in the fictional world depicted onstage. When the play's action began to unfold, it became evident that these stage-set houses also notably lacked fixity. As you witnessed when the scene opened, the houses were able to rotate to offer a suddenly different domestic vantage point, opening up the interior of a room or closing it in one fell swoop. Implied in this design structure was an idea of home as something seemingly solid and fixed but in fact permeable and porous; it appeared both foundational and dynamic. To live in the domestic world depicted here was to be part of an always potentially (and literally!) shifting performance space exposed to viewers on and off stage.

Chicago Shakespeare Theater presented this stage design by James Noone in its 2004 production of *The Merry Wives of Windsor*. Directed by Barbara Gaines, this performance starred Greg Vinkler in the role of Falstaff; Ross Lehman as Mr. Ford; Lise Bruneau as Mrs. Page; and Ora Jones as Mrs. Ford.[1] Windsor life was colored in this production by its autumnal setting.

Amber hues streaked the sky, a huge jack o'lantern dominated the stage in the final scene, and the leaves of the trees had begun to turn for fall. The melancholy tenor of the season was enhanced by added songs—the opening "I Have Been Here Before," a nostalgic piece repeated in the finale, and a poignant love song (with lyrics from Christopher Marlowe's famous love poem, "Come Live with Me and Be My Love") sung by male cast members after the intermission. This latter musical addition emphasized the longing, rather than the satisfaction, of love that pervaded a society notably comprised of sundry classes and peoples who seemed to have very different aspirations and kinds of *longing*. The variety of people in the village was signaled in this performance by their assortment of eighteenth-century costumes: Falstaff sometimes wore a red colonial military uniform but also had velvet jackets and a powdered wig. While the elite Fenton boasted richly brocaded outfits, the citizens' almost equally ornate fashions indicated that a wealthy, upwardly mobile middle class could be confused with nobility in Windsor. Plainer servants' outfits were sometimes muddied by their grimy labors; the social misfit Mr. Ford alone wore black. While this performance emphasized the farcical hilarity of this comedy, it also allowed for a poignant undercurrent that acknowledged the emotional costs and difficulties of its vexed and assorted relationships.

Throughout the performance, the immense visual icons signifying home life rotated strategically to denote shifts from outdoor to interior scenes. Through the deliberate presentation of domestic rooms and objects, Barbara Gaines invited her audience to visualize and indeed experience a crucial point about Shakespearean drama, and about *Merry Wives* in particular: that early modern people saw themselves as theatrically performing everyday acts in ways that defined the boundaries of their communities and families. In *Merry Wives*, household tasks, spaces, and goods serve as the central grammar through which characters register emotion, shape the community, and establish its values. The 2004 production made this point in part by elaborating scenes of high comedy in which characters wrenched domestic items out of context—literally and rhetorically—to redraw social fault lines. Set in a contemporary England and saturated with references to laundry, pumpkins, home remedies, burnt sack, cabbages, turnips, Dutch stews, fritters, possets (curdled milk-ale drinks), pippins, venison pasties, puddings, and cheese, *The Merry Wives of Windsor* is generally considered Shakespeare's most domestic play.[2] It presents a story of financial and marital crises in a small town, where a déclassé knight attempts to seduce two bourgeois wives in order to replenish his coffers, while rival suitors vie for the daughter of a rich businessman. In *Merry Wives* Shakespeare transplanted the highly successful character of Sir John Falstaff from the London tavern milieu in the historical *Henriad* to small-town village life in the world of comedy. The play explicitly stages a "war between the sexes," with two wives effectively using their conventional roles as housewives to exercise their authority in the home and community. When Mrs. Page receives a love letter from Falstaff, she reacts, for instance, by identifying him not as a run-of-the-mill flawed person but specifically as representative of his gender. "Why, I'll exhibit a bill in the parliament for the putting down of men!" Mrs. Page cries, "Revenged I will be, as sure as his guts are made of puddings."[3] It is Mrs. Page's move from parliamentary politics to the stuff of puddings that I find so striking, for the battles that she launches are clearly waged on and through the home front. While Mrs. Ford and Mrs. Page repeatedly dupe Falstaff and assert their rights as wives, other social tensions come to light—the fraught economics of the marriage market, conflicts over who has the authority to settle local legal matters, class tensions between profligate noblemen and prudent citizens, and concerns about how people of varying national and ethnic backgrounds can unite to form a community. As the play's title insists, these tensions emerge—and are managed—through the lens of domesticity. "Wives may be merry, and yet honest too," the titular duo declare (4.2.100). For them, being "merry" means having the freedom to use trickery and performance to redefine what they see as a restrictive family and social role—the Renaissance role of the "good wife."[4]

When Chicago Shakespeare Theater (CST) staged *Merry Wives* in 2004, I had just completed a scholarly book about the relationship of domesticity to national identity in early modern England.[5] I was interested in how early printed recipe books and domestic manuals joined stage representations to nominate the household as a key site for transmitting a middle-class version of English culture. I had been drawn to *Merry Wives* precisely because of its joint interest in household labor and national belonging. During this same period, I regularly offered a course for advanced university undergraduates on performance as a persistent and fascinating theme in Shakespeare's plays. Reading texts such as *A Midsummer Night's Dream*, *The Merchant of Venice*, and *Hamlet*, students in this class investigated how and why so many Shakespearean plays refer to life as akin to theatrical role-playing. "What does it matter for the world to be declared a stage in Shakespearean drama?" I asked, as the starting point for interpreting plays in their historical contexts. Attending CST's production of *Merry Wives* was an epiphany for me, for its presentation of the play allowed me to connect my scholarly research to the ideas underwriting this course. In presenting Shakespeare's story of jealousy, community squabbling, and hidden romance in provincial village life, CST used its particularly configured stage set and an array of domestic stage props to pose questions about performance in everyday life: how was domesticity *staged* in and beyond the home in the early modern world? How did people role-play in order to define the roles of husband and wife, citizen and aristocrat, native and foreigner? How could sport, fun, and merriment allow people to remake the fabric of their daily lives? In this essay, I examine the way that CST's performance not only presented domestic spaces, objects, and practices for its audience but also accentuated the characters' performance and reperformance of their domestic worlds as a means of establishing their identities and the borders of their community.

Merry Wives of Windsor opens with a local dispute about deer-stealing between a local justice of the peace and an aristocrat. It is soon clear that this delicate matter involves everyone in the community, from local businessmen to the parson to the town doctor. As characters attempt to resolve and deflect this initial quarrel, two central plots emerge: Falstaff plans to get out of debt by seducing a rich citizen's wife, while everyone in the town chimes in to decide whom the heiress Ann Page should marry. What we might expect to be private domestic matters are clearly affairs involving all of Windsor—from the tavern owner to servants to housekeepers. Keeping the peace in Windsor is no easy feat, and it certainly seems to take a village to do so.

In representing small-town relationships in this manner, Shakespeare was, in part, reflecting one central way that household life was widely perceived in Renaissance England. Certainly, the architectural layout of early modern homes alerts us to the inhabitants' very different expectations for privacy. Many rooms in Elizabethan houses did not have specialized functions, such that one might eat in a room that then served as a sleeping chamber for several family members and/or servants.[6] Married couples often slept in rooms that also included portable beds for servants or children. The fact that the hallway had not been invented as a modern architectural feature meant that people walked through rooms sequentially to access other rooms; consequently, there were few private spaces for dressing, bathing, sleeping, or generally withdrawing from view. Only in the seventeenth and eighteenth centuries would hallways be added to ensure a measure of privacy for particular spaces, and only then did servants begin to be segregated into different domains of the house. Indeed, Lena Cowen Orlin's work on early modern London unearths court records indicating that people routinely spied into their neighbors' houses through gaping holes in the walls.[7] This is all to say that the interior of homes in the Renaissance suggests that the early modern world did not assume—or welcome—notions of privacy that would become important in later times.

Early modern indifference to creating private spaces reflected the way that communities conceived of their responsibilities and rights. A foreign visitor to London in 1602 commented on this very issue: "In England every citizen is bound by oath to keep a sharp eye at his neighbor's house, as to whether the married people live in harmony," he declared.[8] Communities felt a mandate to monitor and regulate the "private" behaviors carried out within households. They needed to be able to *see* into a home—to keep a vigilant "sharp eye"—to maintain social order. Sermons, conduct books, and household manuals specifically directed people to "get into each other's business," as we might say today, as part of their civic obligation.

It was in part through popular rituals, festivities, and performances called charivari that early modern townspeople sought to enforce proper gender roles and proper behaviors at home.[9] One such practice, inherited from medieval times, was the skimmington ritual, a stylized public rite designed to humiliate a husband who allowed himself to be beaten, domineered, or governed by his wife. In the skimmington, the targeted man would be paraded through town riding backward on a horse while holding a distaff (an implement from a spinning wheel) or a skimming ladle (a kitchen utensil); crowds would create what was called "rough music" to accompany the spectacle by banging pots, skillets, and pans. Often the chastised man would be dressed in women's clothing and domestic aprons to emphasize the gender inversion occurring in his home. And sometimes he wouldn't ride on a real horse at all but instead be carried by a cowl-staff, a long pole used for domestic chores such as carrying laundry baskets. Part of the sport involved dirt and fabricated acts of cleaning: the victims might be smeared with mud and then dunked in ponds, as crowds jeered and mocked. Sometimes the offending husband and wife would be made to act out scenes repeating their transgressions, with the wife beating her husband with a pot, pail, or broom. Occasionally it was assumed that a henpecked man must also be a cuckold (a man whose wife was unfaithful), so the victim would be made to wear horns on his head, the standard sign of cuckoldry. Through these boisterous shaming rituals, the community unofficially censured people who transgressed norms. While scholars have pointed out how complicated these rituals were (in terms of their expressions of inversion, reversal, rule, misrule, order, and disorder), I bring them up simply to point to the fact that people's private lives were not really that private at all. The home and its implements—the cowl-staff, skimming ladle, distaff, pots, and pans—played an important role in a public sphere, where they staged, in stylized ways, the domestic underpinnings of social order.

I was struck by CST's stage set for *Merry Wives of Windsor* in part because it seemed to recognize the fluidity between early modern domestic and public spaces. In fact, in forcing the audience to witness that fluidity in action throughout the performance, it raised questions about when and whether these domains could be distinguished, decisively or at all. Yet the architectural magic of the stage also brought out a perhaps more complex point that *Merry Wives* vividly makes about the time in which it was written: the Renaissance was precisely the moment when a more modern divide between public and private began to be introduced.[10] In numerous episodes in this play, characters *worry* about the fact that they are not allowed to keep secrets, conceal information, or handle issues privately. Fear that something will be suddenly exposed to the view of others riddles the language and action of the play. One of the first scenes turns on the comedy created when Mistress Quickly hides a servant in Dr. Caius's closet, only to have him discovered by her boss. Soon thereafter we see the wives hiding Falstaff behind a curtain and then secreting him in a large laundry basket to evade the scrutiny of a jealous husband. Mr. Ford's unfounded yet hysterically funny jealousy takes the form of him repeatedly searching his own house so as to expose every nook and crevice to view. He stages the spectacle of his own humiliation by repeatedly gathering the men of the town to watch him pry into the private recesses of his house, urging them to search for a sexual intruder in his family's trunks, chests, coffers, ovens, and presses (recesses in the wall for storing linen, clothes, and plateware). Promising to reveal some clandestine "monster" that he suspects to lurk in his domestic space (3.2.73), he neurotically peers into what he admits are "impossible places," a tiny "half penny purse" or "pepper box" obviously too small for a person to hide in (3.5.136). When the wives tell Falstaff, "There is no hiding you in the house," they register their sense that nothing in their sphere is, in fact, private (4.2.59–60). Ford's compulsive desire to expose his wife's sexual infidelity to the world is satirized in this play and marked as a problem: his attempt to erode the already porous walls of the house is presented as Ford's moral failing, and not a simple feature of the Renaissance world. In this sense, this play joins a host of other domestic dramas of the day to hint at a new and more modern public/private divide that is emerging historically.

In CST's production, Barbara Gaines highlighted the themes of exposure and voyeurism in several ways, including through one comic scene in which the exterior of the house rotates to exhibit Falstaff giving a diatribe while taking a bubble bath. Immersed in a large tub (with a bubble poised on his head), he complains about his mistreatment at the hands of the merry wives to Mistress Quickly, who attempts throughout the scene to peek into the frothy bubbles to spy his naked body. Mistress Quickly's knack for getting words wrong—her tendency to unearth unwittingly errant and bawdy meanings—is used to comic effect in this scene. Apologizing for Mrs. Ford's servants, she blunders when seeking the word "direction": "They mistook their erection," she admits. Falstaff responds wittily, "So did I mine to build upon a foolish woman's promise."[11] Gaines heightened the sexual innuendo of the dialogue by choosing to stage the scene in the bathtub, where the possible exposure of Falstaff's body became a source of humor. Vinkler improvised quips to accentuate this theme, making jokes about the fun of bobbing for apples in the bath, or muttering to his servants as he dressed behind a large sheet that they used to shield him from the audience's view ("Don't dry that"; "It's a small thing, I know"). The humor of the scene turned on Quickly's (and the audience's) embarrassing voyeurism, as well as the suggestion that unsavory dimensions of Falstaff's being were always just about to be exposed to view. In Windsor, the bathtub scene suggests, one should think twice about keeping a "sharp eye" fixed on the world. You might not like what you see.

In fact, the play shows how complicated the act of looking can be. When Falstaff decides to seduce Mrs. Ford and Mrs. Page, he takes encouragement from what he (mis)interprets as their aggressive gazes at him. "She gives the leer of invitation," he says of Mrs. Ford (1.3.42). She "gave me good eyes too, examined my parts with most judicious *oeillades* [glances]." "Sometimes the beam of her view gilded my foot, sometimes my portly belly," he says of Mrs. Page, before continuing, "O, she did so course o'er my exteriors, with such a greedy intention, that the appetite of her eye did seem to scorch me up" (1.3.62–64). In Falstaff's view, the women's scorching-hot gazes powerfully act on their objects—scorching and gilding things in their leering purview. The wives respond to Falstaff's overture by turning the lens of scrutiny on themselves. Could hospitality be misread as lasciviousness? they wonder. Clearly the way that one sees is a source of concern in this play. Through this motif, we are thus introduced to a glaring contradiction: early modern English people were encouraged to undertake constant surveillance and to keep a "sharp eye" on their neighbors, but they were anxious about the very nature of visual scrutiny.

The play's merry wives in fact seem determined to draw a sharp line to separate public and private spheres in Windsor. When Falstaff steps over the line and tries to seduce both wives with the exact same love letter (causing them to be indignant on many grounds), they do not set the rumor mill into action and alert the community about his transgressions. They do not organize a public shaming ritual. Instead, they keep the scandal private by devising ways to handle the matter "in-house." The two wives drum up a

29. Greg Vinkler in *The Merry Wives of Windsor* (2004), directed by Barbara Gaines. Photo by Dan Rest

plan in which Mrs. Ford seems to agree to Falstaff's advances and arranges a sexual rendezvous at her house. By ingeniously reconfiguring key elements from the Renaissance skimmington ritual to suit their own purposes, they tellingly claim its power for themselves. They plan to hide Falstaff in a large laundry basket and pretend that he must escape the clutches of a jealous husband. By having servants carry Falstaff in a laundry basket suspended by a cowl-staff, and by having Falstaff dumped with grimy laundry into the river at Datchet Mead, the wives transform the elements of a community sanction into their own private joke. When Falstaff perseveres with his plans for seduction and attempts yet a second rendezvous with Mrs. Ford, the wives again adapt the charivari: they disguise him as an old woman and arrange for him to be beaten with a broom. Mrs. Ford cues her husband to undertake the beating, first informing him that an old woman he despises has dared to enter his house. Then, in the CST production, she actually handed her husband the broom while stating histrionically "Let him NOT strike the old woman" (4.2.167; emphasis in production). When Ford took the hint and dutifully beat the transvestite Falstaff, he became an unwitting collaborator in the wives' spectacle. By manipulating and appropriating elements of shaming rituals, the wives thus scripted Falstaff as an "old wife" within a domestic drama of their own making; they craftily reshaped a community ritual that was used largely to restrict a wife's liberties and enforce strict gender norms. In their privatized version, the skimmington reprimands a man, and an aristocratic man to boot, for daring to question a non-noble woman's sexual and moral control. As they insist that wives can be "merry" and honest without supervision from husbands or neighbors, they seem to make the walls of their households just a tad more opaque. No one is truly privy to the complex plotting going on in the Windsor kitchens.[12]

CST's production emphasized two of the wives' techniques for asserting their authority. First, as the title of the play suggests, the two women used their power specifically as "wives" (another word for "housewives" in the Renaissance) to control wayward men. When Mrs. Ford entertained Falstaff at her house, they flirted in front of a clothesline on which an embarrassingly private display of laundry hung—including undershirts, slips, and long johns. As Mrs. Ford coyly led Falstaff on and then evaded his sexual advances, she used household props strategically. She sat on the large, square laundry basket prominently set to the side of the stage to show off the shapely curve of her leg; in attempting to embrace her, Falstaff ended up getting his face caught in the undershirts, aprons, and linens hanging on the laundry line. In this scene, Mrs. Ford not only eroticized her domestic work but used her ability to manipulate everyday objects to her advantage.

It's worth comparing this scene with its counterpart in Gaines's earlier 1997 version of *Merry Wives*, mounted when CST's home was at the Ruth Page Theater. This first production turned on a similar interpretation of domesticity in *Merry Wives*, but it conveyed that theme very differently; the stage set was largely bare, with only a few isolated objects, such as a chair or table, to signify the domestic space. In the first courtship scene between Mrs. Ford (played by Joan Schwenk) and Falstaff (played by Peter Van Wagner), laundry proliferated and took center stage. As in the later production, a colorful array of aprons, dresses, and undershirts dangled from a line suspended by two tall wooden poles, and the laundry basket to the side overflowed with soiled linens. As Falstaff wooed Mrs. Ford, she coyly ducked in and out of the clothes, alternating between leading him on and thwarting his advances. More so than in the later production, laundry became the central tool of a courtship that depended on role-playing: Mrs. Ford blindfolded Falstaff with a napkin so that he could prance about her like a puppy; they played peek-a-boo with the linens; she held up a sheet so that he could pretend to be a horned bull and charge at her; she physically rebuffed him by piling dirty clothes between them and then proceeded to pole-dance around the props. In short, their coy games—of dependence and conquest—fetishized laundry. Menial domestic work turned into the centerpiece in the nobleman's farcical yet high-stakes attempts at seduction, as well as in the housewife's strategic manipulation of that attempt. In the 2004 production, vestiges of this sexualized domestic life remained, but the vast stage set carried the burden that individual props in the earlier performance had undertaken—that of showing how the stuff of everyday life could be suddenly and unexpectedly taken out of its context and manipulated to manage vexed (though comic) problems.

Throughout the play, the wives take pleasure in rhetorically translating Falstaff into the household goods that are assumed to be under their management and supervision. When Mrs. Page is first alerted to Falstaff's intentions, she roundly declares him to have "guts ... made of puddings," thereby reducing him to the entrails of animals that housewives routinely stuffed with minced meat (2.2.26). Mrs. Ford's initial response to Falstaff's duplicate love letters suggests that he has only insufficiently been subject to housewifery, for she proposes a plot to "entertain him with hope, till the wicked fire [sic] of lust have melted him in his own grease" (2.1.60). When the wives mock Falstaff's girth by saying that he has "many tuns of oil in his belly," they imagine him as the whale oil commonly used to make household items such as candles or medicines (2.1.57); they later label him a "gross pumpion" (pumpkin) that needs to be dried (3.3.36). Their pièce de résistance comes when they convert Falstaff into dirty laundry onstage so that he can be violently and thoroughly washed in the river. Pretending that a jealous husband is at the door with a gang of men (a pretense that turns out to be true), the wives sneak Falstaff into a large buckbasket, or laundry basket, where he is covered with fouled linens, greasy aprons, and sheets. As I noted in *Staging Domesticity*, the verbal wit of this conversion comes to light when the jealous Mr. Ford sees the laundry basket at his door and offers a jealous rant about the word *buck*: "Buck! I would I could wash myself of the buck! Buck, buck, buck! ay, buck! I warrant you, buck, and of the season too, it shall appear" (3.3.144–46). Obsessively repeating the word *buck*, Ford puns on its contradictory meanings—as laundering and as the highly symbolic horned deer, a symbol of both the disempowered cuckold and the lusty sexual rival (a rutting deer). In wanting to "wash" himself of cuckoldry and lust, Ford figures housecleaning as an act that can safeguard and protect the family. Yet he is too caught up in his clever word associations and rage to consider that Falstaff is literally hiding *in* the buckbasket. This funny scene thus exposes two toxic types of male fantasy: Falstaff's narcissistic overconfidence in seducing prominent wives and Mr. Ford's pathological mistrust of his wife (notably revealed in his failed attempts to play the role of "good husband" or "good housewife"). Both men are forced to think through the meaning of domesticity as they attempt to grapple with their faulty tendencies and desires; and they largely do so, in this production, by becoming too intimately involved with laundry.

After Falstaff has been stuffed into the buckbasket and dumped into the river, he describes his traumatic experience in a way that exposes some uneasiness about the housewife's domestic power. Imagining himself as buttered with greasy napkins, "half-stew'd," sandwiched into a distillation tube (which housewives used to make medicines and waters) and almost liquefied, he cries:

> I suffer'd the pangs of . . . several deaths: . . . To be stopp'd in like a strong distillation with stinking clothes that fretted in their own grease. Think of that—a man of my kidney. Think of that—that am as subject to heat as butter; a man of continual dissolution and thaw. It was a miracle to scape suffocation. And in the height of this bath (when I was more than half stew'd in grease like a Dutch dish) to be thrown into the Thames, and cool'd, glowing-hot, in that surge, like a horseshoe; think of that! (3.5.107–22)

In Falstaff's imagination, the buckbasket mutates into an all-purpose kitchen torture chamber populated by cookpots, butter churns, bathtubs, and limbecks (used in distilling). As I have observed in my scholarly work, his physical cleansing, at the wives' behest, makes housework seem a social enterprise and moral art. Ford's desire to "wash himself of the buck" and Falstaff's buckwashing transform mundane acts like bleaching and scouring into techniques for social and spiritual purification. Gaines's production emphasized the physical reality of these rich metaphors, as servants opening the laundry basket held their noses from the horrific smell of festering laundry and Falstaff's sweating body. The servants, groaning under the weight of the basket, highlighted the comedy of a heavy body attempting to be camouflaged as airy linens. And in situating Falstaff in a bathtub in the very scene in which he gives this speech about his previous, dangerously liquefying "bath," Gaines visually accentuated Falstaff's connection to filth and failed cleansing.

When Ford (played wonderfully by Ross Lehman) then attempted a second time to catch his wife being unfaithful, laundry again visually dominated the action of the scene. After devising a female disguise for Falstaff, the wives positioned a decoy laundry basket for Ford to see, so that he would suspect a repeat of their previous plot. In Gaines's production this turned into a scene of laundry gone wild, in a world where Mr. Ford seemingly lost all semblance of rationality. Over and over he deliriously attempted to wrestle with the clothes that he imagined to be hiding a household scandal. Ranting almost incoherently, Ford first aimed to shoot his gun at the laundry basket (as if it were an adversary on the battlefield), only to be restrained by his friends. He then emptied the basket, strewing clothes all over the stage, the other cast members, and himself. "Are you not ashamed?" Mrs. Ford implored him; "Let the clothes alone," she ordered (4.2.127). To punctuate the lunacy of his behavior, Gaines had Ford leap into the now empty basket, where he sat defeated in his attempts to materialize his own worst nightmare. "Well he's not here," Ford admitted sadly, to the audience's laughter (4.2.145). His action picked up metaphors from elsewhere in the play, where Ford is described as "sullied" by his own paranoid suspicions. The inappropriateness of Ford mistrusting his wife fused with his unsuitable meddling into household work, both of which were visually signified by the pathos of a man sitting alone in a laundry basket while friends and neighbors gaped in horror.

Mr. Ford is fascinating precisely because his obsessions show him to be a "bad" husband in two senses of the term: he wrongly steps on his wife's toes in managing the household, and he repeatedly tries to expose intimate details of his marital life to the public. In combining these two issues, Shakespeare touches on several pressing cultural debates about the protocols for proper household governance. How much "supervision" (meaning overseeing or surveillance) should the husband have over a wife? Conduct manuals and household guides of the day debated this issue, alternating between urging a vigilant overseeing of the household and warning of the economic risks of meddling too much into a wife's domain. One Renaissance domestic manual entitled *The Ladies' Dictionary* cautioned husbands: "they must be accounted over-curious . . . that cannot let a Woman alone with Pipkins [apples], Pyes and Puddings, but must be peeping, prying, and finding fault with the Feminine Jurisdiction."[13] Ford's hypervigilance about his wife's affairs, which in the play turns into his single-minded interest in laundry, makes him a perfect negative example of this behavior. *The Ladies' Dictionary*, we might note, also implicitly separates a "feminine jurisdiction" from some other sphere. As part of its affirmation of a wife's autonomy over this domain, *Merry Wives* endorses the idea that some parts of domestic life should remain private. Strewing linens all over the stage, Ford spectacularly violates this newly emerging idea. The scene becomes even funnier when we consider the culturally widespread fear, awe, and contempt that surrounded the figure of the laundress, the lower-class woman who had unusually in-timate access to strangers. John Taylor's poem "The Praise of Cleane Lin-nen" describes her as an intimidating, industrious, and fierce persona whose "foaming froth doth lighten / The whilest her tongue doth thunder & af-frighten, / The totall is a tempest full of chiding."[14] With clear innuendo, he compares her to a

> Commandresse, using martiall Lawes,
> She strikes, she poakes and thrusts, she hangs and drawes,
> She stiffens stiffly, she both opes and shuts,
> She sets, and out she pulles, and in she puts.[15]

Early modern writers joked that the laundress was bawdy and filthy (or contradictorily, purifying) because of her profession but also because she had "dirt" on other people; she knew the stories marked on clothing and sheets and had access to a family's deepest secrets. A Renaissance character book called *The Whimzies* warned that the laundress, a potentially "tatling Titmouse," should be "silent": she "must indent with her brest to bee secret, with her tongue to be silent, and with her countenance to bee constant. She must not tell what shee sees; dictate on what she hears; nor blush at what she enjoyes," the text advises.[16] When Ford threw laundry all over the stage, he seemed to assume the role of laundress and to air the family's dirty laundry to the community. Prying into his wife's domain and attempting to micro-manage her labors, Ford exhibited a behavior that the play clearly mocks.

As it brought out the important role that household work is made to play, the CST production simultaneously made the wives into playwright figures who converted mundane tasks into theatrical events. Mrs. Page and Mrs. Ford were shown positioning particular props in the home, directing servants about their cues for exits and entrances, rehearsing their actions, and devising costuming. "Mistress Page, remember your cue," Mrs. Ford warned her friend as they plotted their adventure with Falstaff; "I warrant thee; if I do not act it hiss me," Mrs. Page responded (3.3.33–34). Deliver-ing these lines with relish, CST's wives not only practiced their parts but suggested that *they* were the ideal audience for their playlet. They delighted in creating and witnessing their own performances.[17] Mrs. Page indicated that she would *act* but also be the critic who might "hiss" or boo a bad performance. Mrs. Ford also emphasized her pleasure in taking creative license. "Marry, as I told you before," she loudly called to her servants John and Robert. "Be ready here hard by in the brewhouse, and when I suddenly call you, come forth and without any pause or staggering take this basket on your shoulders." She then sighed in an exaggerated way as she reassured Mrs. Page, "they lack no direction" (3.3.8–11, 16–17).

Although they labeled themselves as ministers of justice, the wives envisioned chastising Falstaff as a festive theatrical entertainment rather than an act of angry vengeance. When the CST's wives hid Falstaff behind hanging laundry, they delivered words expressing alarm, fear, and disapproval with smiles on their faces, hamming it up so that their acting was clearly seen as acting—by the audience and each other. "O how have you deceived me," Mrs. Page scolds, with a wink to her friend. Mrs. Ford stepped in at one point to "direct" Mrs. Page's performance while the scene unfolded; "speak louder," she whispered, enjoying her role as stage director and prompter. Even Falstaff hinted at the theatrical nature of the episode. When jealous men were about to storm the house, Falstaff cried to the two women in panic, "Devise something!" (4.2.65). In early modern parlance, "devise" meant to create a plan but also specifically to invent, forge, or create a fictional pretense. Part of the comedy of the wives' "device" was that Falstaff was already starring in a drama that he didn't know had been plotted. The wives then admitted to themselves that they had savored the opportunity "to act" so as to kill two birds with one stone: they were able to chastise Falstaff while also reprimanding an overly domineering husband. Refusing to allow the community to take charge of correcting the behavior of its citizens, they transformed their domestic space into private theater.

CST's production added a comic scene that extended and complicated the presentation of domesticity as spectacle. Ford, armed with a broom, chased the cross-dressed Falstaff all over the stage, suspecting that the meddlesome "old wife" who had escaped might be his wife's lover. During this screwball comedy, Falstaff seized the broom from Ford and then later handed it to an audience member with an ironic assurance: "no one will bother *you*!" After failing to catch Falstaff in a Keystone Cops–like chase that rampaged around the house set, through its openings and windows, and up to the second level, Ford spied the broom in the audience, seized it, and pretended to strike the unwitting holder ("She knows!" he cried hysterically, before setting off again on his wild goose chase). The scene turned to pathos when Ford, tired from running, insisted on searching the laundry basket yet again, only to find himself covered once more in dirty clothes. After Ford exited, Falstaff ran onto the stage chased by angry dogs; he begged the audience member to give his broom back so that he could ward off the dogs. When she came up empty-handed, he reluctantly climbed back into the laundry basket for protection. Ford entered one final time—exhausted and emotionally drained ("I need a hug," he ad-libbed)—and tried one final time to make for the basket. His friends dissuaded him and led him offstage to complete his nervous breakdown. A relieved Falstaff then crept out of the basket, having just missed being exposed. Gaines's visual additions in this scene—of the broom that implicated the audience in the action and the return of the laundry basket—hit home the play's domestic emphasis. Banal items became trigger points for comic violence, identification, and refuge. The scene also complicated our understanding of Ford's psychology; he was presented as pathologically single-minded, but—for one fleeting moment—he was ironically *correct* in his suspicions (there was a man in the basket!).

At the end of the play, the wives disclose their secrets to the community, and everyone joins in a final public ritual designed to scold Falstaff once and for all. Purchasing props such as vizards (masks) and writing parts for the children and citizens, the wives allow others to take part in crafting a piece of community theater in which Falstaff will be dressed in horns and ritualistically pinched by fairies. Continuing Ford's pun on "bucking," and adapting other elements from the skimmington ritual, Falstaff is visually transformed into the deer or "buck" that Ford had evoked in his jealous rant. As the citizens devise their fairy pageant, they make themselves into spiritual housecleaners, scouring "sluttery" or bad sexual conduct. At the end, the townsfolk claimed the right to put aristocrats in their proper place, building on the wives' besting of their husbands. With this ending tableau, the "unclean" knight is laundered, and the community joins as one, with the result that the wives' household labors extend outward into the community. The household's walls are again, as the stage set signals, transparent, or at least porous. The private problems of one home again become the business of the entire town, though housewives are now firmly in control of community ritual, namely, the skimmington that has been completely renovated in their hands.

Windsor, which includes the French physician Dr. Caius, the Welsh parson Hugh Evans, the un-Latined Mistress Quickly, a whole host of rich citizens, servingmen, local politicians, and two courtly noblemen, continuously seeks to define and refine the boundaries of its community. In a play that uses comic accents and bawdy malapropisms to mock those who "abuse the King's English," the word *domestic* stretches to mean "non-foreign" as well as household matters. Ford expresses this directly when he meditates on how household goods are subject to foreign threats: "I will rather trust a Fleming with my butter, Parson Hugh the Welshman with my cheese, an Irishman with my aqua-vitae bottle, or a thief to walk my ambling gelding than my wife with herself," he muses, thus thinking of the theft of his goods (including his wife!) as foreign incursions on "domestic"

223

turf (2.2.286–89). Patrolling property and safeguarding household goods shores up the boundaries of the community as a whole. Ford's comment underscores a point made throughout the play, as characters insult and pull rank on each other by confusing particular ethnic groups with foods they typically eat. Thus, when Falstaff is exposed to public ridicule at the end, he craftily tries to redraw the lines so that foreigners are the ones on the margins: "Have I lived to stand at the taunt of one that makes fritters of English," he mutters to the Welsh Evans (5.5.141–42). I think it no coincidence that Falstaff chooses a domestic foodstuff, "fritters," to mock those who mock him. The play ends on a conciliatory note, with citizens, gentlemen, foreigners, and housewives joining together to share a homey snack: "let us every one go home, / And laugh this sport o'er by a country fire / Sir John and all," declares Mistress Page (5.5.235–37). In the CST performance, the cast members joined to repeat the opening wistful song, "We Have Been Here Before." Windsor muddles along, it seems, conveniently translating household objects and spaces into games that include, exclude, and position members of the community. And "going home" turns out to be a highly theatrical process.

CST's monumental stage set for *Merry Wives of Windsor*, like the memorable swimming pool in their production of *Twelfth Night*, commanded the audience's attention.[18] Slowly but surely it intervened and shaped the action of the play, almost making "Domesticity" an added character in this drama. Revolving dramatically to open an interior to view, the set also hinted that much was at stake in guarding who could see into the domestic space. The semitransparent gabled houses raised some knotty questions: who is on the outside looking in at the seemingly private actions of our everyday world? Who controls that act of gazing? When is the home (and community) permeable and when is it sealed off? These issues were especially pressing in the Renaissance, when definitions of public and private life were in the process of undergoing significant if gradual transformation. Before seeing this production, I was well aware that Shakespeare's plays tended to scrutinize the very act of performance in complex ways: with history plays showing kings who performed—and thus risked undermining—their royal identities; cross-dressing comedies exploring the stage practice of boys dressing as women in the early London theaters; and tragedies pointing to the vexed problem of verifying a reality separate from illusions. This production helped me to see in striking ways how vital theatricality and performance were to *Merry Wives'* comic exploration of the shaping power of domesticity.

With its unusually complex stage set as a starting point, CST put domesticity center stage. Characters used household objects as toys in erotic games, as props in skits designed to best others, and as projections of deep-seated fears about sexual betrayal and loss. The audience laughed at Mr. Ford's failed attempt to create spectators to his own marital betrayal. They delighted in seeing him draped in the trappings of domestic life in humorously inappropriate ways. While the characters created fabricated realities out of the stuff of domestic life, the performance itself strategically capitalized on domestic props as relay points to position the audience in relation to the comedic action. The broom, circulating from Ford to Falstaff to audience member and back again to Ford, created comically shared betrayals and alliances. The reintroduction of the laundry basket in the chase scene made the audience exquisitely aware of knowledge that characters did not have. And, more abstractly, the production's own moving stage set demonstrated how things that we classify as "the everyday" could be suddenly and imaginatively estranged for viewers.

Falstaff's closing gesture in the performance added a final whimsical and lighthearted layer to the play's scrutiny of public and private domains. Although he had been brutally humiliated for his failings and publicly made to confess, Greg Vinkler's Falstaff refused to be cowed by the town's authority. At the end of the play, he refused to "go home" and instead slipped out of the crowd to present yet another love letter—this time, offered to a female audience member. This gesture not only softened the severity of the play's preachy reprimand and affirmed the mischievousness of Falstaff's plots; it also served as Gaines's parting move to unsettle the line separating the audience from the represented space. In this self-conscious gesture, the audience was drawn in to act as a spotlighted participant in the stage action, no longer an unseen spectator "spying" onto the domestic stage space. This shift in sightlines was important, especially when we remember that Falstaff originally targeted the wives because he wrongly interpreted their looks as sexual encouragement. Looking—revealing the "appetite" of "the eye," super-*vising*, prying—these remain powerful but potentially dangerous actions. Falstaff's last comic overture wryly made us as audience self-conscious of our (intrusive?) gaze onto the spectacle onstage. We seemed to be caught out in the act of watching what we paid to see. And this last humorous gesture was amusing in part because it implied a sly question: "Who is watching *you watch* when you act the part of spectator?" Peering into the transparent walls of (play) houses, spectators were made only too aware of their roles as collaborators in the business of theater, where even seemingly mundane actions don't escape the demands of performance.

NOTES

1. Chicago Shakespeare Theater performed *The Merry Wives of Windsor* in its Navy Pier location September 3–November 21, 2004. The play was directed by Barbara Gaines, with scene design by James Noone, lighting by Anne Militello, costumes by Mariann Verheyen, and sound by Lindsay Jones.

2. Recent critics interested in the play's domestic themes include Richard Helgerson, "The Buckbasket, the Witch, and the Queen of Fairies: The Women's World of Shakespeare's Windsor," in *Renaissance Culture and the Everyday*, ed. Patricia Fumerton and Simon Hunt (Philadelphia: U of Pennsylvania P, 1999), 162–82; Natasha Korda, *Shakespeare's Domestic Economies: Gender and Property in Early Modern England* (Philadelphia: U of Pennsylvania P, 2002), 76–109; and Wendy Wall, *Staging Domesticity: Household Work and English Identity in Early Modern Drama* (Cambridge: Cambridge UP, 2002), 90–93, 112–26.

3. William Shakespeare, *The Merry Wives of Windsor*, ed. Giorgio Melchiori, Arden third series, ed. Richard Proudfoot, Ann Thompson, and David Scott Kastan (London: A & C Black, 2000). All subsequent parenthetical citations of the text will be to this edition. *Merry Wives* exists in two early variants, the 1602 Quarto and the 1623 Folio versions.

4. On Renaissance ideas about the "good wife," see Margaret Ezell, *The Patriarch's Wife: Literary Evidence and the History of the Family* (Chapel Hill: U of North Carolina P, 1987), 36–61; and Frances E. Dolan, *Dangerous Familiars: Representations of Domestic Crime in England, 1550–1700* (Ithaca: Cornell UP, 1994).

5. Wall, *Staging Domesticity*.

6. On architecture, see Mark Girouard, *Life in the English Country House: A Social and Architectural History* (New Haven: Yale UP, 1978); and Alice Friedman, *House and Household in Elizabethan England* (Chicago: U of Chicago P, 1989).

7. Lena Cowen Orlin, *Locating Privacy in Tudor London* (Oxford: Oxford UP, 2008).

8. Philip Julius, "Diary of the Journey of the Most Illustrious Philip Julius, Duke of Stettin-Pomerania . . . 1602," ed. Gottfried von Bulow, *Transactions of the Royal Historical Society*, n.s. [2d ser.] 6 (London, 1892), 65. Orlin discusses this passage in *Private Matters and Public Culture in Post-Reformation England* (Ithaca: Cornell UP, 1994), 7.

9. On charivari and early modern shaming rituals, see Martin Ingram, "Ridings, Rough Music and the Reform of Popular Culture in Early Modern England," *Past & Present* 105 (November 1984): 79–113; Natalie Zemon Davis, *Society and Culture in Early Modern France* (Stanford: Stanford UP, 1975), esp. 97–100.

10. On domesticity's shifting and contested meanings in early modern England, see Dolan, *Dangerous Familiars*; Susan Amussen, *An Ordered Society: Gender and Class in Early Modern England* (Oxford: Basil Blackwell, 1988); Orlin, *Private Matters and Public Culture*; Mary Beth Rose, *The Expense of Spirit: Love and Sexuality in English Renaissance Drama* (Ithaca: Cornell UP, 1988); Susan Cahn, *Industry of Devotion: The Transformation of Women's Work in England, 1500–1650* (New York: Columbia UP, 1987); Korda, *Shakespeare's Domestic Economies*; and Wall, *Staging Domesticity*.

11. On Mistress Quickly's errant speaking, see Patricia Parker, *Shakespeare from the Margins: Language, Culture, Context* (Chicago: U of Chicago P, 1996), 116–48; and David Landreth, "Once More into the Preech: The Merry Wives' English Pedagogy," *Shakespeare Quarterly* 55.4 (2004): 420–49.

12. On the charivari in *Merry Wives*, see Ann Parten, "Falstaff's Horns: Masculine

Inadequacy and Feminine Mirth in *The Merry Wives of Windsor*," *Studies in Philology* 82.2 (1985): 184–99.

13. N. H., *The Ladies' Dictionary, Being a General Entertainment of the Fair-Sex* (London: John Dunton, 1694), 203. Korda, *Shakespeare's Domestic Economies*, discusses this passage on p. 93.

14. John Taylor, *All the Workes of John Taylor the Water Poet* (London: J. B. for James Boler, 1630), 169.

15. Ibid.

16. Richard Brathwaite, *The Whimzies: Or, a New Cast of Characters* (London: F. K., 1631), 83, 85.

17. On performance as a theme in *Merry Wives*, see Leslie S. Katz, "*The Merry Wives of Windsor*: Sharing the Queen's Holiday," *Representations* 51 (Summer 1995): 77–93.

18. In spring 2009, CST staged *Twelfth Night* using a 7,000-gallon swimming pool. See Alicia Tomasian's and Wendy Doniger's essays in this volume for full discussions of that production.

BIBLIOGRAPHY

Amussen, Susan. *An Ordered Society: Gender and Class in Early Modern England*. Oxford: Basil Blackwell, 1988.

Brathwaite, Richard. *The Whimzies: Or, a New Cast of Characters*. London: F. K., 1631.

Cahn, Susan. *Industry of Devotion: The Transformation of Women's Work in England, 1500–1650*. New York: Columbia UP, 1987.

Davis, Natalie Zemon. *Society and Culture in Early Modern France*. Stanford: Stanford UP, 1975.

Dolan, Frances E. *Dangerous Familiars: Representations of Domestic Crime in England, 1550–1700*. Ithaca: Cornell UP, 1994.

Ezell, Margaret. *The Patriarch's Wife: Literary Evidence and the History of the Family*. Chapel Hill: U of North Carolina P, 1987.

Friedman, Alice. *House and Household in Elizabethan England*. Chicago: U of Chicago P, 1989.

Girouard, Mark. *Life in the English Country House: A Social and Architectural History*. New Haven: Yale UP, 1978.

Helgerson, Richard. "The Buckbasket, the Witch, and the Queen of Fairies: The Women's World of Shakespeare's Windsor." *Renaissance Culture and the Everyday*. Ed. Patricia Fumerton and Simon Hunt, 162–82. Philadelphia: U of Pennsylvania P, 1999.

Ingram, Martin. "Ridings, Rough Music and the Reform of Popular Culture in Early Modern England." *Past & Present* 105 (November 1984): 79–113.

Julius, Philip. "Diary of the Journey of the Most Illustrious Philip Julius, Duke of Stettin-Pomerania . . . 1602." Ed. Gottfried von Bulow. *Transactions of the Royal Historical Society*, new series [2d ser.] 6. London, 1892.

Katz, Leslie S. "*The Merry Wives of Windsor*: Sharing the Queen's Holiday." *Representations* 51 (Summer 1995): 77–93.

Korda, Natasha. *Shakespeare's Domestic Economies: Gender and Property in Early Modern England*. Philadelphia: U of Pennsylvania P, 2002.

Landreth, David. "Once More into the Preech: The Merry Wives' English Pedagogy." *Shakespeare Quarterly* 55.4 (2004): 420–49.

The Merry Wives of Windsor. Dir. Barbara Gaines. Chicago Shakespeare Theater, September 3–November 21, 2004.

N. H. *The Ladies Dictionary, Being a General Entertainment of the Fair-Sex.* London: John Dunton, 1694.

Orlin, Lena Cowen. *Locating Privacy in Tudor London.* Oxford UP, 2008.

———. *Private Matters and Public Culture in Post-Reformation England.* Ithaca: Cornell UP, 1994.

Parker, Patricia. *Shakespeare from the Margins: Language, Culture, Context.* Chicago: U of Chicago P, 1996.

Parten, Ann. "Falstaff's Horns: Masculine Inadequacy and Feminine Mirth in *The Merry Wives of Windsor.*" *Studies in Philology* 82.2 (1985): 184–199.

Rose, Mary Beth. *The Expense of Spirit: Love and Sexuality in English Renaissance Drama.* Ithaca: Cornell UP, 1988.

Shakespeare, William. *The Merry Wives of Windsor.* Ed. Giorgio Melchiori. Arden third series. Ed. Richard Proudfoot, Ann Thompson, and David Scott Kastan. London: A & C Black, 2000.

Taylor, John. *All the Workes of John Taylor the Water Poet.* London: J.B. for James Boler, 1630.

Wall, Wendy. *Staging Domesticity: Household Work and English Identity in Early Modern Drama.* Cambridge: Cambridge UP, 2002.

Two *Merchants*
The Glow of the Roaring Twenties and the Shadow of 9/11

MICHAEL SHAPIRO

In the twenty-five-year period under review in this volume, Barbara Gaines, Artistic Director of Chicago Shakespeare Theater and its predecessor, Shakespeare Repertory Theater, has directed two productions of *The Merchant of Venice*. The first was in 1997, when the company was called Shakespeare Repertory Theater; it ran from October 10 to December 7 at the Ruth Page Theater on Dearborn Avenue. The second was performed in 2005 by Chicago Shakespeare Theater at its new home on Navy Pier and ran from September 2 to November 12. Both productions were well reviewed, although, as we shall see, they offered contrasting interpretations of this difficult and troubling play, setting it in different historical moments, employing different theatrical styles, and working in different tonal registers.

One key to those differences is the relationship of the two versions, directed by the same director, to the tragic events of 9/11. The 1997 production, four years *before* 9/11, encapsulates anti-Semitic 1920s New York, a world characterized by naive frivolity and unaware of the Holocaust to come. The 2005 production, four years *after* the planes hit the Twin Towers and the Pentagon, not only reflects but addresses a world in which ethnic, political, and religious conflicts threaten to engulf us all.

The "Time and Place" for the 1997 productions was, as the program states, "the financial district of New York City and the Hamptons, Long Island, 1925."[1] The production's representation of Venice captured the self-indulgent exuberance of the Roaring Twenties, the cut-and-thrust of the New York business world, and the aristocratic ease of the Hamptons, then as now a summer playground for the rich. For Joel Henning, reviewer for the *Wall Street Journal*, this "Gatsbyesque backdrop of uneasy opulence" also evoked social tensions of the period with unerring precision.[2] Despite the fact that the country was then living under Prohibition, or perhaps because of it, alcohol flowed freely, whether brought by servants on trays or, as in Gratiano's case, carried in a leather-covered hip flask. Historically, the mass immigration from eastern and southern Europe of the previous several decades had slowed to a trickle, due to changes in the immigration laws made in the early 1920s aimed at Italians, Greeks, Slavs, and Jews. The opening music and ensemble scene evoked both the presence of these immigrant "Others" and the carefree partying of the elite. The first sounds the audience heard while the stage was still dark were the slow, plaintive, klezmer-inflected notes of a violin, the production's "Jewish motif." As it died out, it was replaced by shrieks of laughter, whoops of joy, and wild Charleston music, while lights came up on a raucous party of men in formal evening wear dancing wildly with young women in brightly colored flapper-type dresses.

The production also caught the tone of American upper-class anti-Semitism during the twenties, a tone marked by innuendo and subtle gestures, rather than by harangue and violence. It conveyed a tone of genteel prejudice, innocent of the racist hatred to be unleashed by fascism in the next decade. It was a time, as a friend of mine rather mordantly put it, before the Nazis gave Jew-baiting a bad name. In 1925, it seemed, even nice people like Portia and her friends felt free to give public expression to a mild distaste for immigrant Jews, as Portia (played by Jennifer Erin Roberts) did when she welcomed Jessica to Belmont with chilly correctness and had trouble remembering her name later in the same scene. One reviewer felt that Portia viewed Shylock's daughter as "some kind of alien creature, the Jew girl that Alonzo [sic] brought home with him as a kind of pet or toy."[3] Indeed, the 1997 Jessica, played by Susan Moniz, started out as a frumpily dressed immigrant, who later "paints her face, . . . tries to smoke from a long cigarette holder,"[4] and who appeared in Belmont with grotesque spit curls on her brow, but who in the play's final moments seemed fully assimilated into Venetian high society, as she congratulated Antonio on his good fortune and accepted her own without the slightest twinge of remorse about her father or regret over her elopement with Lorenzo. Shylock's insistence on his bond eventually brought out a more virulent strain of anti-Jewish feeling, but it subsided once he was rendered harmless and his daughter was finally accepted into Belmont society.

The 1920s look of the production was the work of Neil Patel and Nan Cibula-Jenkins as, respectively, set and costume designer. The equivalent of the Rialto was the lobby of an office building, evoked economically by art deco glass and metal doors on the rear wall, through which, when they opened, the audience could hear the buzz of cars and the honking of horns. The Long Island shore was suggested in 1.2 by a beach scene—Portia and four or five friends in period bathing suits, their hair tied up in colorful strips of cloth, as they lolled on blankets surrounded by beach umbrellas and beach balls, sipping tall drinks, waving their cigarette holders, and cattily mocking Portia's suitors. Portia was set off from the group, as she alone wore a white beach robe, with a collar of artificial white feathers. The later Belmont scenes, inside Portia's residence, were populated by liveried servants, while the final scene, set on a terrace around a small decorative pool, was introduced by Jessica and Lorenzo and two other couples dancing to Alaric Jans's original tango music. The Venetian men were all clean-shaven and were dressed either in business suits or blue or colorfully striped double-breasted blazers, while the more sporty Gratiano, a "chattering drunk"[5] jauntily played by Brad Armacost, at one point appeared in a checked suit, knickers, and a white linen cap. Most of the Venetian men wore or carried panama hats or straw boaters, while Portia and her friends changed from bathing suits into elegant cocktail dresses, subtly accessorized by pearl necklaces. Shylock and Tubal, both fully bearded, stood out in their old-fashioned attire—somber three-piece suits with knee-length jackets, wing collars, and broad-brimmed fedoras, under which they wore yarmulkes (skullcaps worn by observant Jews).

Some reviewers contrasted the production favorably with one directed a few years earlier by Peter Sellars, which had visited Chicago. Whereas Sellars heavily stressed a homosexual relationship between Antonio and Bassanio,[6] Gaines (as she was to do again in 2005) imagined the two men, one younger and one older, as devoted friends without any suggestion of erotic attraction on either side. Antonio, played by Roger Mueller, stood out in the opening scene in a red dinner jacket as he stoically described his mysterious melancholy, whereas David New's Bassanio had the classic good looks often seen in 1920s ads for Arrow dress shirts[7] and exuded "the preppy charm [of] . . . an intellectually torpid lad who had a few bad days trading pork bellies."[8]

Shylock, played by Richard Russell Ramos, appeared as a robust and vigorous man in his fifties. He enjoyed himself in 1.3, where he savored the rare chance to wield power over Christians who needed a loan, one of whom had taunted him in the past. As Ramos's Shylock recalled Antonio's past insults, he adopted "a bondsman's key"[9] of false humility, relishing this "rare chance . . . to play cat to Antonio's mouse."[10] He almost seemed to be daring Antonio to accept his offer of an interest-free loan as an act of friendship, and he further amused himself, and eventually Antonio, over the odd penalty for forfeiture in this "merry bond" (2.1.169): a pound of the borrower's flesh.

A few scenes later, Shylock's world was invoked by a few bars of the "Jewish" violin music that opened the play, and the lights came up on him seated at a table with Jessica standing next to him. The prompt book indicates that she was to bless the candles, evidently in preparation for the Sabbath, but in the DVD that I watched she cut bread and poured wine but uttered no blessings and lit no candles (as she was to do in the 2005 production). Shylock seemed to be counting money and making entries in a ledger, quite contrary to the spirit of the Sabbath, but it was nonetheless a moment of cozy domesticity. Christian–Jewish tensions were underscored in the next scene when Lorenzo gave Launcelot a letter to give Jessica, as stipulated in the text, but also handed him a gold necklace bearing a cross, which Jessica would be wearing when she arrived in Belmont.

Before Shylock's reaction to her elopement is seen, it is reported by Salario and Salanio, two of the possibly three "Salads," as some actors call these indistinguishable minor characters.[11] In Gaines's 1997 production, they mocked Shylock's ostensible words, "My daughter! O my ducats!" (2.7.15), between swigs from hip flasks, in high nasal voices and exaggerated singsong Jewish accents, neither of which Ramos employed. They further mocked Shylock by using their carnival masks or pocket handkerchiefs as yarmulkes to cover their heads. Some spectators seemed to enjoy this highspirited mockery of Shylock (as they would again in 2005). Reflecting on this moment in both productions, Gaines welcomed such laughter, trusting that the ridicule of Shylock would turn sour and the laughter sound hollow shortly after Shylock came onstage.[12] Indeed, the laughter quickly diminished once Ramos's Shylock entered and took command of the scene. As the "Salads'" ridicule modulated into affected nonchalance at his first threats of revenge, he snatched the newspaper one was pretending to read and closed in on the other as he launched into "Hath not a Jew eyes . . . " (3.1.49–50). In the end, the "Salads" were frightened and intimidated as they scurried away, leaving Shylock alone onstage, his final threats of vengeance hanging in the air.

Shylock seemed virtually alone in the trial scene. Although the text does not specify Tubal's presence, some productions have him accompany Shylock. He could not do so in this production, as the actor who played Tubal, Neil Friedman, was now playing the Duke, a bit of doubling that perhaps subliminally underlined Shylock's isolation. When Portia entered, in a red judicial robe, with hair back and rimless glasses, she assumed a brisk, businesslike air as she offered Shylock the chance to end the matter by showing mercy. Henning captured the moment:

> Her offer rejected, however, she demonstrates, with all of the others, an unsettling disdain for Shylock the Jew that leads to her triumph and his undoing. We see his zeal for the pound of flesh growing out of the scorn they all share for him. In this wonderfully theatrical scene, Ms. Gaines makes clear that this Shylock is reflecting the worst that his adversaries think of him.[13]

Awarded the pound of flesh, he made a move with his large, pointed knife toward Antonio, who was trying to be brave with his suspenders down and his shirt fully opened to reveal his naked breast. Shylock's lunge was stopped by Portia's first command to "tarry" (4.1.341). As the tables turned, Ramos's Shylock began to deflate, until he was ordered by Portia to kneel before the Duke and beg for the mercy he refused to show to Antonio, remaining on his knees to hear the revised terms proposed by his erstwhile victim. Stripped of at least half of his wealth and ordered to convert to Christianity, he started to crawl away on his hands and knees, then haltingly rose to his feet and staggered offstage. Henning again caught the mood: "He knew he couldn't win, and, as movingly played by Mr. Ramos, he slinks off with no more than a quiet 'I am not well.'"[14]

In Shakespeare's day, his exit might have been cheered by spectators who lived in a world virtually devoid of Jews as the well-deserved discomfiting of the play's comic villain. For the last two centuries, most productions of the play have responded to changes in demography and a growing tolerance of outsiders throughout the West by turning Shylock into something of a tragic victim. In the Victorian period, great actor-managers like Edwin Booth and Henry Irving sometimes ended the play with Shylock's departure from the stage.[15] The modern director is thus left with a problem: how is it possible to give full weight to Shylock's tragic trajectory and at the same time to embrace the rich romantic comedy of the wooing of Portia and her union with Bassanio?

In 1997, Barbara Gaines certainly did not hold back on comedy, romantic or farcical. She did cut the scene with Launcelot Gobbo and his father (as she would do again in 2005), but she gave the former (played by Jeffrey Hughes) free comic rein in his soliloquy about whether to leave Shylock's employ.

As Shylock's servant, he wore suspenders and a collarless shirt, but once he entered Bassanio's service, he appeared in "a livery more guarded than his fellows" (2.2.139–40)—a yellow sport coat and later a chauffeur's uniform. With his moustache tinged bright yellow by the mustard from his lunch, he staged the debate between the Fiend and his Conscience as a debate between the hot dogs he held in either hand. Portia's suitors came across to one reviewer as a pair of "spoiled, rich, slightly exotic Harvard men."[16] The second suitor, the Prince of Aragon, played by the versatile Neil Friedman, was a stereotypical stage Spaniard, complete with thick Castilian accent. He dressed even more formally and archaically than Shylock and Tubal, in a double-breasted long coat, red silk ascot, tall hat, spats, red lapel flower, and cane. Morocco was treated less comically: Leonard Roberts played him as an athletic, serious, and dignified young man with no stereotypical features. When it came time for the suitors to make their choices, each casket was held by one of Portia's girlfriends, who tried hard not to show their own opinions of the wooers.

As Portia and Bassanio, Jennifer Erin Roberts and David New seemed quite comfortable as part of the Smart Set, and their romance blossomed . . . until the business of the ring. Portia, still in male disguise, was clearly pleased when Bassanio refused to give her the ring immediately after the trial, but she was soon disappointed to learn that he had changed his mind. Antonio's urging of Bassanio to give up the ring was quick and urgent, and it seemed to both men the obviously right thing to do. Once back in Belmont, Gaines extracted maximum comic value from the confusion engineered by the women. Playing space was slightly restricted by a small decorative pool in the center of the stage, which had the comic effect of forcing the two sets of lovers into symmetrical positions on either side, thus underscoring the parallels and differences in the skirmishing that took place. The skirmishing ended with Portia and Nerissa seated on benches flanking the pool with their husbands supplicating for forgiveness. Exemplifying "the quality of mercy" defined by Portia in the trial scene, both she and Nerissa granted full pardons to their erring husbands, while Portia graciously welcomed Antonio as her husband's friend, and Jessica seemed happily married to Lorenzo and fully accepted as part of the joyous throng. Forgiveness, welcome, happy marriage, and acceptance would all be somewhat more precarious in 2005, but in the 1997 production, Gaines switched Gratiano's and Portia's final speeches, so that Portia had the last word, to which Gaines added the phrase, "Let's dance." Alaric Jans's Charleston music broke out again, and the cast reprised the acrobatic dancing that opened the show, while servants offered drinks on trays as girls in flapper dresses were again tossed from man to man, carefully avoiding the pool stage center.

Whereas many productions have ended the play on the joyous note struck here at the conclusion of the final scene, Gaines clearly felt that the production would lose its integrity if it did not in some way acknowledge the Venetians' cruelty toward Shylock and his agonized departure from the courtroom and from the world of the play. Increasingly, directors have used Jessica's reaction to the deed of gift to allude to Shylock (as Gaines would do in 2005), but in 1997, with Jessica happily married and integrated in Christian Venice, that choice was foreclosed. So, Gaines brought Shylock himself back in a coda to the play. As the Charleston music and raucous dancing began to wind down, a spotlight revealed Shylock on the upper level, wearing his *tallit* (prayer shawl) and reciting a Hebrew prayer: "*Sh'ma Yisroel Adonai Eloheinu Adonai Echod*" ("Hear, O Israel, the Lord is Our God, the Lord is One"). By reciting the Sh'ma, a reaffirmation of monotheism included in all Jewish services, Shylock nullified his consent to undergo conversion to Christianity, with its triune god (as Gaines would have him do again in the 2005 production). As she explained in an interview eight years later, and surely felt strongly at the time of the earlier production, no forced conversion can ever be authentic.[17]

Christiansen did not feel that Gaines's ending fully resolved the tension between Shylock's discomfiting and the lovers' reunions: "After the final scene, in which the gloating Christian lovers play their silly little games of deception, she sets them dancing one more frantic round of the Charleston. In the background we see poor, mournful Shylock, in prayer shawl, bowed down before his god. It's an obvious contrast that looks just plain awkward."[18] My own reaction to this final vignette of Shylock at his devotions, both when I attended the production in 1997 and when I saw it again on DVD, was that it was ambiguous, if not confusing. From whose perspective were we now seeing him? Were we seeing Jessica's remorseful vision of her father as she remembered him earlier in her life, before they became Christians? Or was the play reassuring us that Shylock never went through with the conversion, was still a Jew, and had recovered from his painful ordeal well enough to return to his religion and actively practice it? I also felt this last glimpse of Shylock at prayer was actually an evasion of the anti-Semitic attitudes the production had unleashed and that Gaines might have done better to have shocked the audience into a recognition of those attitudes by bringing Shylock back in effigy, a caricature of the Jew as seen by the Venetians who had destroyed him. In the 2005 production, Gaines would confront the tonal disparity between Shylock's pain and the lovers' rejoicing more directly, as we shall see.

In an interview published in the *Playbill* for the 2005 production, Gaines acknowledged her determination to press harder in this version on the question of the hatred and savagery that she now saw at the heart of the play.

> I directed *Merchant* for the first time close to 10 years ago. I remember hearing the characters' words and being shocked at their cruelty, but I didn't explore it far enough because I suppose I denied what I was hearing. And I probably lacked the confidence then, or maybe even the energy, to get to the bottom of it. But this time there's no escaping the raw hatred that permeates this play because our world is now more dangerous, and we can't avert our eyes from our own racism. And by "racism" I mean all of the "isms" by which people dismiss, hate and exclude other people. It's as though somebody has sprayed gasoline made of prejudice and there are fires raging around the globe.[19]

In the aftermath of the suicide attacks on the Twin Towers and Pentagon, which for Gaines included the backlash against Muslims in this country and abroad, she was determined to address the extremist hatred "which resides in the underbelly of the play."[20] Although the Jew is the primary symbol of the "Other" in the play, she believed that it "taps into *all* of our irrational fears—of strangers, of exclusion, of humiliation, of losing control."[21] Chris Jones of the *Chicago Tribune* rejected the concept outright, on the grounds that the text is not about religious tolerance in general but "an authorial feast of anti-semitism in particular."[22] Lawrence Bommer of the *Chicago Free Press* objected to Gaines's approach for "pronouncing a plague on all parties . . . that leaves no one to care about."[23] However, most critics were willing to grant Gaines license to mount a production in accord with her own vision of the play, and some, even if unconvinced by the concept, applauded her for the execution. As Terry Teachout of the *Wall Street Journal* put it: "I can't imagine what Shakespeare would have made of it all, but I was thrilled—and moved."[24]

To underscore the common if flawed humanity of both opposing factions of the play, she chose to deploy a presentational style: the entire cast was visible at all times, seated on chairs below the level of the playing area upstage and downstage when not performing. Although some critics understood her staging to represent a rehearsal in street clothes before the back brick wall of the theater, Gaines's intent, as she later explained, was to suggest that a small group of actors had gathered to put on a show that revealed their deeper human identities through whatever role they happened to play at any given moment.[25] To achieve this effect, Gaines not only doubled such roles as Antonio and Aragon, or Morocco and the Duke, but sought and found opportunities for ensemble work in which featured actors took mute minor roles: "The actor playing Shylock [Mike Nussbaum] will be playing a servant in the opening scene. The actor playing Portia [Kate Fry] will be playing a waitress, and a Muslim woman. I want the boundaries that keep us apart to become blurred."[26]

In visual terms, the production would also blur the distinction between Venice, as the place of economic and commercial rivalries, and Belmont, as the locus of love, romance, and unstinting generosity: "Our set will be very simple—just a floor, simply there so we can tell the story by peeling away everything that's nonessential [to reveal] our interior landscape"[27] The Rialto, that is, the place of business, was briefly identified in one scene as the Stock Exchange, complete with a siren to start the day's trading and send clerks scurrying. Jewish and Christian characters dressed as all Americans did in 2005—casual if not scruffy attire for the lesser Venetian men, business suits for Antonio, Bassanio, and Shylock, which led to a witty picture caption in one review: "Hath Not a Jew Armani?"[28] The women (including Jessica) wore stylishly elegant attire, though only Portia wore a particularly elegant combination of "palazzo pants,"[29] that is, long, wide-cut culottes, and a jacket she later shed to reveal a backless blouse.

In auditory terms, the distinctions between Venice and Belmont were blurred. Instead of using Alaric Jans's original "Jewish" motifs for Shylock's world and swing and tango to characterize Portia's domain, as in the 1997 production, the 2005 production eschewed music entirely. As Gaines remarked in an interview, "I just wasn't hearing any music when I read this play in 2005."[30] Instead of music, she relied on Lindsay Jones's metallic soundscape, a "hair-raising 'score' made up of electronically distorted gongs and chimes."[31] The only music in the production occurred in an inserted scene designed to stress the universality of the impulse underlying religious expression. More or less simultaneously, in pools of light in various parts of the stage, a Muslim unrolled his prayer rug and then chanted his devotions, an African American Christian knelt and crossed himself in response to the strains of a Gregorian chant, and Jessica intoned the Jewish blessings over the Sabbath candles. Hedy Weiss, critic for the *Chicago Sun-Times* objected to this moment of "ecumenical 'equal time'" as "unnecessary and intrusive."[32] Given Gaines's concept for the play, it could also be read as a moment of *convivencia*, the term historians use for the short-lived period of peaceful coexistence of Muslims, Christians, and Jews in parts of medieval Spain, a vision of a world in which differences could be respected and "Others" accepted without hatred or demonization. Her intention, as she later explained it, was for this moment to represent the world as it should be.[33]

Shylock was played by Mike Nussbaum, a much-beloved Chicago actor in his early eighties, still very much at the top of his game. He was clearly older and thus more vulnerable than Ramos's Shylock of 1997, yet just as capable of hatred and rage. Gaines had great confidence in Nussbaum and told one interviewer that the 2005 Shylock was "Mike's creation."[34] She especially valued his ability to convey outrage, to which, as she later put it, "Shylock was certainly entitled."[35] He carried a cane, more as a sign of age than as a fashion statement, and his only concessions to "Otherness" were a slightly archaic Homburg and a barely perceptible roll to his "r"s, most notably on the frequently uttered word *Christian*. One critic described him as "an actor of arresting gravitas who plays Shylock as an old-world grandpa who worked for everything he's got and has no intention of giving up a shred."[36] Like Ramos, he enjoyed toying with the loan-seeking Christians and savored the opportunity to make them grovel or to provoke Antonio to near violence when Shylock recalled being insulted and spat upon. Despite the malice vaguely contemplated in his aside "How like a fawning publican he looks . . ." (1.3.37), he seemed genuinely amused in seeing the bond as "merry sport" (1.3.141), a chance to "gain the favor of an important Christian businessman," in Nussbaum's words,[37] or perhaps to humiliate Antonio into accepting his friendship, rather than to lure him into a lethal trap.

Despite his daughter's complaints about him, mostly cut in this version, he seemed a doting father, beaming as she performed the Sabbath rites, which partly explained his powerful reaction when she eloped with her Christian boyfriend. Indeed, Nussbaum himself was quoted as defining Jessica's betrayal as the turning point for Shylock.[38] But Gaines had given Shylock other reasons to be angry at the Christian world. In the scene after he leaves home to dine with Antonio and Bassanio, he was accosted by the masquers, who crowded around him and enjoyed frightening him from behind their identical metal masks with sinister whisperings, from which the word *Christkiller* clearly emerged. In a kind of reprise of this scene before the intermission, Shylock tried to exit upstage immediately after his scene with Tubal but could only do so by running a gauntlet of all of the other actors, who struck and spat at him as he passed.

His vulnerability had been underscored earlier in the scene in his confrontation with Salario and Solanio just before the "Hath not a Jew eyes" speech. He entered disheveled, shirttail out, tieless, with one cuff dangling out of the sleeve of his suit jacket. One of the "Salads" punched him in the stomach, and he fell to the ground, raising himself to his knees on "to feed my revenge." At "I am a Jew," a Salad removed Shylock's yarmulke and threw it to the ground, later spitting into it before replacing it on the

Jew's head. Whereas Ramos intimidated the Salads with the threat of revenge against Antonio in 1997, the 2005 Salads became enraged: one beat
Shylock with his rolled-up newspaper, then tried to throttle him. As alarm
bells rang, they rushed upstage, then returned to the prostrate Shylock as
though to finish the job, when they were stopped by a summons delivered
by Antonio's servant. "The villainy you teach me" (3.1.60) had been graphically displayed.

Shylock found great solace in Tubal's report of Antonio's likely forfeiture.
Whereas some productions use Tubal as a foil for Shylock (a moderate, gentle or gentlemanly fellow Jew somewhat disapproving of the moneylender's
furious determination to collect his pound of flesh), this Tubal—played by
Bruce Young, a burly African American actor who also doubled as Morocco
and the Duke—enjoyed inciting Shylock to vengeance and shared his mali-
cious glee at the prospect of killing Antonio. Egged on by a sinister Tubal, the
victim became the victimizer, or as another critic noted, "Mike Nussbaum's
characteristic plaintive dignity soon degenerates into a lone wolf snarling
against a greater pack."[39] Nussbaum, who is Jewish, spoke of the difficulty
facing "any Jew in the post-Holocaust period who plays Shylock." As he saw
it, "the task becomes to find the humanity in what was written to a certain
extent as a caricature."[40] In Gaines's view of the play, that "humanity" also included a capacity for homicidal, self-destructive revenge, which Nussbaum
played successfully even if he somewhat soft-pedaled it in an interview with
a reporter for the *Chicago Jewish News* by emphasizing Shylock the victim
rather than the avenger, and universalizing the theme of victimization: "everybody is a victim . . . [we] are all victims when there is this kind of hatred
around us."[41]

It was not as a victim that Nussbaum brought the snarling lone wolf to
the first part of the trial scene. The scene opened with the Duke and Antonio
in warm and intimate conversation, indicating that the cards were stacked
against Shylock from the start. That impression was reinforced by the large
white screen on the back wall, seen only once before, in the "gauntlet" scene
that preceded intermission. Nussbaum's Shylock was coldly implacable each
time he was asked to show mercy or accept money in lieu of his collateral.
Antonio was stripped to the waist and handcuffed by court officers to his
chair; he seemed to be reciting prayers as Shylock approached him. As he
raised his knife to strike, Antonio screamed, at which Shylock drew back,
while Portia, who seemed in absolute control, as if she could predict each
move, coolly urged him to "tarry," the first time over the issue of blood, and
the second time over the question of an alien intending to seek the life of a
Venetian citizen.

Now the snarling lone wolf would once again become the victim. Antonio giggled over each of Portia's legalistic gambits and even expressed a mock-sorrowful "Aw" at Shylock's sudden peril. Sternly, and with a nasty edge, Portia ordered the Jew "down" to beg mercy of the Duke, but it was clear that Antonio had no intention, despite Portia's prompting, of extending anything like mercy to Shylock, once again vulnerable and on his knees. His intention in dedicating his half of Shylock's wealth to Lorenzo and Jessica was clearly an act of vengeance. Then, and with a villainous chuckle, he added the stipulation of Shylock's conversion, took a cross on a chain from around his own neck, placed it over Shylock's head, and made the sign of the cross over the Jew. Still on his knees, Shylock softly uttered, "I am content," and finally rose to leave. In the performance recorded on DVD, Gratiano snatched the yarmulke from his head, while Nussbaum waited a beat and then recited the *Sh'ma*, the same prayer Shylock recited in the coda of the 1997 production. On the night I saw the production of 2005, I recall that Shylock retrieved the yarmulke, waited a beat, and shambled downstage center as if to leave the court but stopped at the edge of the stage, put the yarmulke back on his head, and then recited the prayer.[42] In any case, Shylock's exit was powerful. Shaken by the turn of events and fleeced of much of his wealth, he nonetheless had no intention of becoming a Christian. Bloodied but unbowed, Nussbaum's Shylock emerged—barely—as a survivor. He had passed through the pain of Jessica's betrayal and the humiliation inflicted on him by the Venetians, to say nothing of his own dark night as a hater, to regain his "plaintive dignity."[43]

Given the production's heavy stress on mutual and reciprocal nastiness, Gaines set herself a challenge as to how to handle both the romantic plot and the comic relief provided by Launcelot Gobbo. She did not address these issues at all in her *Playbill* interview but did comment on the lovers in an interview with Novid Parsi in *Time Out Chicago*. She challenged Parsi's assertion that "the Christians do end up happily married."[44] She not only cited the opening expressions of sadness by Antonio and Portia but pointed out that Portia's chief attraction for Bassanio was her wealth and that Jessica was unlikely to be accepted in the Christian world: "I don't think anyone will walk away from this production thinking it's anything other than a tragedy."[45]

In fact, the 2005 production opened with Antonio, played by Scott Jaeck, not merely sad but undergoing a tearful breakdown, an issue the production never explored. As for Bassanio's fortune-hunting, while one reviewer described him (along with Antonio) as "trust-fund babies out of touch with the way the world actually works,"[46] most critics found him acceptable, and the majority bought Kate Fry's portrayal of Portia. Katherine Bourke found

30. Mike Nussbaum in *The Merchant of Venice* (2005), directed by Barbara Gaines. Photo by Liz Lauren

her "multifaceted"—"sweet, desirable, clever, and playful,"—but also capable of handing Shylock "the ultimate blow."[47] For Hedy Weiss, she was "a woman in her 30s who is fiercely independent but aching to be married, and trapped by a constricting inheritance clause in her father's will."[48] In her scenes with the first two suitors, where Morocco was played with a touch of comic menace by Bruce Young, and Aragon was performed deliciously if stereotypically Castilian by Scott Jaeck, who doubled as Antonio, she projected, in Weiss's words, a "sharp biting quality,"[49] though she also appeared convincingly in love in her scenes with Bassanio. In the trial scene, where she appeared in nerdy rimless glasses and a navy blue suit unbuttoned to reveal suspenders, she avoided the clichés of "the heroine in male disguise" and subordinated any potential comic moments to her ruthless pursuit of Shylock. In other words, the romantic comedy of Portia and her suitors was well served despite Gaines's skeptical if not jaundiced view of the lovers. Indeed, she still views Portia as cold and cruel and Bassanio as a "gigolo," who first exploits his friend and then his wife.[50]

Low comic relief was provided by Launcelot Gobbo (played by Blaine Hogan). His entrance was preceded by the opening of a trap door through which three black garbage bags were tossed onstage. Launcelot had, to judge from the sound effects, just missed the passing garbage truck, a disappointment that seemed to be the catalyst for his debate over whether to leave Shylock's employ. Wearing suspenders and a backward baseball cap, he seemed to Hedy Weiss like a modern-day Huck Finn.[51] On the DVD that I watched, there was no scene with Old Gobbo, his father, although the *Playbill* listed Mike Nussbaum in the role, which had obviously been cut late in the rehearsal process.[52] Hogan's Launcelot displayed a kind of boyish charm, as he strutted about in the new yellow linen blazer given to him by Bassanio, and had a good-natured if curtailed relationship with Jessica. In this production, as in 1997, there was no mention of his having gotten the Moor (whoever *she* might be) with child.

Coming on the heels of Nussbaum's powerful performance at the end of the trial scene, the return to Belmont, the play's concluding scene, must have been a particular challenge for Gaines. In the interview with Novid Parsi, she professed not to like it: "[The actors and I] discovered that there's a flatness to the last scene. No one's saying anything interesting, there's no electricity."[53] Nevertheless, there were some sparks of comedy in it, though it finally sputtered to an end in a way that oddly enough pulled together the whole production.

The opening of the scene, featuring Jessica and Lorenzo, was subdued and seemed to run out of steam. Jessica was now wearing a sleeveless dress and had shed her glasses. Her initial welcome in Belmont had been somewhat chilly. Gratiano referred to her as "infidel" and "stranger," and at one point she seemed thoroughly deflated and left the stage. The "outnighting" duet suggested neither playful teasing banter nor growing tension. Comic energy began to pick up when Portia and Nerissa entered, and it went into a higher gear when Antonio, Bassanio, and Gratiano arrived. Kate Fry's Portia handled the dispute over the rings with verve and authority. She rebuffed Antonio's first intrusive attempt to make excuses for Bassanio—"I am th'unhappy subject of these quarrels" (5.1.237)—by uttering words of welcome but pushing him upstage out of her way. On his second foray, his offer to stand surety for his friend, she gave him the real ring to deliver to her husband, which he did by pretending to scold Bassanio, with a wink and a nod, urging him to keep it better than he did the first. In short, although the production did not play up the rivalry between Portia and Antonio over Bassanio, Kate Fry's Portia gracefully and efficiently established her supremacy in her husband's affection, although significant pauses from Bassanio and Gratiano suggested some lingering resentment over their wives' deceptiveness. When she revealed the truth behind the confusion of the rings, she did so with an almost giddy joy, which persisted as she passed out letters to Antonio and to Lorenzo and Jessica.

At this point, the tone began to shift. Nerissa handed the letter to Jessica, who began to read it avidly but with obvious distress. At the mention of "the rich Jew" (5.1.290), Lorenzo snatched it from her hands and then hugged and lifted her in celebration of the "manna [dropped] in the way / Of starved people" (5.1.293–94). Clearly, Jessica did not share his delight. She fought her way free of his embrace, looked even more troubled as she pointed to the letter, staggered a little, and covered her mouth with her hand. On the DVD, I seemed to hear a whimper and perhaps the words, "Oh, no!" Then she fled offstage, followed by Lorenzo. In her wake, Gratiano and Antonio burst into coarse, triumphant male laughter and gave each other a playful or congratulatory slap on the arm, something in the spirit of a high five. Their macho rejoicing at her distress over her father's fate sounded a disturbing note, as it brought back the whole story of her betrayal of her father, his attempt to take revenge by killing Antonio, and his agonizing defeat in the courtroom.

Portia's last speech, an invitation to "Let us go in" (5.1.296) and a promise to "answer all things faithfully" (5.1.298), seemed like an irresistible offer to Bassanio, who somberly responded with what is actually Gratiano's line, "Let it be so" (5.1.299), and then followed her downstage and off to the seats reserved for the actors. But he was several paces behind her and still seemed to harbor some resentment amid his relief. Gratiano's sexual advances toward

Nerissa fell flat and were rebuffed, and he, like Bassanio, followed his wife down- and offstage to their seats, muttering his lame bawdy joke about keeping safe Nerissa's "ring." The last person left onstage, as is often the case, was Antonio, more or less as he was at the start of the play, sad and lonely, covering his face with his hands as if on the verge of breakdown again, then looking up and staring ambiguously out at the audience as the stage went dark, save for one candle left burning, which one critic read as "perhaps . . . a beacon of hope and a challenge to change the status quo."[54] In short, the production deliberately avoided the celebration of the three marriages, instead offering a bittersweet finale whose joy, diminished by the subtle allusion to Shylock through Jessica's reaction, could never be rekindled.

In recent years, viewers have become used to such bleak if not sour endings. Joshua Sobel, an Israeli director who produced the play for the Illinois Shakespeare Festival in Normal, Illinois, in 2002, set the play in Italy in 1943–1944, after German and Italian Fascists began rounding up Jews for deportation, and simply trashed the entire romantic-comedy dimension of the work through extreme gender bending: Antonio was revealed in the courtroom scene to be Antonia, a woman, while Portia turned out to be male, which made no difference to Bassanio, who fully enjoyed his bisexual ménage a trois. Sobel's Jessica, as her father had planned, escaped from Venice with a casket of gold and jewels he had prepared for her to "steal" from him and so was not present in the final scene.

Two productions involving Al Pacino as Shylock also opted for endings devoid of delight. In the film directed by Michael Radford and released in 2004, the entire final scene was underlit and slowly paced, and the business of the rings seemed so lugubrious that Jessica could hardly be blamed for walking out of the house and down to the lagoon. There as the rising sun gilded the shore, she watched something far more interesting—fishermen standing in boats and shooting waterfowl with bows and arrows, just as seen in a painting by Canaletto, as the camera zoomed in on her finger, which bore the turquoise ring Tubal had reported (erroneously? maliciously?) that she had exchanged for a monkey in Genoa.

Pacino also appeared in a recent stage production (2010–2011) directed by Daniel Sullivan. In the reunion scene of this production, the two Venetian couples could not patch up their squabble over the rings, so that all four of the lovers, one by one, left the stage in a snit, just as Lorenzo did when he was unable to make Jessica enjoy the prospect of their future wealth at her father's expense. She and Antonio remained alone on stage, staring silently at each other. Jessica continued to scan the deed of gift Shylock had signed but eventually crumpled it up and tossed it onto the surface of a pool, the same pool that in the previous scene had served as the baptismal font where her father, converted by a Latin-speaking priest, was forcibly submerged by Gratiano and another Venetian witness. One might conclude, from this highly selective survey, that twenty-first-century directors can no longer celebrate these unions with a clear conscience, though only Barbara Gaines explicitly used the play as a way of responding to the state of the world after 9/11, in bold contrast with the Roaring Twenties version she had mounted less than a decade earlier.

In studying these two productions, one comes away yet again with a sense of the richly suggestive power of Shakespeare's language, that is to say, with his plays' potential to evoke a vast range of ideas and images in the minds of subsequent theater artists. In studying two versions of a single play directed by Barbara Gaines eight years apart, one also catches a glimpse of the way one such artist, working with the same company but with an entirely different cast and crew, developed a new vision of the play in response to a social and political environment that had been vastly altered by 9/11.

NOTES

1. *The Merchant of Venice, Playbill*, Shakespeare Repertory Theater, 1997. I wish to thank Marilyn Halperin, CST's Educational Director and her assistant Kate Meyers for access to CST's archives, which contain DVDs of both productions, as well as promptbooks, playbills, and reviews. I am also grateful to Barbara Gaines, who was kind enough to meet with me.

2. Joel Henning, "Shakespeare Redeemed," *Wall Street Journal*, November 7, 1997.

3. Richard Christiansen, "Shakespeare Repertory's 'Merchant' Delivers Sparks," *Chicago Tribune*, October 20, 1997.

4. Ibid.

5. Ibid.

6. Ibid.; Henning, "Shakespeare Redeemed."

7. Christiansen, "Shakespeare Repertory's 'Merchant.'"

8. Henning, "Shakespeare Redeemed."

9. William Shakespeare, *The Merchant of Venice*, in *The Norton Shakespeare*, ed. Stephen Greenblatt (New York: W. W. Norton, 1997), 1.3.119. Subsequent citations will appear in the text.

10. Henning, "Shakespeare Redeemed."

11. Early editors, following the second quarto publication of the play (Q2), listed three characters: Salerio, Solanio, and Salerino. Modern editors usually retain only the first two names. See J. R. Brown, ed., *The Merchant of Venice*, Arden Shakespeare, 7th ed. (London: Methuen, 1955; reprinted 1977), 2.

12. Barbara Gaines (Artistic Director, Chicago Shakespeare Theater), discussion with the author, September 22, 2011.

13. Henning, "Shakespeare Redeemed."

14. Ibid.

15. Toby Lelyveld, *Shylock on the Stage* (London: Routledge and Kegan Paul, 1961), 71, 81, 92–93.

16. Henning, "Shakespeare Redeemed."

17. Gaines, discussion, 2011.

18. Christiansen, "Shakespeare Repertory's 'Merchant.'"

19. *The Merchant of Venice, Playbilll*, Chicago Shakespeare Theater, 2005, 19.

20. Gaines, discussion, 2011.

21. *Playbill*, 2005, 20 (my emphasis).

22. Chris Jones, "Tidied 'Merchant' Is Compelling and Conflicted," *Chicago Tribune*, September 12, 2005, Tempo, 1.

23. Lawrence Bommer, "Mutual Detestation," *Chicago Free Press*, September 21, 2005.

24. Terry Teachout, "Above and Beyond," *Wall Street Journal*, September 3, 2005.

25. Gaines, discussion, 2011.

26. *Playbill*, 2005, 20.

27. Ibid., 21.

28. Christopher Piatt, "The Merchant of Venice," *Time Out Chicago*, issue 29, September 15–22, 2005.

29. Hedy Weiss, "Anti-Semitism, Chick-Lit Bite in This 'Merchant,'" *Chicago Sun-Times*, September 12, 2005.

30. Gaines, discussion, 2011.

31. Teachout, "Above and Beyond."

32. Weiss, "Anti-Semitism."

33. Gaines, discussion, 2011.

34. Pauline Dubkin Yearwood, "Shylock, circa 2005," *Chicago Jewish News*, September 2–8, 2005, 11.

35. Gaines, discussion, 2011.

36. Piatt, "Merchant of Venice."

37. Yearwood, "Shylock, circa 2005."

38. Ibid.

39. Bommer, "Mutual Detestation."

40. Yearwood, "Shylock, circa 2005."

41. Ibid.

42. The promptbook is unclear about the blocking at this moment. Gaines suggested in my conversation with her that the blocking might have been modified for the camera on the night the production was filmed for the DVD. It is also possible that my memory has reshaped the scene to make Shylock's last utterance more prominent.

43. Bommer, "Mutual Detestation."

44. Novid Parsi, "Venetian Mines," *Time Out Chicago*, issue 27, September 15–22, 2005.

45. Ibid.

46. Piatt, "Merchant of Venice."

47. Katherine Burke, "*The Merchant of Venice*," Backstage.com, September 17, 2005.

48. Weiss, "Anti-Semitism."

49. Ibid.

50. Gaines, discussion, 2011.
51. Weiss, "Anti-Semitism."
52. *Playbill*, 2005, 8.
53. Parsi, "Venetian Mines."
54. Burke, "Merchant of Venice."

BIBLIOGRAPHY

Bommer, Lawrence. "Mutual Detestation." *Chicago Free Press*, September 21, 2005.
Brown, J. R., ed. *The Merchant of Venice*. Arden Shakespeare. 1955. 7th ed. London: Methuen, 1977.
Burke, Katherine. "*The Merchant of Venice*." Backstage.com, September 17, 2005.
Christiansen, Richard. "Shakespeare Repertory's 'Merchant' Delivers Sparks." *Chicago Tribune*, October 20, 1997.
Henning, Joel. "Shakespeare Redeemed." *Wall Street Journal*, November 7, 1997.
Jones, Chris. "Tidied 'Merchant' Is Compelling and Conflicted." *Chicago Tribune*, September 12, 2005. Tempo, 1.
Lelyveld, Toby. *Shylock on the Stage*. London: Routledge and Kegan Paul, 1961.
The Merchant of Venice, Playbill, Shakespeare Repertory Theater, 1997.
The Merchant of Venice, Playbill, Chicago Shakespeare Theater, 2005.
Parsi, Novid. "Venetian Mines." *Time Out Chicago*, issue 27, September 15–22, 2005.
Piatt, Christopher. "The Merchant of Venice." *Time Out Chicago*, issue 29, September 15–22, 2005.
Shakespeare, William. "The Merchant of Venice." In *The Norton Shakespeare*. Ed. Stephen Greenblatt. New York: W. W. Norton, 1997.
Teachout, Terry. "Above and Beyond." *Wall Street Journal*, September 3, 2005.
Weiss, Hedy. "Anti-Semitism, Chick-Lit Bite in This 'Merchant.'" *Chicago Sun-Times*, September 12, 2005.
Yearwood, Pauline Dubkin. "Shylock, circa 2005." *Chicago Jewish News*, September 2–8, 2005. 11.

Gender Blending and Masquerade in *As You Like It* and *Twelfth Night*

WENDY DONIGER

INTRODUCTION: SHAKESPEAREAN GENDER BENDING

In Shakespeare's day, the parts of women were played by men, so that when a woman in a Shakespeare play masqueraded as a man, a man was playing a woman playing a man. Gender has a penchant for the theater, and the theater for gender, particularly for this sort of triple cross-dressing. Shakespeare explicitly acknowledges this gendered triple cross at the end of *As You Like It*, when Rosalind, *as a male actor*, speaks the Epilogue, beginning: "It is not the fashion to see the Ladie the epilogue" and continuing, contradictorily, "If I were a woman . . ."[1] In the 2011 Chicago Shakespeare production of *As You Like It*, Orlando joined Rosalind for the Epilogue, and they alternated the verses.

> ORLANDO: It is not the fashion to see the Ladie the Epilogue:
> ROSALIND: But it is no more unhandsome, than to see the
> Lord the Prologue. If it be true, that good wine needs
> no bush, 'tis true, that a good play needes no Epilogue.
> ORLANDO: Yet to good wine they do use good bushes: and good
> playes prove the better by the helpe of good Epilogues:

ROSALIND: What a case am I in then, that am neither a good Epilogue,
nor cannot insinuate with you in the behalfe of a good play?
ORLANDO: Our way is to conjure you, and Ile begin with the Women.
I charge you (O women) for the love you beare to men,
to like as much of this Play, as please you.
ROSALIND: And I charge you (O men) for the love you beare to women
(as I perceive by your simpring, none of you hates them)
that betweene you, and the women, the play may please.
ORLANDO: If I were a Woman, I would kisse as many of you as had
beards that pleas'd me, complexions that lik'd me, and breaths
that I defi'de not.
ROSALIND: And I am sure, as many as have good beards, or good faces,
or sweet breaths, will for our kind offer, when we make curt'sie,
bid us farewell.
[Exit. Finis.] (5.4.198–220)

Giving the "If I were a Woman" line to Orlando is a stroke of genius,
which seems to me brilliantly to embody one of the points of the play: just
as Rosalind must learn what it is to be a woman by pretending to be a man,
so too Orlando must learn what it is to be a man by falling in love with a
woman whom he mistakes for a man. And, as we shall see, the "If I were"
refrain is one of the recurrent leitmotifs of *As You Like It*; a great deal of the
play is played in the subjunctive mode.

Explicit acknowledgments of cross-gendered casting, like this one, abound
in Shakespeare. In *Antony and Cleopatra*, the male actor playing Cleopatra
complains, "I shall see / Some squeaking Cleopatra boy my greatness / I' the
posture of a whore."[2] And in *Hamlet*, Hamlet says to the player who is to play
the Queen, referring to the habit of casting as women young boys whose voices
had not yet changed, "Pray God your voice like a piece of uncurrent gold be not
cracked within the ring."[3] In *A Midsummer Night's Dream*, when Peter Quince
tells Flute to play the part of Thisbe, a woman, Flute objects, "Nay faith, let me
not play a woman, I have a beard coming," to which Quince replies, "That's
all one. You shall play it in a mask, and you may speak as small as you will."
Whereupon Bottom breaks in, saying, "An I may hide my face, let me play
Thisbe too. I'll speak in a monstrous little voice."[4] At the start of *The Taming of
the Shrew*, a page is dressed as a woman to trick a man—an episode that was
cleverly revisited in the 2010 production of *The Taming of the Shrew* at Chicago
Shakespeare Theater, directed by Josie Rourke. Echoing Neil LaBute's revised
frame, in which the audience watched a lesbian couple navigate the mirroring
of their vexed personal relationship dynamic in their professional dynamic

(the Director, who wanted a lesbian partnership cast in a conventional het-eronormative mold, was romantically involved with her Kate, who wanted to sleep around), Petruchio arrived for his wedding to Kate wearing lipstick and a bridal veil over ass-less chaps, Grumio cavorting behind him cross-dressed as a bridesmaid, tossing rose petals out of a basket.

In *The Comedy of Errors, Much Ado About Nothing, A Midsummer Night's Dream, As You Like It, Twelfth Night, All's Well That Ends Well, Measure for Measure,* and *A Winter's Tale* (to put them in roughly chronological order), gender masquerades proliferate at the drop of a curtain. Clearly, Shakespearean audiences were aware that men were playing the parts of women—sometimes the parts of women playing men. Yet audiences suspended that awareness, or rather, half-suspended it, enjoying the frisson of "conscious illusion" and "double pleasure" that Goethe said he enjoyed in operas in which men played the part of women or women played the "trouser roles" of men.[5]

Often, Shakespeare uses the gender masquerade to express androgyny or even that elusive homosexuality that so often underlies the joy of cuckold-ing, the cuckolder making sexual contact with the husband by seducing the wife. The gender masquerade also served Shakespeare as a magnet for two of his favorite themes: madness and dreams. Faced with apparently inexpli-cable situations in which A expects B to be C, who (unbeknownst to A or B) is a dead ringer for B, the central characters think they are mad or dreaming, or others accuse them of madness.

Marc Norman and Tom Stoppard's film *Shakespeare in Love* (dir. John Madden, 1998) adds yet another twist to the spiral: a woman (Gwyneth Paltrow) plays a woman (Viola de Lesseps) playing a man (Thomas Kent) playing a man (Romeo) and then playing a woman (Juliet), the final twist inspiring Shakespeare (in the film) with the idea for *Twelfth Night,* in which a male actor played a woman (Viola) playing a man (Cesario). It might bet-ter have inspired the earlier counterpart to that play, *As You Like It,* where that final man doubles back yet again to play a woman (male actor playing Rosalind playing Ganymede playing Rosalind). Perhaps the inevitable twist to this tangled skein was provided in 2003 by the playwright actor David Greenspan in his play *She Stoops to Comedy,* in which an actress who has decided to audition for the role of Orlando in a production of *As You Like It* spends most of the first scene offstage, preparing her disguise in the bath-room. When she finally emerges in slacks, a short-sleeved shirt, furry arms and a butch haircut, she is most convincingly male, for the simple reason that David Greenspan plays this part, "without a stitch of drag."[6] Rosalind-as-Ganymede-as-Rosalind, meet Greenspan-as-actress-as-male-actor-as-Orlando.

31. Kate Fry and Matt Schwader in *As You Like It* (2011), directed by Barbara Gaines. Photo by Liz Lauren

TWELFTH NIGHT

Twelfth Night (1601–1602), the younger, later twin of *As You Like It* (1598–1602), has less convoluted gender twists, though it also has a more serious sounding of the theme of the gender masquerade, the blacker comedy. Here is a summary of that central plot (omitting several political and comic subplots): Viola, separated from her brother Sebastian by a shipwreck, fears that he is dead. She dresses as a man, calling herself "Cesario," and in this form is employed at the court of Duke Orsino. Orsino woos Olivia, who, mourning her dead brother, rejects him—but now falls in love with Viola-as-Cesario; Viola rejects the love of Olivia and falls in love with Orsino. When Sebastian appears, he is at first mistaken for Cesario, but when Sebastian and Viola are revealed to be two separate people, male and female, Olivia marries Sebastian and Orsino marries Viola.

Viola explicitly constructs her gender ambiguity: she plans to present herself to Orsino neither as a man nor as a woman, but as a eunuch.[7] Yet clearly no one takes her to be a eunuch: first she is a woman, then a boy, and then a woman. She engages in two overlapping masquerades: she pretends to be a boy in general, and to be her own brother in particular. The first layer of the disguise has an ambiguous success: Orsino remarks to Viola, "They shall yet belie thy happy years / That say thou art a man: Diana's lip / Is not more smooth and rubious; thy small pipe / Is as the maiden's organ, shrill of sound, / And all is semblative a woman's part" (1.4.30–34). The voice betrays the person where the eye is still deceived, and femininity and youth take each other's places; they think she is just young (and male, with a still unbroken voice), but she is female (and mature, a soprano). Malvolio, similarly mistaking femininity for youth, quips that Viola-as-Cesario is "not yet old enough for a man, nor young enough for a boy; . . . 'tis with him in standing water, between boy and man. He is very well favoured, and he speaks very shrewishly: one would think his mother's milk were scarce out of him" (1.5.153–58). But we know that the standing water is not between boy and man, but between boy and girl.

Josie Rourke's 2009 production of *Twelfth Night* for Chicago Shakespeare Theater set the whole action of the play around a 7,000-gallon pool of what was literally standing water. At the beginning of the play's second scene, Viola (played by Michelle Beck) dramatically plunged from the fly system down into the pool, simultaneously bereft of her brother and her "woman's weeds"—her corset, streaming water, rose up into the spotlight emptied of her, leaving Viola to crawl ashore in Illyria stripped of her past, her family connections, and most of her clothes. Once in Illyria, she took on the clothing style and manners of her brother, Cesario. In Rourke's production, for the duration of her cross-dressed performance as Cesario, Viola always appeared only on the periphery of the pool of water until her joyous reunion with her brother and the revelation of her female self to her beloved Orsino. Thus, she could be in the standing water only when she was able to be fully Viola, rather than her divided, dual-gendered identity, Viola-as-Cesario.

Olivia's infatuation with Viola-as-Cesario is an instance of the folk theme of the love-messenger who woos for himself, somewhat complicated by the fact that this messenger, not being a man like the man for whom "he" woos, does not wish to woo and is unwillingly wooed in return. Viola-as-Cesario teases Olivia cruelly, perhaps out of her uneasiness at the (unconsciously) homosexual advance, telling her what "he" would do, "If I did love you in my master's flame," to which Olivia eagerly replies, "Why, what would you?" (1.5.259, 263). (There's that subjunctive again.) God knows, Viola-as-

Cesario drops heavy enough hints to Olivia: "What I am, and what I would, are as secret as maidenhead" (1.5.211), and "I am not that I play" (1.5.180), lines echoed later, when Viola-as-Cesario warns Olivia, "I am not what I am" (3.1.141–42), to which Olivia replies passionately, "I wish you were, as I would have you be!" (3.1.143). (More subjunctives.) In desperation, Viola-as-Cesario tells her, "I have one heart, one bosom, and one truth, / And that no woman has; nor never none / Shall mistress be of it, save I alone" (3.1.158). This is the claim of narcissism (or unconscious assertion of the narcissistic aspect of homosexuality): I will love no one but someone just like me.

The cruelty is, however, turned back on Viola-as-Cesario when he falls in love with Orsino, the man on whose behalf he woos, and tells him, "I'll do my best / To woo your lady: (*Aside*) Yet a barful strife! / Whoe'er I woo, myself would be his wife" (1.4.42–44). Viola-as-Cesario tells Orsino that he (Cesario) is in love with a woman who is of the same complexion, and the same age, as Orsino, whereupon Orsino tries to talk him out of loving a woman so old (2.4.29–35): it is wrong for the male Cesario to love an (imaginary) old, female Orsino, but right for the male Orsino to love a young female Viola-as-Cesario. Of course, since the male Cesario seems younger than the female Viola of the same age (femininity standing in for youth, as usual), the May–September gap is also wider between the imagined older woman and the younger man (Ms. Orsino and Cesario) than between the older man and the younger woman (Orsino and Viola).

The family resemblance between Viola and Sebastian, despite the differences in their sexes, is easily transformed into an explanation for the physical resemblance between Viola-as-Cesario and Sebastian. Sebastian himself first remarks upon it: "A lady, sir, though it was said she much resembled me, was yet of many accounted beautiful" (2.1.24–25). And when Viola sees Sebastian, she says, "I my brother know / Yet living in my glass; even such and so / In favour was my brother; and he went / Still in this fashion, colour, ornament, / For him I imitate" (3.4.381–85). So they look alike both because they share the same genes—indeed, they are fraternal but not identical twins—and because one of them is trying to look like the other.

When Orsino sees both Viola and Sebastian he cries out, in a quasi-liturgical formula, "One face, one voice, one habit, and two persons" (5.1.215). Olivia simply croons, "Most wonderful!" (5.1.225), both because she realizes that Cesario is male after all, and because there are two of him (and, as Mae West once remarked, too much of a good thing can be wonderful). Sebastian's friend Antonio remarks, "An apple cleft in two, is not more twin / Than these two creatures" (5.1.223–24). But the twins are in fact far more unlike each other than are the two halves of an apple. Are we to assume, for instance, that their voices and bodies and personalities as well as their faces are the same? If not, then how can Olivia love Sebastian? He is entirely different from Cesario—a different gender—which becomes vividly apparent when Viola-as-Cesario runs away from a swordfight (3.4.301–12) that Sebastian aggressively welcomes (4.1.25). If, in her temporary, grief-induced misanthropy, Olivia loved Cesario's gender (feminine) as well as his apparent sex (male), has she really gotten what she wants in Sebastian, who has the sex but not the gender? That is the crux.

When, after Olivia has married Sebastian, Viola-as-Cesario denies her (5.1.132–69), Olivia experiences, momentarily, the same rejection that the wife experiences in *Comedy of Errors* (2.2.111–82), and for the same reason: she doesn't realize that she is talking to her husband's double, who naturally doesn't recognize her. Antonio, who loves Sebastian, experiences the same rejection from Viola, in a scene (much like several in *Comedy of Errors*) (3.2, 4.1, 4.3) in which money, rather than love, is what is demanded and refused (3.4.334–72). Indeed, just as Viola is sandwiched between Olivia, who loves her as Cesario, and Orsino, whom she loves as Viola, so too, Sebastian is sandwiched between Antonio, who loves him as Sebastian, and Olivia, who loves him as Cesario.

Near the end, Viola and Sebastian test each other's identities through facts: the father's mole, the day of his death, the captain's confirmation, and so forth. The drawing out of this scene makes us wonder why so many people who were *not* in love with Viola-as-Cesario were so easily fooled by the masquerade, but there is no point in treating the play like a murder mystery, let alone a legal case. It is a recognition play, which requires us to suspend our disbelief. When the victim of the masquerade finally recognizes the masquerader ("Oh, it's Viola!"), the audience recognizes the plot ("Oh, it's one of those recognition plays!").[8] That moment brings with it the same satisfaction as the moment when the last piece of the jigsaw puzzle—or the last line connecting the dots—slips in to reveal the total image.

AS YOU LIKE IT

Let us turn now to the gender masquerade in *As You Like It*: Orlando and Rosalind have fallen in love, but both are banished from the court to the Forest of Arden. Rosalind disguises herself as a boy, Ganymede, ostensibly to avoid being raped or otherwise attacked if it is known that she is a mere woman, and also to escape a malevolent ruler. In Arden, Rosalind-as-Ganymede encounters Orlando, for whom Rosalind-as-Ganymede openly "pretends" to be Rosalind, in order, he says, to dissuade Orlando from the love of women in general and the love of Rosalind in particular—all the while, of course, using his wit and charm to make Orlando fall deeper and deeper in love with him in his male persona. Rosalind-as-Ganymede also inadvertently attracts the love of a shepherd girl, Phoebe, whom he tries in vain to dissuade and to encourage to marry Silvius, the shepherd boy who loves her. In the end, Rosalind reveals herself and marries Orlando, and Phoebe marries Silvius.

As in *Twelfth Night*, the awkward fact that a woman (Phoebe) falls in love with a woman (Rosalind-as-Ganymede), while the putative man (Rosalind-as-Ganymede) falls in love with a man (Orlando), allows the play to express a complex series of meditations on androgyny. On the outside, it would seem that a male Ganymede is in love with a male Orlando; on the inside, a female Rosalind is in love with a male Orlando. Rosalind-as-Ganymede thus experiences simultaneously two different sorts of gender/sex asymmetry, one public, one private (rather like the quandary of cross-dressed characters in plays and films who must choose between using the men's room or the women's room).[9] And the same asymmetry prevails in both plays: since we know that Rosalind and Phoebe, like Viola and Olivia, are sexually the same (women), the play denies the possibility of their encounter even though they appear to be of two different genders; since explicit homosexuality plays no part in Shakespeare's official world onstage, Rosalind's and Viola's uneasiness is an expression of the embarrassment that they as heterosexuals feel in response to what is perceived, on some level, as a homosexual attraction. But since we know that Rosalind and Orlando, like Viola and Orsino, are sexually different (a woman and a man), the play affirms their encounter even though they appear to be of the same gender.

Ganymede's name—the name of the boy lover of Zeus—signals his mythological sexual ambiguity, a broad hint that the putatively false homoerotic passions in *As You Like It* are for real. Later writers certainly took the hint: Oscar Wilde's Dorian Gray, otherwise thoroughly embroiled in homoeroticism, falls in love with a woman when he sees her playing Rosalind, and Virginia Woolf's bisexual Orlando begins life as an Elizabethan man but becomes a woman who, on occasion, cross-dresses and passes as a man among women.[10]

Despite the playfulness of the plot, which might encourage a reader to ignore the illogical or irrational success of the masquerade, Shakespeare tackles head-on the real problems posed by the fact that no one notices that Ganymede is Rosalind. Rosalind's disguise, like Viola's, has two layers: she pretends to be, in general, someone of the other gender, a boy, and she pretends to be a particular individual of the other gender, Ganymede. The first part of Rosalind's disguise has the same ambiguous success as Viola's. The more general gender passing is made possible, as she tells us from the very start, because she is unusually tall, and her height is noted at once, although people still remark upon Rosalind-as-Ganymede's femininity. Orlando's brother, Oliver, comments, "The boy is fair, / Of female favour, and bestows himself / Like a ripe sister" (4.3.85–87). She is a boyish woman who passes herself off as a girlish boy, as another cross-dressing actress was once described.[11] And when Rosalind-as-Ganymede faints (or, as she puts it, counterfeits [or feints] a faint) in front of Oliver, who says, "Counterfeit to be a man," she lamely remarks, "I should have been a woman by right" (4.3.175). Here, Oliver is asking a man (or so he thinks) to pretend to be a man. Adding this to the tab we've been running, you have a male actor as a woman (Rosalind) as a boy (Ganymede) as a boy (the counterfeited man).

The second, more particular masquerade is noted when Rosalind's father thickly remarks of Rosalind-as-Ganymede, "I do remember in this shepherd boy / Some lively touches of my daughter's favour," and Orlando replies, "My lord, the first time that I ever saw him, / Methought he was a brother to your daughter" (5.4.26–29). Family resemblance to the rescue, as usual in the recognition comedies. But Rosalind and Orlando have met and fallen in love before she starts wearing trousers, which makes more problematic the fact that Orlando does not see through the gender masquerade. Orlando's uneasiness is expressive of the latent androgyny of both Rosalind and himself, but it is also a powerful testimony to a love that transcends gender but not sexuality.

And then a third masquerade occurs, when Orlando tells Rosalind-as-Ganymede of his love for Rosalind and she promises to cure him of his love "if you would but call me Rosalind and come every day to my cote and woo me." And when he says, "With all my heart, good youth," she reminds him, "Nay, you must call me Rosalind" (3.2.415–22). This is an inversion of the scene in *Twelfth Night* in which Viola-as-Cesario tells Orsino that he is in love with a woman who is of the same complexion and the same age as Orsino, which is to say, Orsino (male) imagined as Orsino (female).

Rosalind-as-Ganymede-as-Rosalind is not the same person as Rosalind-as-Rosalind. Rosalind-as-Ganymede-as-Rosalind is more daring, more playful, more flirtatious, more confident than Rosalind *tout court* (or Rosalind-as-Rosalind), emboldened both by the double mask and by the masculinity embedded in the mediating second personality, able to say things to Orlando that she was not able to say to him when she met him as Rosalind.[12] She cannot become herself except by going through Ganymede. Rosalind at the start is fond of word games, but she plays them only with her friend

Celia. Face-to-face with Orlando, Rosalind-as-Rosalind is almost as tongue-tied as he is (she speaks only short sentences, which lack wit though they are still eloquent), and their romance goes nowhere at all. At Chicago Shakespeare Theater, Kate Fry portrayed these transformations through eloquent acting; in Justin Schaltz's view, her "expressive Rosalind, more refined and mature than is typical of the role, is graceful in speech and poised in action, then somewhat awestruck in love-at-first-sight jitters in the presence of Orlando."[13] Her masquerade changes her and transforms her entire world.[14]

And it changes Orlando, too. At first, in Rosalind's presence, Orlando is mired down in his own paralyzing and verbally graceless love-sickness: "What passion hangs these weights upon my tongue? / I cannot speak to her, yet she urged conference," he moans to himself (1.2.248–49). Later, he can express his love for Rosalind-as-Rosalind only in her absence and in poems so bad that even Rosalind mocks them, though not to Orlando's face (3.2.161–75). Still later, he tells Rosalind of his love for Rosalind only when she is in her double drag. For Rosalind-as-Ganymede-as-Rosalind uses her witty wordplay to draw him out, and it is to Rosalind-as-Ganymede-as-Rosalind that he can say, "Why blame you me to love you?" (5.2.106).

That line occurs near the end of the play, when the supple verbal devices of Rosalind-as-Ganymede-as-Rosalind trick Orlando into admitting his love for both Rosalind-as-Ganymede-as-Rosalind and Rosalind-as-Rosalind, expressing in words his subconscious realization that Ganymede is Rosalind. There is a series of three verbal duels in which double entendre comes into play in more senses than one.

First, Rosalind-as-Ganymede half hypnotizes Orlando through a repetitious series of formulas in which each of the three lovers—the shepherd Silvius (in love with Phoebe), the shepherdess Phoebe (in love with Rosalind-as-Ganymede), and Orlando (in love with Rosalind)—declares three times that each one is made of sighs and tears, and passion and fantasy, for his or her beloved ("And I for Phoebe," "And I for Ganymede," "And I for Rosalind"), each time naming the object of this passion, while Rosalind-as-Ganymede, making up the quartet, resolutely declares, "And I for no woman" (5.2.82–101). (This is a lighter variant of the unconscious assertion of the narcissistic aspect of homosexuality that we saw in *Twelfth Night*).

Finally, when Orlando is caught up in the rhythm somewhat in the manner of a game of Simon Says, after the other two have said to their physically present lovers (Silvius to Phoebe and Phoebe to Rosalind-as-Ganymede), "If this be so, why blame you me to love you?" [5.2.106]), substituting for the specific name the second-person pronoun, Orlando blurts out, "If this be so, why blame you me to love you?" Immediately, Rosalind-as-Ganymede pounces: "Who do you speak to?" she asks, forgetting her grammar, and he replies, lamely and with a very poor pun, "To her that is not here, nor doth not hear" (5.2.106–7). But of course, she is here, and she hears. In the 2010 production at Chicago Shakespeare, the question of whether Orlando recognizes her or not was left delightfully up in the air: he did not look at her when he said, "you."

The pronoun "you" is ambiguous: unlike most proper names (including those in question), it can refer to either gender. But, unlike a name, it must refer to someone present, within earshot (in this case, Rosalind-as-Ganymede). Orlando rather lamely claims that he meant it to refer to Rosalind (allegedly absent, actually present). This Freudian slip therefore may or may not mean that Orlando knows that Rosalind-as-Ganymede is Rosalind.

The ambiguity of "you" is matched by the ambiguity of the gender of the actor Orlando is addressing, whom the audience may or may not perceive, at any given moment in the play, in terms of physical sex or conventional gender. Each flickers back and forth between levels of reality. When, therefore, Orlando says "you" to Rosalind-as-Ganymede-as-Rosalind, he is speaking to a character that is two parts male (the gender of the actor and of Rosalind-as-Ganymede) and two parts female (the gender of Rosalind and of Rosalind-as-Ganymede-as-Rosalind). Of course, Phoebe (played by a boy), in love with Ganymede (played by a boy playing a woman), is also present at the charade, adding yet another point of view to the contrasting views of the audience (who know all four layers of Rosalind's masquerade: actor, Rosalind, Ganymede, Rosalind) and Orlando (who knows some and suspects others): Phoebe sees only the surface.

The second dialogue of double entendre occurs when Rosalind-as-Ganymede, with the same echoing rhetoric that we have just seen, makes Orlando promise to marry Rosalind, and her father promise to give Rosalind to Orlando; then, changing from "Rosalind" to "me" (Ganymede), she makes Phoebe promise "to marry me if I be willing" and makes Silvius promise to marry Phoebe (5.4.5–25). Here again the move is from the name (Rosalind) to the ambiguous pronoun ("me"), and back to the name (Phoebe). It is after this exchange that Orsino and Orlando comment on the startling resemblance between Rosalind-as-Ganymede and Rosalind; they are beginning to get the joke but have not quite figured it out.

This rhetoric is then echoed yet again in the third passage, later in the same scene, when Rosalind returns, now dressed in her own clothing, women's clothing, and mocks the earlier dialogue. Now all the masks are about to be stripped off, and Rosalind herself—revealed as who she really is, actually present—gives herself first to her father and then to Orlando, but not to Phoebe. Where Orlando, who wanted Rosalind-as-Ganymede to be a female and wrongly thought he was not, was the one who did not fit in the previous set of repeated phrases ("Why blame you me to love you?" [5.2.84–101]), Phoebe, who wanted Rosalind-as-Ganymede to be male and now knows that he is not, is the one who does not fit in this set.

And where the first and second passages moved from proper names to the ambiguous pronoun, this third passage moves from ambiguous pronouns to unambiguous proper nouns and names. Rosalind says the same thing to both her father and Orlando: "To you I give myself, for I am yours"; but both "give" and "yours" have very different meanings in the two phrases. And the two men respond by clarifying that difference. Her father says, "If there be truth in sight, you are my daughter" (not "you are mine," which would have remained ambiguous), and Orlando says, "If there be truth in sight, you are my Rosalind" (again, not "you are mine" but not quite "you are my love / my wife," which would have been entirely unambiguous) (5.4.117–18). The name removes the ambiguity of identity but not that of relationship.

But now Phoebe says, "If sight and shape be true, Why then, my love adieu!" (5.4.119–20). Where vision confirms a welcome truth to Rosalind's father and to Orlando, it brings a most unwelcome truth to Phoebe, who was far happier with the now shattered illusion. For, since Rosalind's male persona remains entirely imaginary, Phoebe does not get to have her true love. The triangle (Phoebe and Orlando love Rosalind, Rosalind loves Orlando) is resolved into one pair (Rosalind and Orlando) and an extra woman, Phoebe (who settles for Silvius). Phoebe is not one of the central characters, though she is in love with one of the central characters; she is just a small loose thread. But the final quartet of Rosalind and Orlando, Phoebe and Silvius, does come out neatly, the rustics doubling the nobles. (They are tripled when the reformed Oliver marries Rosalind's companion Celia, a numerical excess that prompts Jacques to remark, "There is sure another flood toward, and these couples are coming to the ark" [5.4.35–36]).[15]

Jacques then goes off to renounce the world, a relatively mild parallel to Malvolio in *Twelfth Night*, who at the end rushes offstage screaming for revenge. In Rourke's 2009 production of *Twelfth Night* for Chicago Shakespeare Theater, Malvolio was played with brilliant comic austerity by CST veteran Larry Yando; he frequently carried an umbrella as he stalked the set's centerpiece pool, and he wore a severe, buttoned-up outfit, complete with covered buttons on his boots. He was the lone character who never interacted with the "standing water." While Malvolio shares with Orsino and the clownish Sir Andrew Aguecheek a longing for Olivia, Malvolio is able to express emotions only in a manner scripted and stage-managed by his fellow household servant, the wily

Maria, wonderfully portrayed in this production by Ora Jones.

Ironically, Maria and Sir Toby, Olivia's uncle, are brought romantically together as a result of their collaboration in the plot against Malvolio. They excoriate him for believing that his mistress could love him, but, by marrying Olivia's uncle, Maria ultimately rises socially in exactly the manner that Malvolio hoped to do. While they exuberantly plunged into the pool in Rourke's production even as they plunged into vengeful cahoots against Malvolio and into love with each other, their punishment of Malvolio physically demonstrated his removal from their community. As Malvolio, Yando was suspended, blindfolded, hovering in a swing suspended over the pool of water in an isolation spotlight, his toes dangling just above the water's undulating surface. There, Ross Lehman's wickedly witty Sir Topas catechized him to cure the "madness" with which the conspirators Maria, Sir Toby, and Feste (Lehman) had diagnosed him. (This "madness" consisted in his dressing in the weird manner that Maria's letter posing as a missive from Olivia had directed.) In Rourke's production, Malvolio's abhorrence of the water signified his radical inability to love, to throw himself unreservedly into emotion as the other characters, one by one, did so boisterously.

The fun is in the joke, but who is in on the joke, and who is its butt? Everyone on stage in *Twelfth Night* (except Malvolio) is in on the joke against Malvolio; the audience and Viola/Rosalind are very much in on the joke against Olivia/ Phoebe and Orsino/Orlando. Noting this, Marjorie Garber complained that Rosalind's superior knowledge of the actual state of affairs "did not mitigate, but rather confirmed, the remanding of women back to their proper places at the end of the play."[16] But that moment at the end of the play also explicitly acknowledges the outermost frame of the play, the fourth wall of the theater, and that is what really put women in their places. For Shakespeare's audience alone was in on the ultimate joke, of which Viola/Rosalind is the butt: for they knew that she was being played by a male actor; where she thought she had the last laugh by pretending to be Rosalind pretending to be Ganymede, the audience knew that she was in fact merely the penultimate masquerader, since yet another person, of another gender, was framing her. And the women in the audience could certainly be heard laughing just as hard as the men at the tales of duped men and women.[17]

THE REVERSAL OF NATURE AND GENDER IN THE FOREST OF ARDEN

There really is today, and was in Shakespeare's time, a large forest called the Forest of Arden, west of Shakespeare's home at Stratford-upon-Avon, but he may have made the name up by combining the classical region of Arcadia (a rustic, idyllic paradise, whose inhabitants were thought to be simple and blissfully happy) and the biblical garden of Eden (ditto). Shakespeare's Forest of Arden is a place of magical transformation, like the forest in *A Midsummer Night's Dream*, where false love (or hate) is replaced by true love, and nature and culture trade places.

In both *As You Like It* and *King Lear* (composed a few years later, 1603–1605), the protagonists flee from the court to the world al fresco, from culture to nature, more precisely to human nature (in geographical nature). But that nature is "red in tooth and claw,"[18] like something out of Thomas Hobbes, in *Lear*, where human nature seems at first polite enough at court but is revealed in all its savagery stripped naked on the naked heath; by contrast, it is far closer to Jean-Jacques Rousseau's innocent state of nature in *As You Like It*, where the court is brutal while life in the sheltering forest brings out a kindness and camaraderie. The parallels grow closer if we accept the view of some scholars that Cordelia is double-cast as the Fool (they never appear on stage together),[19] giving her, like Rosalind, a male alter ego in the forest.

The first act of *As You Like It*, at court, is *Lear*-like in its human darkness and bleak, brutal hypocrisy; but in the rest of the play, life in the sheltering forest brings out a noble savagery that is kind and gentle. As Duke Senior insists, "Are not these woods / More free from peril than the envious court?" (2.1.3–4). If the truer self is discovered through the masquerade in nature, when artifice is stripped away, then all of the characters in *As You Like It* are really at heart forest people who usually pretend to be courtiers and now pretend to be (courtiers pretending to be) forest people, as Marie Antoinette played at being a shepherdess. Stanley Cavell likens this "green world" in Shakespeare to Connecticut (sometimes called "Conneckticut") in Hollywood's early romantic comedies, the magic forest where a dead marriage is brought back to life.[20]

The very first scene of *As You Like It* sets the stage for a reversal of (cultured) humans and (natural) animals, when Orlando tells us that his brother Oliver feeds and educates his horses better than he treats Orlando. Then we see Oliver call the good old servant, Adam (Adam! Shades of Eden!), an "old dog" (1.1.81). Soon after, in Arden, the good Duke Senior speaks of "books in the running brooks, sermons in stones"—a metaphor that Orlando later seems to take literally, proclaiming, "O Rosalind! these trees shall be my books," as he carves his rather lame poems on their bark (2.1.16–17, 3.2.5). Corin, a shepherd, then argues that human behavior is inevitably reversed from court to country: "Those that are good manners at the court are as ridiculous in the country as the behavior of the country is most mockable at the court" (3.2.45). But something deeper than mere behavior is transformed in the Forest of Arden.

At the end of the play, a snake and a lion conspire to kill the wicked Oliver; the animals remain in their natural state, cruel and fierce, but Orlando's intervention makes them the fable-like instruments of the sudden, miraculous conversion of the cruel and fierce Oliver. The forest similarly reverses, miraculously, the cruel character of Duke Frederick the moment he sets foot in its outskirts. The ending is pure carnival, mocking its own too easy resolutions, its unbelievable instant conversions of all the villains. At the end there are so many romantic happy endings, so many weddings, that Jacques makes his joke about all the couples heading for the ark (5.4.35). Lewis Carroll in *Through the Looking Glass* depicts a magic forest in which creatures forget their names and therefore their natural enmity. I wonder if he had Shakespeare's Forest of Arden in mind.

Angela Carter's *The Passion of New Eve* evokes Rosalind in the magic forest when Eve (a transsexual transvestite, formerly a man, now a woman wearing a man's costume) looks in the mirror and sees

> the transformation that an endless series of reflections showed me was a double drag. . . . It seemed at first glance, I had become my old self again in the inverted world of the mirrors. But this masquerade was more than skin deep. Under the mask of maleness I wore another mask of femaleness but a mask that now I would never be able to remove, no matter how hard I tried, although I was a boy disguised as a girl and now disguised as a boy again, like Rosalind in Elizabeth Arden.[21]

Eve in Eden thus becomes Rosalind in (The Forest of/Elizabeth) Arden. As Marjorie Garber remarks, "'Rosalind' becomes here a sign word for that reflecting mirror, that infinite regress of representation, of which the transvestite (*always*, in one sense, 'in double drag') is a powerful and inescapable reminder."[22]

WHY IS THERE NO BEDTRICK?

Shakespeare may have based *Twelfth Night* on one or both of two stories by Barnabe Riche (1540–1617). One of the stories was "Apollonius and Silla," in which the widowed Julina becomes infatuated with Silla, who is disguised in the clothes of her brother Silvio. When Silvio arrives in town, Julina, mistaking him for Silla-as-Silvio, invites him to dinner and later slips into bed with him. The other story, "Of Phylotus and Emelia," is more complex:

A rich old Roman named Phylotus fell in love with a young virgin named Emelia, whose equally old father forced her to submit to the marriage; she escaped by wearing a suit of men's clothing, and when her brother, Phylerno, who had been raised from birth at Naples, came now to Rome to seek his father for the first time, Phylotus assumed he was Emelia (in the expected drag). Phylerno-as-Emelia married Phylotus in church, but when they were alone in the bridal chamber, Phylerno-as-Emelia left the room and sent back a whore to take his place. Eventually they sorted it all out: Phylerno married Phylotus's beautiful daughter, and Emelia married her beloved young man.[23]

These stories make use of the plot device known as the bedtrick, sex with a partner who pretends to be someone else:[24] you go to bed with someone you think you know, and when you wake up you discover that it was someone else—another man or another woman, or a man instead of a woman, or a woman instead of a man, or a god, or a snake, or a foreigner, or an alien, or a complete stranger, or your own wife or husband, or your mother or father.

Shakespeare used bedtricks when he wanted to (in *All's Well That Ends Well* and *Measure for Measure*),[25] but there is no actual bedtrick in *Twelfth Night* or *As You Like It*. As Marliss C. Desens remarks of *Twelfth Night*, "Olivia may marry Sebastian without knowing his true identity, but Shakespeare structures the action so that only after his identity has been revealed and she has accepted the substitution will the marriage be consummated."[26] If either of the two Barnabe Riche plays was in fact Shakespeare's source, then he had to go out of his way to cut the bedtrick out of *Twelfth Night*.[27] Why? Perhaps because he wanted to preserve the innocence of the fantasy in *Twelfth Night* and *As You Like It* and hesitated to darken it with the bedtrick, which is always somewhat sinister in Shakespeare.

Yet all the other accoutrements of the bedtrick (save the consummation) are there in the acts and words of Rosalind and Viola. The implicit bedtrick in *Twelfth Night* was made explicit in the 1998 production by David Bell at Chicago Shakespeare Theater, in which Sebastian staggers out, more or less naked, from the house of the presumably bedtricked Olivia. So, too, in Barbara Gaines's production of the *Comedy of Errors* in 1998, the "wrong" twin comes out of a long, long lunch with the apparently bedtricked lady, hastily buttoning up his pants. In this way, the director can choose to play the offstage private conference with Olivia and Sebastian as chaste or consummated.

CHICAGO SHAKESPEARE THEATER

HOW DOES *TWELFTH NIGHT* MASQUERADE AS *AS YOU LIKE IT*?

The names of the brothers in *As You Like It,* Orlando and Oliver, are strongly reminiscent of the names of the lovers in *Twelfth Night,* Orsino and Olivia, while Viola is (but for one "i") an anagram for Olivia. The names of both of the male doubles, Ganymede and Cesario, imply mythological gender ambiguity, Ganymede as the boy lover of Zeus, Cesario with overtones of a Caesarian section that would make him what Shakespeare elsewhere called "not . . . of woman born" (*Macbeth* 5.8.13). In both plays, a woman (Phoebe/Olivia) falls in love with the heroine's male persona (Ganymede/Cesario), and in both plays, a man (Orlando/Orsino) is attracted to a woman (Rosalind/Viola) whom he mistakes for her male double or brother. In both, a woman (Olivia/Viola) mourns excessively for a dead brother. The uneasiness of Orlando/Orsino is expressive of the latent androgyny both of their love-objects and of themselves, as well as a powerful testimony to a love that transcends gender but not sexuality, a love made all the more titillating by the woman's safe hiding place behind man's clothing.

But there are significant differences: where Viola gives no reason for dressing as a boy, other than her desire to be with Olivia (though Olivia has "abjur'd the company and sight of men" [1.2.39–40]), Rosalind cross-dresses explicitly in order to avoid being raped (and robbed). And where Viola had never met Orsino in her female persona before she met him in her male persona, Rosalind and Orlando have met, and fallen in love, before she starts wearing trousers. This may explain why Orlando is more quickly attracted by Rosalind-as-Ganymede than Orsino is by Viola-as-Cesario, but it makes even more problematic the fact that Orlando does not see through the gender masquerade.

The most important difference of all, I think, is the fact that Rosalind has no competition, while Viola does (Olivia). The corollary to this aspect of the plot is the fact that Olivia's apparently dead brother really is dead, while Viola's is not, so that Viola is eventually able to supply her competitor (Olivia) with another, identical lover (Sebastian), putting Olivia forever after out of the running for Orsino. In *As You Like It,* by contrast, there is no real counterpart to Rosalind-as-Ganymede.

Some gender tricksters pretend to be persons who exist, while others pretend to be persons who do not. *As You Like It* is of the second type, for Rosalind invents the nonexistent, indeed purely mythological, Ganymede. But the two types exist side by side in *Twelfth Night,* where Viola pretends to be the nonexistent Cesario, but then Viola-as-Cesario is mistaken for Viola's very real brother, Sebastian; thus, Viola knowingly pretends to be Cesario but does not at first know that Sebastian has been, unknowingly, mistaken for Cesario. *Twelfth Night* is therefore able to resolve the triangular tangle by squaring it, adding a fourth person, Sebastian, to make it come out even, like a good dinner party. And this is necessary because, in *Twelfth Night*, the extra woman is a major character, a noblewoman, not just a disposable comic rustic like Phoebe. Sebastian materializes the dream figure of Cesario, who has existed only in the infatuated imagination of both Olivia and Orsino but now proves actually to exist, so that Olivia can have him. By contrast, Rosalind's male persona in *As You Like It* remains stubbornly imaginary, so that Phoebe can never have her true love and must settle instead for Silvius, a last-minute replacement far less satisfactory (to her) than Sebastian; since Phoebe is of a class below that of Rosalind-as-Ganymede (and, related to her class, ugly), she cannot have Sebastian but must have someone of her own class.

The pure fantasy in *As You Like It* becomes imitation in *Twelfth Night* as in *The Comedy of Errors*, where the actual existence of the other brother "solves," at least for the moment, the wife's problem of her straying husband: the one who does not love her is actually not her husband. Marjorie Garber suggests that "Rosalind differs from Viola in a crucial way: she returns to the stage dressed as a woman."[28] But even more crucial is the fact that Viola, who is merely imitating a real brother, remains purely female, while Rosalind, who has no brother, therefore becomes both people, male and female. In place of Viola's simpler imitation, borrowing from her brother the qualities that make Cesario, Rosalind must conjure up from within herself the male qualities that she uses to create Ganymede.

GENDER AND CULTURE IN THE TWO PLAYS

We might view both variants of this story as expressing a kind of gender essentialism: Orsino/Orlando knows, somehow, that underneath the clothing there really is someone of the opposite sex: gender is natural, rather than cultural. But we might, on the other hand, view the point as just the opposite, exposing gender as a purely superficial cultural construct: Orsino/Orlando takes the culturally constructed Cesario/Ganymede to be male and loves him, or loves the male aspect of Viola/Rosalind. Gender turns out not to be natural at all, but purely cultural.

Or we might view it as a story that denies gender altogether. Nothing in the actual lines of the plays indicates that Orsino returns Viola-as-Cesario's love, or Orlando Rosalind-as-Ganymede's, but most productions play it that way, with Orsino/Orlando increasingly fond of, if not actually in love with, Cesario/

Ganymede. Eventually Orsino/Orlando comes to understand that he loves that person, male or female, in a way that makes gender irrelevant. Gradually we in the audience share Orsino/Orlando's confusion: was this a boy or a girl? And *did it matter?* In this protean world where evil can instantly be transformed to good, female can easily be transformed to male and back again.

Twelfth Night is more fantastic than *As You Like It*, more like *The Tempest*, but both are fantasies, and one should not look too closely at a fantasy. Or, perhaps, we should grant to the characters in the inner frame the same "double pleasure" and "conscious illusion" that we grant to ourselves, the right both to see through the trick and to be taken in by it. The alternate title of *Twelfth Night* is *What You Will*, linking it to *As You Like It* in its very indecisiveness as to what the play purports to (re)present. As Bruce Smith puts it: "Desire of male for female (Orsino for Olivia, Sebastian for Olivia), of female for male (Olivia for "Cesario," Viola for Orsino), of male for male (Antonio for Sebastian, Orsino for "Cesario"), of female for female (Olivia for Viola) or male for either, of female for either, of either for either: the love plots in *Twelfth Night* truly offer 'what you will.'"[29]

NOTES

1. William Shakespeare, *As You Like It*, ed. Agnes Latham, Arden Shakespeare, 2nd series, ed. Una Ellis-Fermor, Harold F. Brooks, Harold Jenkins, and Brian Morris (London: Methuen, 1975), 5.4.198. Subsequent citations to this edition will appear parenthetically in the text.

2. William Shakespeare, *Antony and Cleopatra*, in *William Shakespeare: The Complete Works*, ed. Charles Jasper Sisson (New York: Harper & Brothers, 1953), 5.2.20–21.

3. William Shakespeare, *Hamlet*, in *William Shakespeare: The Complete Works*, ed. Charles Jasper Sisson (New York: Harper & Brothers, 1953), 2.2.47–48.

4. William Shakespeare, *A Midsummer Night's Dream*, in *Four Comedies*, ed. David Bevington (New York: Bantam Books, 1988), 1.2.42–46. Subsequent citations to this edition will appear parenthetically in the text.

5. Goethe, cited by Margaret Reynolds, "Ruggiero's Deceptions, Cherubino's Distractions," in *En Travesti: Women, Gender Subversion, Opera*, ed. Corinne E. Blackmer and Patricia Juliana Smith (New York: Columbia UP, 1995), 138.

6. Don Shewey, "A Man Plays a Woman, without Any Disguise," *New York Times*, April 13, 2003, sec. 2, p. 5.

7. *Twelfth Night*, in *Four Comedies*, ed. David Bevington (New York: Bantam Books, 1988), 1.2.56 and 62. Subsequent citations to this edition will appear parenthetically in the text.

8. Terence Cave, *Recognitions: A Study in Poetics* (London: Oxford UP, 1988).

9. Wendy Doniger, *The Bedtrick: Tales of Sex and Masquerade* (Chicago: U of Chicago P, 2000), 427.

10. Oscar Wilde, *The Picture of Dorian Gray*, ed. Donald L. Lawler (New York: Norton, 1988); and Virginia Woolf, *Orlando: A Biography* (New York: Harcourt Brace, 1928).

11. This was said of Katharine Hepburn in *Sylvia Scarlet* by Claudia Roth Pierpont, "Born for the Part: Roles That Katharine Hepburn Played," *New Yorker* (July 14 & 21, 2003): 56.

12. Chris Jones found Chicago Shakespeare Theater's Rosalind up to the task: "There is no more appealing Shakespearean heroine than Rosalind. . . . And there is no better Rosalind than Kate Fry, an actress able to play the entire seven ages of women and men without any stretch of credulity, and who invariably encapsulates on stage those very same and very beguiling qualities." Jones went on to identify those beguiling qualities as Fry's warmth, crispness, intermittent insouciance, and perpetual lack of irony. Chris Jones, "At Chicago Shakespeare, Delightful Rosalind Makes for Shakespeare Done 'As You Like It,'" *Chicago Tribune*, The Theater Loop, January 14, 2011.

13. Justin Schaltz, Review of *As You Like It*, Chicago Shakespeare Theater, February 17, 2011, SchaltzShakespeareReviews.com.

14. Chicago Shakespeare Theater's Rosalind, Kate Fry, conveyed these qualities clearly, in the estimation of reviewer Lawrence Bommer, who found that her "electric Rosalind fascinates with every quicksilver, gender-shifting mood swing, capricious whim, resourceful quip or lyrical rhapsody. Fry also plays her as postmaturely young, a woman who was happy enough to be a maiden but won't become a wife without a complete guarantee of reciprocal adoration." See Lawrence Bommer, "An Ardent Arden Blooms Beautifully," Chicago Theater Beat, January 14, 2011.

15. Interestingly enough, Laura Kolb likened Lucy Osborne's set for Josie Rourke's production of *Twelfth Night* at Chicago Shakespeare Theater to Noah's ark: "Upstage, in what looks like a gigantic heart-shaped ark, the actors range themselves in decorous groupings like Noah's animals. Downstage: the flood." See Laura Kolb, "Gender Bending, Shakespeare Style," Centerstage, April 8, 2009.

16. Marjorie Garber, *Vested Interests: Cross-Dressing and Cultural Anxiety* (New York: Routledge, 1992), 72.

17. Wendy Doniger, *The Implied Spider: Politics and Theology in Myth* (New York: Columbia UP, 1998; paperback, 1999), 109–36.

18. The line is from Alfred, Lord Tennyson's poem "In Memoriam A. H. H. [Arthur Henry Hallam]" (1850), canto 56. It is often quoted to express the philosopher Thomas Hobbes's attitude toward "wild violence" as natural to human beings.

19. William J. Lawrence, *Pre-Restoration Stage Studies* (Cambridge: Harvard UP, 1927), in ch. 3, "The Practice of Doubling and Its Influence on Early Dramaturgy"; and David M. Bevington, *From Mankind to Marlowe* (Cambridge: Harvard UP, 1962), esp. ch. 5, "Four Men and a Boy," and ch. 7, "Doubling Patterns in the 1580s and 1590s."

20. Stanley Cavell, *Pursuits of Happiness: The Hollywood Comedy of Remarriage* (Cambridge: Harvard UP, 1981), 49.

21. Angela Carter, *The Passion of New Eve* (London: Bloomsbury, 1993), 132.

22. Garber, *Vested Interests*, 76.

23. Barnabe Riche, "Of Phylotus and Emilia," in *His Farewell to Military Profession*, ed. Donald Beecher (Ottawa: Dovehouse Editions, 1992), 291–314.

24. Doniger, *Bedtrick*. It is often spelled "bed trick" or "bed-trick," but I will use the simpler form, "bedtrick."

25. William Witherle Lawrence, *Shakespeare's Problem Comedies* (New York: Frederick Ungar, 1960), 51. First published 1931 by Macmillan. The term "problem comedy" was coined for *All's Well That Ends Well*.

26. Ibid., 33.

27. Marliss C. Desens, *The Bed-Trick in English Renaissance Drama: Explorations in Gender, Sexuality, and Power* (Newark, NJ: U of Delaware P, 1994), 33.

28. Garber, *Vested Interests*, 72.

29. William Shakespeare, *Twelfth Night, or What You Will: Texts and Contexts*, ed. Bruce R. Smith, Bedford Shakespeare Series (Boston: Bedford/St. Martin's, 2001), 15.

BIBLIOGRAPHY

Bevington, David M. *From Mankind to Marlowe*. Cambridge: Harvard UP, 1962.

Bommer, Lawrence. "An Ardent Arden Blooms Beautifully." *Chicago Theater Beat*, January 14, 2011.

Carter, Angela. *The Passion of New Eve*. London: Bloomsbury, 1993.

Cave, Terence. *Recognitions: A Study in Poetics*. London: Oxford UP, 1988.

Cavell, Stanley. *Pursuits of Happiness: The Hollywood Comedy of Remarriage*. Cambridge: Harvard UP, 1981.

Desens, Marliss C. *The Bed-Trick in English Renaissance Drama: Explorations in Gender, Sexuality, and Power*. Newark, NJ: U of Delaware P, 1994.

Doniger, Wendy. *The Bedtrick: Tales of Sex and Masquerade*. Chicago: U of Chicago P, 2000.

———. *The Implied Spider: Politics and Theology in Myth*. New York: Columbia UP, 1998; paperback, 1999.

Garber, Marjorie. *Vested Interests: Cross-Dressing and Cultural Anxiety*. New York: Routledge, 1992.

Jones, Chris. "At Chicago Shakespeare, Delightful Rosalind Makes for Shakespeare Done 'As You Like It.'" *Chicago Tribune*, The Theater Loop, January 14, 2011.

Kolb, Laura. "Gender Bending, Shakespeare Style." Centerstage, April 8, 2009.

Lawrence, William J. *Pre-Restoration Stage Studies*. Cambridge: Harvard UP, 1927.

Lawrence, William Witherle. *Shakespeare's Problem Comedies*. New York: Frederick Ungar, 1960. First published 1931 by Macmillan.

Pierpont, Claudia Roth. "Born for the Part: Roles That Katharine Hepburn Played." *New Yorker*, July 14 & 21, 2003, 53–63.

Reynolds, Margaret. "Ruggiero's Deceptions, Cherubino's Distractions." *En Travesti: Women, Gender Subversion, Opera*. Ed. Corinne E. Blackmer and Patricia Juliana Smith, New York: Columbia UP, 1995. 132–51.

Riche, Barnabe. "Of Phylotus and Emilia." *His Farewell to Military Profession*. Ed. Donald Beecher. Ottawa: Dovehouse Editions, 1992. 291–314.

Schaltz, Justin. Review of *As You Like It*. Chicago Shakespeare Theater, February 17, 2011, SchaltzShakespeareReviews.com.

Shakespeare, William. *Antony and Cleopatra*. In *William Shakespeare: The Complete Works*. Ed. Charles Jasper Sisson. New York: Harper & Brothers, 1953.

———. *As You Like It*. Ed. Agnes Latham. Arden Shakespeare, 2nd series. Ed. Una Ellis-Fermor, Harold F. Brooks, Harold Jenkins, and Brian Morris. London: Methuen, 1975.

———. *Hamlet*. In *William Shakespeare: The Complete Works*. Ed. Charles Jasper Sisson. New York: Harper & Brothers, 1953.

———. *A Midsummer Night's Dream*. *Four Comedies*. Ed. David Bevington. New York: Bantam Books, 1988. 163–264.

————. *Twelfth Night. Four Comedies.* Ed. David Bevington. New York: Bantam Books, 1988. 409–551.

————. *Twelfth Night, or What You Will: Texts and Contexts.* Ed. Bruce R. Smith. Bedford Shakespeare Series. Boston: Bedford/St. Martin's, 2001.

Shewey, Don. "A Man Plays a Woman, without Any Disguise." *New York Times*, April 13, 2003.

Wilde, Oscar. *The Picture of Dorian Gray.* Ed. Donald L. Lawler. New York: Norton, 1988. First published 1890 in *Lippincott's Monthly Magazine.*

Woolf, Virginia. *Orlando: A Biography.* New York: Harcourt Brace, 1928.

Notes on Contributors

Jonathan Abarbanel is theater critic for Chicago Public Radio and the weekly *Windy City Times* newspaper. He is senior writer for *Chicago Footlights* magazine and Chicago correspondent for *Back Stage*, the national trade paper. His own plays, libretti, lyrics, and revue sketches have been performed in Chicago at the Center for New Music, Court Theatre, Bailiwick Repertory, Theatre BAM! and The Second City. His work also has been produced at the Milwaukee Repertory Theatre, the Westside Theatre (Off-Broadway), and London's Royal Festival Hall, and broadcast on WFMT.

Michael Billington is the longest-serving theater critic in the history of *The Guardian* UK. He has also blogged for *The Guardian* and Whatsonstage. com and has taught theater at King's College London as a visiting professor since 2002. Billington is the author of several critical biographies of British actors such as Peggy Ashcroft and playwrights such as Tom Stoppard. He is the authorized biographer of Harold Pinter.

Regina Buccola is Associate Professor of English at Roosevelt University, where she also serves as Core Faculty in Women's and Gender Studies. She is the author of *Fairies, Fractious Women, and the Old Faith: Fairy Lore in Early Modern British Drama and Culture* and the editor of *A Midsummer Night's Dream: A Critical Guide*. Buccola is the Scholar in Residence at Chicago Shakespeare Theater.

Simon Callow is a British actor and director of stage, screen, television, and radio. He is the author of numerous books, including *Charles Laughton: A Difficult Actor* (for which Callow also directed the documentary film adaptation) and the autobiographical works *Being an Actor* and *Love Is Where It Falls: The Story of a Passionate Friendship*.

Gina M. Di Salvo is a doctoral candidate in the Interdisciplinary PhD in Theatre and Drama program at Northwestern University. Her dissertation examines saints' plays after the English Reformation.

Wendy Doniger [O'Flaherty] is the Mircea Eliade Distinguished Service Professor of the History of Religions at the University of Chicago and the author of *The Bedtrick: Tales of Sex and Masquerade* and *The Woman Who Pretended to Be Who She Was.*

Jeffrey Gore completed his dissertation on John Milton and Renaissance education in 2008. His research interests include the response by writers to the emerging middle class in the early modern period and contemporary film adaptations of Shakespeare's plays. He teaches courses on Shakespeare and literary theory at the University of Illinois at Chicago.

Bradley Greenburg is Associate Professor of English at Northeastern Illinois University in Chicago. His articles on Shakespeare and literary periodization have appeared in *Criticism, Shakespeare Studies, Studies in Medieval and Renaissance History, Quidditas,* and elsewhere.

Clark Hulse is Emeritus Professor of English and Dean of the Graduate College at the University of Illinois at Chicago. His books include *Elizabeth I: Ruler and Legend; Early Modern Visual Culture: Representation, Race and Empire; The Rule of Art: Literature and Painting in the Renaissance;* and *Metamorphic Verse: The Elizabethan Minor Epic.*

Peter Kanelos is Associate Professor of Theater at Loyola University Chicago. His publications include *Thunder at a Playhouse: Essaying Shakespeare and the Early Modern Stage, The New Kittredge Much Ado About Nothing,* and articles and chapters in *Early Modern Studies Journal, Shakespeare's Language, Culinary Shakespeare, Quidditas, Hamlet Studies,* and elsewhere. He is also a general editor of the book series *Shakespeare and the Stage.*

Richard Ouzounian is the chief theater critic for the *Toronto Star* and the Canadian theater correspondent for *Variety.* He wrote the book and lyrics for the musicals *Dracula: A Chamber Musical, Emily,* and *Larry's Party* with Marek Norman. He is also the author of the theater histories *Are You Trying to Seduce Me, Miss Turner? Stars Talk to the "Star,"* and *Stratford Gold.*

Peter Sagal is the host of *Wait Wait . . . Don't Tell Me!*, one of the most popular shows on National Public Radio. A playwright and a director, Sagal has won numerous awards for his theatrical work, including a DramaLogue Award for directing, grants from the Jerome and McKnight Foundations, and a residency grant at the Camargo Foundation in Cassis, France. He has been commissioned to write new plays by the Seattle Repertory Theater and the Wind Dancer Theater and has been invited to work on his plays at Sundance, the Eugene O'Neill Theater Center, and the New Harmony Project.

Michael Shapiro taught for many years at the University of Illinois in Urbana-Champaign, where he was a member of the English Department and Director of the Program in Jewish Culture and Society. He is currently Visiting Professor at Loyola University Chicago. He is the author of *Children of the Revels: The Boy Companies of Shakespeare's Time and Their Plays* and *Gender in Play on the Shakespearean Stage: Boy Heroines and Female Pages*.

Terry Teachout is the drama critic of the *Wall Street Journal* and the author of *Pops: A Life of Louis Armstrong*. He wrote the libretto for Paul Moravec's *The Letter*, an operatic version of Somerset Maugham's play, which was premiered by the Santa Fe Opera in 2009. *Satchmo at the Waldorf*, his first play, opened in 2011 in Orlando, Florida.

Alicia Tomasian is Assistant Professor of English at William Rainey Harper College. Her work has appeared in the *Ben Jonson Journal*, and she is currently completing a book on criminal women in Renaissance drama.

Jonathan Walker is Associate Professor of English at Portland State University. In addition to coediting a collection of essays titled *Early Modern Academic Drama*, Jonathan has published in *Exemplaria*, in *Comparative Literature*, in *Theatre Survey*, and elsewhere.

Wendy Wall is Avalon Foundation Professor of the Humanities at Northwestern University. Author of *The Imprint of Gender: Authorship and Publication in the English Renaissance* and *Staging Domesticity: Household Work and English Identity in Early Modern Drama*, she is currently at work on a book entitled *Strange Kitchens: Knowledge and Taste in Early English Recipe Books*.

Index